Managing High-Tech Services

Using a CRM Strategy

Donald F. Blumberg

Managing High-Tech Services

Using a *CRM Strategy*

S^t_L

ST. LUCIE PRESS

A CRC Press Company
Boca Raton   London   New York   Washington, D.C.

Library of Congress Cataloging-in-Publication Data

Blumberg, Donald F.
  Managing high-tech services using a CRM strategy / Donald F. Blumberg.
    p. cm.
  Includes bibliographical references and index.
  ISBN 1-57444-346-1 (alk. paper)
  1. Customer services—Management. 2. Strategic planning. I. Title.

  HF5415.5 .B57 2002
  658.8′12—dc21   2002031761

Visit the CRC Press Web site at www.crcpress.com

© 2003 by CRC Press LLC
St. Lucie Press is an imprint of CRC Press LLC

No claim to original U.S. Government works
International Standard Book Number 1-57444-346-1
Library of Congress Card Number 2002031761
Printed in the United States of America 1 2 3 4 5 6 7 8 9 0
Printed on acid-free paper

THE AUTHOR

 Donald F. Blumberg is an internationally recognized authority on the service and support industry and market, as well as the design, operation, service, and support of computer, telecommunications, process control and plant automation, and related high-technology equipment and software service. Blumberg is the president, chief executive officer, and founder of Blumberg Associates, Inc. (BAI). Blumberg received his Bachelor of Science degree in electrical engineering, with a major in computer science, from the University of Pennsylvania in Philadephia in 1957 and his Master's of Business Administration degree, with a major in management and operations research, from the Wharton School of Business in Philadelphia in 1958. In 1963, he also completed all course work leading to a Ph.D. in applied economics, with a major in microeconomics and business planning, from the Graduate School of the University of Pennsylvania.

Blumberg has more than 40 years of experience in strategic planning, market research, and management of service operations in the data processing, office automation, and telecommunications industries. He has served as a consultant to a broad array of vendors in the high-technology service industry, advising on how to organize, operate, direct, manage, and market their hardware and software systems integration, application, installation, and field maintenance and repair organizations. Clients have included such firms as: AT&T, IBM, DEC, GM, Microsoft, Philips, Siemens, ABB, Picker, Technicon, Technicare, Lucent, GE, Panasonic, Varian, Applied Materials, Anacomp, Agfa, Kodak, Xerox, Square D, Johnson Controls, and Rosemount. He has also been directly involved in assessing and evaluating the ability of firms to meet customer needs and requirements for service and support and to assess, as an expert witness, damage to users and buyers of service.

ACKNOWLEDGMENTS

The concept and analytical framework, technology, and processes for managing service businesses, as outlined in this book, are a result of more than 40 years of management consulting experience in the service field. I would like to credit the staff of D. F. Blumberg & Associates, Inc., particularly Michael Blumberg, its chief operating officer (and my son), who helped in developing many of the concepts and directed much of the market research studies supporting the evaluations. Other members of the D. F. Blumberg & Associates, Inc. staff, including Robert Snyder, Tony Mercogliano, and Gaby Shaw, also contributed to the research and development efforts. I also owe an extreme debt of gratitude to the many service executives with whom I have worked, including Tom Faughnan, chief executive officer of TSI/KPG; Russ Spencer, senior vice president of service at Agfa; Peter van Voorst, managing director at Getronics; Jeff Cramer, chief executive officer at Anacomp; Bill Beaumont, vice president at Decision One; Bob Williams, vice president/general manager at Kodak Service; John Schoenewald, vice president at Imation and chief executive officer at AFSMI; and many others who provided real-world insight and rules of thumb. Finally, my thanks to the Association for Service Management International (AFSMI), the National Association of Service Managers (NASM), the Service Industry Association (SIA), and the editors of *Field Force Automation Magazine* for both their encouragement and the use of their platform to present many of the views and concepts discussed in this book.

As usual, the credit belongs to many, but all complaints, critiques, and suggestions should be directed to me.

Donald F. Blumberg

CONTENTS

APPENDICES

1

MANAGING SERVICE: A GENERAL OVERVIEW AND INTRODUCTION

Managing service activities, in general, and particularly services run as a profit center or line of business requires, almost by definition, a critical focus on the relationship and interaction between the customer and the organization. Such management goes far beyond the basic functions of sales and customer data management normally found in any customer relationship process model. It also involves the need for a high degree of focus on the entire processes associated with receiving calls from customers, handling those calls, dispatching and assigning service personnel and other resources (material) to meet the call needs and requirements, and managing the processes associated with delivery of materials to the customer in the field and their return. These functions all represent primary operational functions and processes in a typical service business.

On the other hand, in the typical product business, these particular service functions (call handling, dispatch, and assignment) are very simple or may not exist, while other functions not found in the typical service business model, such as manufacturing or forward supply chain management, may not exist or may require very different structures. In essence, a real difference exists between managing a general product-oriented business and managing a service business in terms of customer relationship management (CRM) and business strategy. In a product-oriented business,

CRM is an important factor; in a service business, CRM is the strategic factor. Yet, in much of the CRM technology that exists today, CRM system design, concepts, and operational technology tend to presume a product focus or product-based operational environment.

The overall objective of this book is to bring together a full discussion of the issues, models, and operating structure involved in managing a service business and to describe the design, concepts, and applicability of CRM technology and infrastructure in support of this service management process. This general introduction describes the underlying framework and operational structure and models involved in managing service as a profit center or line of business and introduces the key functions and technology required in support of that management process. Subsequent parts and chapters examine, in depth, the application of CRM technology in managing service and the use of supporting specific and critical service management processes and infrastructure. The discussion establishes the critical role of information and data in regard to customers and their relationships to organizations over time and in real time, as well as focusing on the concept that in a service business (unlike a product business) the resources of customer information and data become just as critical as labor and material. Finally, this discussion combines service business models and processes with the technology and systems infrastructure necessary for both CRM and real-time support of the service delivery process to provide an overall framework for managing service in the 21st century.

It is important at this point to define a *service business* and examine how generic the solutions and technologies to be applied are. Unlike most other business activities, such as finance and accounting, manufacturing, marketing, or human relations, service is quite fragmented and lacks a strong structural definition. Services tend to be defined by economists as "not product". Even basic mechanisms for financial control and accounting fail to deal with important measures of service performance and activity, such as time measurement. Many economic and managerial studies tend to be a little vague about when service stops and product starts. This is particularly true in product-oriented/manufacturing-based companies that are involved in both product and service business activities. In essence, our mindset and training tend to focus on describing services in product terms. McDonald's, a fastfood restaurant service, is often thought of in terms of hamburgers, even though it provides more than just hamburger food service. An airline, as a travel and transportation service, is often characterized in terms of its product (airplanes), yet it moves people and freight by more than just planes. Material handling trucks move freight to and from the plane and the cargo warehouse. Passengers arrive and depart via cab, limousine, rail, or another airplane.

Passengers also have a need to eat and drink. Virgin Airlines is a good example of an airline that goes beyond the basic "airplane" concept by also providing limousine services and special walk-up facilities in the terminal.

We suggest that, based on over 40 years of consulting experience, a common structure and function exist across all service businesses and that from this service business perspective the business of funeral directors is the same as the business of locomotive maintenance and repair services. While an obvious similarity exists between banking services and insurance services, does such an apparent similarity exist between banking and healthcare services or between retailing and computer support services? We hope to answer this question in this book and in the following chapters and parts.

Our experience, in a wide variety of different businesses and market segments, strongly suggest that, once you eliminate the specific industry jargon and language, service businesses are all the same. They follow the same rules, use the same practices, and can utilize the same infrastructure and technology. This underlying assumption is critical to understanding and making use of the discussion that follows. We have found that by viewing service management generically and generally, we can more effectively identify the strategic and tactical issues in a given business, rather than viewing the service business through a product orientation. We recognize that it requires a leap of faith to view a service business as structurally different from a product business from a management standpoint; however, we will, through both analysis and anecdotal experience, provide a framework for this transition and attempt to show how this new outlook can improve the business of service management.

In summary, the process of managing a service business from the position of a logical and operational framework is driven by the nature of the service market and customer needs and requirements, rather than from the viewpoint of a traditional product-based business model. We hope that we will be able to provide a new insight, a different perspective, and workable solutions to dealing with service business management optimally using this approach. This first section attempts to deal with the entire concept of service business management. The second part focuses on CRM technology applied to service management, key service management and marketing issues, and new strategic directions.

This book, particularly Parts III and IV, is also designed to focus on crucial issues of marketing and selling service as a strategic business and to provide both the theory and dynamics as well as the practice associated with service-based business, drawing upon extensive market research in a wide variety of markets and industries of a service nature. Through a combination of theory, structural dynamics, case studies, examples, and procedures, we have attempted to provide a clear prescription and workable strategies and tactics for marketing and selling service in a variety of different markets and situations. You will find that many of the same concepts and ideas (particularly market research, segmentation, and the use of public relations mechanisms) also have applicability in product-oriented marketing and selling, but we highlight the reasons why those techniques, methodology, and approach offer such a high payoff when applied to marketing and selling services. We also focus on new technology for managing the total customer information through CRM. Finally, we demonstrate that a service business can be managed, controlled, and delivered optimally, just like a product business, but through the use of different business models, systems, and infrastructure, and marketing and sales concepts. We show that a high-tech approach to service management can pay off, not just for high-tech products, but for any business service.

1

MANAGING SERVICE AS A LINE OF BUSINESS

CONTENTS

The business of service has become a major opportunity in almost every developed or semi-developed country in the world. For example, within the United States over 70% of our total gross domestic product is service or service related. With this already great and continuing growth in service as a business, increasing emphasis is being placed on the need to develop new mechanisms, theory, structure, and practice for management, marketing and selling service as a strategic line of business based upon the underlying concepts and dynamics of service.

Most executives and managers of service businesses would naturally ask a very basic question: why can't we use the traditional management approaches that work so well in product business; in essence, why not treat service as simply another product? The answer, to a large extent, comes from the growing recognition that, while a lot of similarities exist between service businesses and product businesses, so, too, do some extremely important *differences*. These differences were discussed in an earlier book, *The Management of Service as a Strategic Profit Center* (McGraw-Hill, 1990), in which the traditional "economic theory of the firm," which has been built upon the concept of the manufacture and sale of a product, was contrasted with a new theory of the service firm that attempts to embody some very crucial and dynamic differences between a product and service business.

Figure 1.1 illustrates the differences in the dynamic structure of these two theoretical approaches. In a product business, two major resources (people and material) are used in an engine of production to produce units of goods sold to the customer or market for a given unit of value. Profit from the business is the difference between the amount received and the cost of those resources and the engine of production. However,

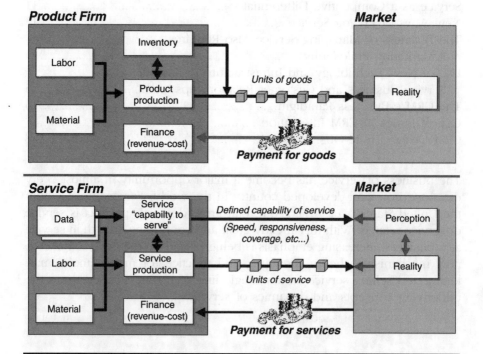

Figure 1.1   Comparison of product and service business models.

in the service firm, three sets of resources (people, material, and data) are utilized through a mechanism of two engines of production (the actual provision of service and the capability to serve). These produce a cluster of "products" consisting of both (1) the *actual service* and (2) the *ability, or perception of ability, to service where and when required.* The payment provided by the market is, in fact, for *both* streams of service rather than the stream of single goods or units generated within the product-oriented firm. The key differences between the product model and the new service model are shown in Figure 1.2.

DATA RESOURCES IN A PRODUCT VS. SERVICE BUSINESS

Data certainly exist in the product model but serve primarily as a control or management mechanism. However, in service, data are as much a resource as labor and material. In a number of service businesses, data are the products being collected and sold. In addition, data (e.g., on customer needs and requirements or problems) become much more important, primarily because of the need for the service organization to react much more rapidly than a product organization to changes in market condition, customer needs, etc. Changes in data and information about the customer in a service environment is measured in terms of seconds, minutes, and hours. This is essentially a "real-time" orientation. A service business must be very flexible and adaptive to market needs on a timely basis. For the product business with its fixed form, fit, and function, changes in requirements will generally occur over months and even years.

Differences in Engines of Production

A pure product business has a single engine of production, but a service business, in addition to the general engine of service production, also has a second engine, the ability to serve. This exists because one cannot stockpile or inventory service. In a product business, goods produced can be set aside and then sold at a later date. While products certainly may be perishable, it is not equivalent to the service environment, where unused service capacity and capability is simply lost. Because of this, the service business must deal directly with managing service response, or the ability to serve. This ability is largely a perception in the mind of the potential customer, but it depends directly on the amount of time it takes to deliver the service to the customer requiring it. As a result, time to serve becomes very critical in the service business model; for the customer requiring it, service delivered in 2 hours is different than service delivered in 24 hours, even though the actual service may be the same. This has very real implications in terms of:

Attitudes and Procedures	Services Orientation	Product Orientation
Attitudes toward customers	Customers' needs determine plan	Try to cut costs and bring out better products
Product/service offering	Company makes what it can sell	Company sells what it makes
Role of market research	To determine customer needs and how well company is satisfying them	To determine customer reaction to product
Interest in innovation	Focus on locating new opportunities	Focus on technology and cutting costs
Importance of profit	A critical objective	A residual; what is left after all costs are covered
Role of customer support	Seen as a customer opportunity	Seen as a necessary evil
Logistics/parts inventory levels	Set with customer requirements and costs in mind	Set with production requirements in mind, with emphasis on cost minimization
Focus on advertising	Need-satisfying benefits of services	Product features and quality; how products are made
Role of sales force	Help customers to buy if services fit their needs, while coordinating with the rest of firm, including production, advertising, logistics, etc.	Sell the customer, the product; do not worry about coordination with other promotion efforts

Figure 1.2 Key differences between services and product business model orientation. (Based on McCarthy, M., Basic Marketing Theory, Ph.D. thesis, 1987.)

■ *Time management.* A service business must manage the time aspects of service products for the potential or actual customer in terms of the ability to provide service within a given time frame and at a certain level of response, when it is required.

- *Financial and cost management.* In general, product-oriented accounting and financial control systems do not deal with the issue of time. For example, the measurement of profitability of 2-hour service vs. 24-hour service is rarely, if ever, calculated. While this issue of time is generally not present in product businesses, management of a service business requires a very careful calculation of the time impact on the service portfolio, its costs, and its profitability. It is also important to recognize the differences in revenue stream and profitability due to the existence of a second engine of production.

As a very real illustration of this difference, it is important to consider the concept of the service contract for maintenance and repair of equipment. In cases involving service, the customer pays both for the actual service, if and when it is needed, but also for the ability to get the service at some point in the future, within well-defined parameters. It may well be that no real service is ever provided over the course of a service contract if the equipment never fails, yet the customer will have paid for a service contract to gain the "warm and fuzzy" feeling that service will be provided if needed. In essence, in this example, customers often wind up paying for the perception that service will be provided, at some point in the future, if and when required. In essence, in service businesses, perceptions, and particularly perceptions related to time, are as important as, if not significantly more important than, the actual service itself. The ability to serve is created through an infrastructure that can collect, collate, and present all of a customer's related data and information in real time to management. This, in essence, is the basis for customer relationship management (CRM) technology, which is discussed in depth in Part II.

Marketing and Selling Service

In the marketing and sale of product, the primary drivers are the form, fit, and function of the product itself; while perceptions do enter into the marketing and selling equation, they are not dominant and at best introduce only a subtle distinction. Of course, this does not suggest that perceptions can be ignored in product marketing and selling, but rather that perceptions are a much more critical issue in the marketing and selling of service. In essence, because service cannot be stockpiled or inventoried and generally cannot be touched or felt, service customers are much more driven by issues of perception in regard to their ultimate decisions to buy and their subsequent evaluations of the quality of the service deliveries (i.e., customer satisfaction). Therefore, marketing and selling mechanisms (both strategic and tactical) that work extremely well in a product-oriented business may not only be not as effective; in fact, they may even be counter-productive in marketing and selling service. This set of issues is discussed in Part III.

SERVICE AS THE KEY TO THE COMPETITIVE EDGE

As the pace of technological change and global competition intensifies, organizations are increasingly looking to the service function as a strategic source of revenue and competitive differentiation. We see this happening across all industries and marketing. One of the most striking characteristics of recent changes in our economy has been the explosive growth in services. In fact, services now account for over 70% of the gross national product. This growth has attracted much attention. Many organizations not previously involved in service are now positioning themselves to take maximum advantage of the opportunities.

Many companies are adopting a new view of service. They are beginning to view service as a strategic line of business, as a viable profit center with strategic value. Investments in service businesses can yield much higher returns than investments in traditional products and operations. The investments are aimed at providing the service function with the tools necessary to improve the effectiveness and quality of service delivery.

It is clear that providing service and support of all kinds and types, such as professional services, healthcare services, maintenance, and repair service, is a growing business. In fact, in many companies, service revenues are overshadowing revenue from products. Research indicates that the amount spent to service and support equipment and technology after the initial product purchase are considerably greater than the product cost, *per se*. Over the life cycle of use of a large item such as an airplane, ship, or locomotive, service support costs are typically up to two and one-half times the original purchase acquisition value. In a series of studies recently completed in the data-processing, office automation, telecommunications, process control, and building automation markets, it was found that the same general ratios apply: For service over the life of the product, the user will typically pay more than two and one-half times the amount paid for the original equipment (hardware) purchase. Thus, more money can be made in equipment service than in equipment product sales over the product life cycle.

An analysis of many companies reveals that the revenue and profit contribution of the service function to total corporate revenues and profits is also increasing at a far more rapid rate than is the contribution from product sales. Typically, anywhere from 25 to 40% of corporate revenues and from 20 to 50% of corporate profits can be generated from the service component of a business, particularly if service is run as a strategic line of business, or strategic profit center, with service transferred to the product line businesses at market price. Several equipment manufacturers, such as GE, Honeywell, Unisys, IBM, and Xerox, are providing service as a separate strategic line of business.

A major study of the economics and profitability of service in over 100 companies developed detailed information on these companies' service costs and revenue contributions, as well as the same information for their product businesses.* The study showed that profit margins of services are about 15 to 25% or more before tax, while those for products are typically only 7 to 11%. More significant is the implication of those figures on the return on investments (ROI) in the product vs. service business lines. For service, ROI is typically in the vicinity of 70 to 80% or more annually. In some cases, cost recovery can be achieved in under a year. By contrast, an investment in product is typically returned in 24 to 36 months or more.

SERVICE AS A COMPETITIVE DIFFERENTIATOR

As products evolve away from the new and unique toward the accepted and familiar, finally achieving commodity status, the level and type of accompanying service may be the real critical market differentiators. Early in the product life cycle, service may consist entirely of timely repair service. Later, ancillary services (such as design, engineering, installation, training, or upgrades) are necessary to make a product more attractive, easier to buy, or more convenient. Service can also inject new life into products that reached maturity and commodity status long ago. That is why forward-thinking companies are investing in technology to support their service management efforts. It is an investment they have good reason to expect will pay off very well in terms of additional product, as well as service revenues.

Service is as much about perception of future performance as it is about current activity. It is what we sometimes call the "warm and fuzzies" — the customers' *certain knowledge* that if something goes wrong or service is needed they can call and get service performed within the time frame required. Most customers not only expect service but also recognize its value and are willing to pay for it.

The service market customer base can be divided into three segments: (1) people for whom product price is important and service is relatively unimportant; (2) people for whom service is very critical and product price is relatively unimportant; and (3) people who have a more balanced view of product purchase price and service price, with both having equal

---

* Unless otherwise identified, all market research studies referenced in this book were carried out by Blumberg Associates, Inc., management consultants, on a standard, random-access telephonic survey basis and using double-blind methodology.

weight. It is interesting to note that the first group, the price-conscious consumers, comprise only about 10% of the population; the second group represents about 40%, and the third group is about half of the population. This information is important, as it suggests that organizations that focus on price and reduce service will not attract as large a market as those that balance their focus on price and service or emphasize service as a key differentiator. Organizations must understand their markets and the potential value of service in reaching those markets.

It is also important to recognize that service marketing and sales are largely based on perception rather than reality. This is particularly true with respect to price. Quite often, customers equate price to service quality. Their perception is that a high price equates to high service quality and performance in the future and that a low price means poor performance and slower response in the future. Thus, pricing services at a higher level could, in some markets, create a strong perception of quality. For example, a patient is more likely to choose a high-priced surgeon to perform open-heart surgery than the least expensive one.

The most important perception about service is related to time for delivery of service: the time that elapses between when the user organization receives a request for service (to make a repair because of equipment failure, for example) and when the task is completed. Market research studies have shown that, for every service task and in every market environment, most customers (typically 80% in any survey) have a very precise view of how long they will (or want to) wait for service. Thus, a company that can determine the customer time-frame requirement, and then commit to and deliver service on the basis of that commitment, can generate the highest level of perceived customer satisfaction. Taking longer will obviously negatively affect service satisfaction levels. Interestingly, improving service (i.e., too rapid a response compared to the optimum customer waiting time) does not improve customer satisfaction perception. Customers do not differentiate between service that meets their time requirements and more rapid service; however, they can, and in fact do, differentiate between good and bad service if they have to wait too long. Thus, service is primarily perceived and the perceptions are largely related to time. The greatest negative impact on customer satisfaction for service occurs in the *absence* of the service being delivered within the required time frame.

Actually, studies have shown that too much service can generate negative customer satisfaction perception, just as too little service can. Think about your perception of service if you enter a store and no sales clerk waits on you (i.e., too little service). On the other hand, what is your reaction if two or three sales clerks immediately pounce on you to make a sale (too much service). Both situations generate negative customer satisfaction. Service has to be strategically designed to just meet customer waiting time requirements in order to optimize customer satisfaction and achieve the highest value-added perceptions.

The soft drink business offers an excellent example of market differentiation through proper management of the service function. Soda is nothing more than a little syrup, water, and some bubbles generated by a drink dispenser and served in a paper cup, for which consumers pay 70¢ to $1.00 or more. You can well imagine the profit margin associated with dispensing that drink. It is very, very high — in the range of 60 to 75%. In many organizations, such as fastfood restaurants or movie theaters, a disproportionate amount of profits in the operation come from selling soda. If the drink dispenser fails, the business stops making money. And right there, at the dispenser, is where service makes a strategic difference.

One of the major soft drink companies recognizes the strategic importance of service. Customers or users of dispensers issued by that company who have a problem, anywhere in the country, dial a single number and arrange for immediate service. All service is coordinated centrally and the dispenser user is assured of standard service response and repair within a 2- to 4-hour time frame. A competitor, not recognizing the strategic value of dispenser service, hands off most of its service business to local contractors. Customers call different numbers across the country, and the various contractor service organizations respond according to their own individual practices and with varying response and repair time commitments. Not surprisingly, the first company has the lion's share of the soda business. At least part of that difference in market share is attributable to the very different ways the two companies organize their service functions to support the drink dispensers on their customer's premises, or at least opt for the retailer offering required service.

Domino's Pizza offers another example. They have experienced very rapid growth, but not because of their pizza. Everybody sells pizza; it is a pure commodity. Years ago, Domino's Pizza added a service component. They discovered that the decision to buy is usually made when customers are at home. They want a service. The service is home delivery and easy ordering. In this case, service redefined the product, and for that new product customers are willing to pay a premium price.

NEW WAYS OF PRICING SERVICE

Forward-thinking companies, recognizing the true nature of service, also look at service pricing differently. For a tangible product, price is typically a function of cost plus a normal markup. For service, the price should be determined by the value in-use as a *function* of the customer who needs the service. One popular pricing scheme is to use labor hours and labor costs and add a percentage for overhead and profit. Another is to price service based on competitive prices. In many cases, neither of these approaches to service activities makes sense.

Consider this example. On the way to a very important meeting in which you will gain a personal commission of $1 million, your car fails. You rush to a phone and call a service mechanic. How much are you willing to pay him to fix your car in order to get you to that meeting before your prospect leaves? The real value depends on what you stand to lose because you cannot use your car. You might be prepared to spend up to $900,000 to fix it on a timely basis. The point is this: The value of the service is derived from what would happen in the absence of the service and not providing the service within the time that it is needed, not from what it costs to provide the service.

Pricing service as a function of the cost of delivery of the service or some percentage of the hardware leads to some strange but common situations. For example, when you ask companies about the delivery of service during off hours (such as on a Saturday or Sunday or after 5:00 p.m.), you will often hear that such service is not offered because it is "too expensive". That does not make any sense. Such thinking represents a failure to recognize that the customer cares less in the long run about costs than what he stands to lose in the absence of the service. If the use of a particular product is critical to a the customer, then the service is also critical. Such a customer needs the service and is prepared to pay to ensure that the service is provided when necessary. In fact, as indicated previously, underpricing service can lead to negative perceptions about future service quality. Service should be priced on the basis of its value in use.*

When the true value of service is understood, it can provide tremendous internal incentives to establish service as a strategic line of business. Many companies have learned that servicing the installed base can often generate more revenue each year than can the sale of new equipment. The classic example is razors and blades. After selling the razor, the real business (and profit) is found in selling the blades. Research indicates that not only is this true for the razor blade business, but it also holds true for most products. After initial product introduction, the real business and profit is in the service. By the end of the product life cycle (i.e., in the mature or commodity state), the business is totally related to service.

THE BUSINESS OF MANAGING SERVICE ALSO REQUIRES A MARKETING PHILOSOPHY

In summary, service is not just an adjunct to a product, it is, or can become, a major strategic line of business and, at the same time, enhances

---

* This will be discussed in depth in Part III.

the product lines of businesses. What is required is a new philosophy toward the customer and to service that, properly implemented, affects all aspects of an organization's business. Such a philosophy would affect the product development and marketing processes, as well as sales, distribution, and logistics functions. The key from a marketing and sales perspective is to focus on the customers' needs for service and to deliver them in a cost-effective manner. Linking all the customer-focused service functions together to ensure that they all have the same information about customers' service needs and that they all are marching to the same customer service "drum" is one of the greatest challenges for today's organization.

Over time, the service function must meet the broadest service needs of the customers. Leading organizations recognize these opportunities and offer an integrated service approach to take advantage of them. Users recognize that it is much more efficient to have one organization servicing a complex system than to have a multitude of individual vendors, each pointing a finger at the other. In addition, focus on the service issues of a product, particularly one at the end of its life cycle of maturing, can lead to a revitalization of the product.

Businesses need to rethink the world and market in service terms. Service can lead to the development of new revenues, new businesses, higher profitability, new products, and new level of market differentiation. Companies that keep their focus on the service needs of their customers and meet those needs strategically are the ones that will succeed in the long run. Those that do not have such a focus or think only about service as a tactical element of product sales will fall by the wayside.

USE OF NEW TECHNOLOGY AND INFRASTRUCTURE TO MANAGE SERVICE BUSINESS AND CUSTOMER RELATIONSHIPS

The management and coordination of service have been the subjects of a great deal of attention over the last 20 years, as customer and field service has moved from its traditional role as a cost center to its current position as a profit center or full line of business. We now see service in its strategic role — providing the customer with full services over the life cycle, a concept sometimes referred to as *strategic service* or *service management*. This view has typically been interpreted as focusing on service at and after the sale, which ignored the need for full management of all the customer interactions, including presales and sales, as well as order processing. This broader concept addressing strategies both before and after the sale is now known as CRM. CRM demands full management of the total relationship between the seller (vendor) and the buyer "(customer). In essence, CRM calls for a seamless interface between the buyer and seller, implemented through advanced e-business and system technologies. This new CRM concept creates both a paradigm and an opportunity for service executives to strengthen the total service management and delivery capability of their organizations. The concept could also cause problems, however, due to the failure to fully recognize all of the CRM implications.

THE CRM/E-BUSINESS PARADIGM

Without question, advanced integrated computer and communication systems and the e-business infrastructure will affect and support the conduct of business in the new millennium. This dictates the use of a full multimedia approach to network communications, including the web, voice, data, video, images, e-mail, chat rooms, etc. Applying the broader concept of CRM in this new world will certainly lead to:

- Rapid increase in the pace of business transactions, with increased demand
- Increased requirement for flexibility and enhanced service reaction time expected by the customers from their vendors
- Realignment, consolidation, or elimination of inefficient sales distribution channels (particularly indirect channels)
- Increased added value of services, primarily in terms of significant changes in time to service
- Full integration and provision of services and support due to the need for full support over the life cycle
- Maximum use of all data and intelligence throughout the integration between company and customer to focus fully on both met and unmet customer requirements
- Ability to rapidly recognize and adjust to new customer requirements
- Need for continuing real-time customer satisfaction measurement
- Ability to accurately recognize customer needs and requirements and willingness to pay by segment and market niches, rather than treating all customers the same

Traditionally, sales and service were generally combined in one organization, with service acting in a subordinate role, often as a cost center. In general, service has been moved out from under sales, as a separately managed business. The move into CRM requires some reintegration of at least the systems infrastructure of both sales and service, with after-sales service being given an equal rather than subordinate role compared to presale functions and support.

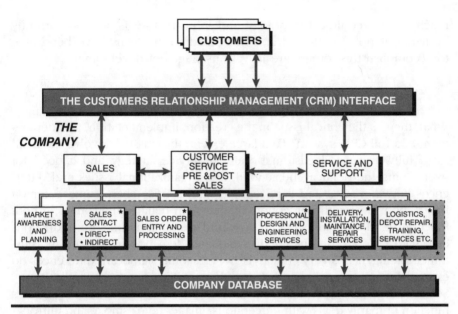

Figure 1.3   The customer relationship management concept.

As shown in Figure 1.3, CRM requires full integration of all before-and after-sales services systems operating off a common database, using a variety of voice, data, and image communication links (wireless, Internet, etc.). As indicated by the arrows, this data flow is often two way, and information flows out of one formation to another in real time. This is designed to create a *seamless interface* for the customer (as perceived by the customer) and a full focus on the current and potential customer service needs and requirements (as perceived by the vendor) in real time. The CRM technology provides the ability to manage the service requests and requirements in real time and provide both the perception and reality required. The entire array of field force automation technology supports this infrastructure, as do other sales automation technologies, such as data mining, data warehousing, and sales planning and scheduling.

CRM calls for a fully integrated real-time, added-value linkage from the customer or potential customer to the company and back again. It also is intended to provide all functions and elements of the company with a common database in real time, allowing continuous tracking, coordination, and control of all interactions with a given customer and customer segment.

If we examine the array of new technologies, software, and systems, such as data warehousing, data mining, call management, logistics man-agement, or integrated wireless field force support, it would appear that much of the required technology and infrastructure is at least currently available, if not fully tested and integrated. Some firms have been able to accomplish this; others are in various stages of development.

CRITICAL ISSUES IN CRM INTEGRATION

What, then, is the critical issue in the creation, implementation, and deployment of a full CRM system? To a large extent, these issues involve the need for a fully articulated customer-oriented service strategy and a need for overcoming the political, behavioral, and organizational issues and differences between sales and service. Sales and service share some common issues; both deal with perceptions, rather than realities. Personnel in both functions tend to be involved in travel and are often mobile. Both functions deal with random, unscheduled events and demands so market and customer intelligence is very critical. However, some significant differences do exist. Sales are often linked to incentives, while service generally is not. Service personnel must deal with reality as well as perceptions. The sales function primarily deals with perceptions, images, and "smoke and mirrors".

These differences are most critical in the management of product businesses vs. service businesses. Products can be stockpiled and inventoried, but services cannot. Our experience indicates that CRM applied to service businesses can have an even higher payoff than CRM applied to product businesses. This is particularly true because the service business salesperson is often selling from an "empty store" and thus must have a full understanding of all customer requirements and relationships in real time to add value to the customer. When sales personnel (selling service) can understand the customers' real needs and requirements for service, the time criticality, the value of the service to the customers, and the customers' willingness to pay, the profit margins from these sales will be greater. Most sales personnel, however, tend to view service as a necessary evil or as a cost of doing business. They have difficulty in seeing services as having real value and often, particularly in product businesses, tend to want to give away the service to sell the product. CRM forces sales personnel (selling service) to fully understand the true service needs of the current or potential customer. However, if the CRM program lacks a full strategy and plan, sales and marketing tend to dominate the design, and less than complete attention is given to the after- sales service and support needs.

CRM DESIGN TRADE-OFFS

In designing and specifying a CRM system, how is it possible to achieve a common ground on the value and return on investment of various systems and technology, some supporting sales and marketing and others

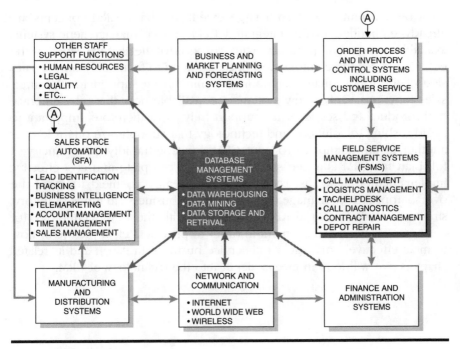

Figure 1.4   Infrastructure technology support for customer relationship management (CRM) strategy.

supporting after- sales service? For a good example of the type of trade-off required, consider data mining vs. call management. In a service business, functional improvements in call management, especially in introducing call diagnostics and call avoidance, can have very high and measurable ROI, whereas data mining may offer only qualitative improvements in the selling process. Thus, a CRM system designed by sales personnel will tend to focus on more qualitative areas of sales support, as opposed to the much more precise measurement needs of the service organization. A good example is data mining done in support of predictive planning and scheduling of sales and service. While to some sales executives both data mining and call management would seem to apply to their product businesses, they may not fully recognize the applicability of data mining to service planning, coordination, and control.

In summary, the technology to create the full CRM model, systems infrastructure, and interface is available now. The critical issue is to overcome the political, administrative, and organizational barriers to a full strategic reintegration of sales, service, and support through a seamless infrastructure and support system. If the company or business is in both product and service businesses, both business models (see Figure 1.4) must be accommodated. To a large extent, the basic CRM concepts are already embedded in the integrated field service management systems available today, but primarily with respect to the service side of the equation. Sales force automation packages tend to focus only on the sales side of the CRM equation, ignoring or minimizing support for the after-sales functions. Only a few systems are available now that fully embrace both product and service sales support fully. It is, therefore, important to avoid rushing to solutions and technology that suboptimize one role over another in an attempt to roll out CRM concepts rapidly. In summary, a full plan for CRM is a necessary first step in complete and cost-effective implementation. The discussion thus far attempts to meld together the overall approach to management of a service business (in terms of theory, structure, marketing, and sales approach) with the new technology for customer relations management in order to provide a clear picture of how to most effectively manage a full-service business. In Part II and its related chapters, we will look in greater depth into the technology of CRM.

2

MANAGING SERVICE IN SPECIFIC MARKET SEGMENTS

CONTENTS

The basic problem in managing service is defining what service is, how to coordinate and control it, how to deliver it, and how to market price and sell it. Little problem with these issues exists in today's manufacturing environment. Full theory, process, and practice concerning product business now exist. It is of interest to note the basic principles of scientific management in terms of a general theory and approach were developed in the late 1880s and early 1900s, in parallel with the industrial revolution, which involved the manufacture of steel and iron products, automobiles, etc. Until that time, except for certain specific professional service fields such as military and civil engineering, architecture, and transportation (navel and railroad), very little study, research, or investigation focused on the general management of service and service-related businesses. As a result, most of our management thinking and concepts and even our financial and accounting structures tend to presume the existence of a tangible product, even in such service-oriented fields such as construction. For example, the tangible results of construction services (buildings, highways, or bridges) tended to focus on management in terms of a specific project tied to that general construction service business, rather than the service itself.

Early economists also typically presumed the existence of a product in their development of market theory and explanations. In fact, in basic economic courses, service tends to be defined as everything other than product production. Supply and demand analysis was typically described in product (as opposed to service) terms.

As we moved from a product- to a service-oriented economy after World War II, improvements in productivity and the efficiency of product production increased the amount of leisure time available. Higher income levels produced economic growth and created the demand for more and more types and categories of services, each with its own jargon and processes. This proliferation of services has made it very difficult to understand and direct service businesses using a general business model and structure. Each individual service industry or market has developed its own descriptive processes, business concepts, and "rules of thumb". A typical view is that the basic process and management model for products applies whether one is producing and selling automobiles, computers, copiers, men's wear, or locomotives. The same cannot generally be said about the existence and acceptance of a similar common structure for apparently disparate service businesses, such as banking, insurance, or retail. In fact, most of the management research and analysis in services tends to be either anecdotal or very industry or market specific.

In the first chapter, a conceptual framework for a general service business model was proposed. This chapter shows how that basic model applies to individual service market segments and industries, as well as in product/manufacturing businesses, which include service. Based on over 40 years of consulting experience in an extremely broad array of service and product-oriented companies, we have developed a reasonable amount of anecdotal evidence that suggests that basic similarities and a general service business model do exist, regardless of the market segments or industries in which the model is used.

One of the problems facing managers in understanding and, more importantly, accepting the existence of this new service business model, as discussed in Chapter 1, is the difficulty of defining even basic terms. To illustrate this critical point, we can think of two broad classes of service:

- *Presale services.* Presale services focus on the normal and general relationship that any formal organization has with its potential and total market and customer base and deals with the general image of the organization, as well as explanations of the business and its capabilities, products, and portfolio. This type of activity is a requirement of, and exists within, any type of organization or business activity regardless of whether it is dealing in products or services. It is generally regarded as a staff function, a part of marketing or sales.
- *At and aftersale service.* The important focus of this analysis is on the service required at or after the sale. These services, for which revenue in one form or another is directly generated and which can be managed as a line of business, are direct equivalents of products yet involve intangibles. The services in this case could be the total output of the company or business (in the case of a full-service business) or could be a part of the revenues of the total business organization (in the case of a product business with services).

In our discussion, the concepts, structure, and models presume the existence of both presales and aftersale service activity; however, we are primarily interested in the "business" of service defined in terms of the sale itself and aftersale activities. While we do include discussion of presale service in the context of managing a service business as a whole, we do not evaluate the general function of presales service, including the general sales function normally found in any product business model. The exception is that we deal with market and sales issues specifically related to service businesses. In essence, it is important to distinguish between presales service, sometimes called customer service, which does not by itself generate revenues and which functionally is a part of any business, and services at and after the sale, sometimes called field service, or services for which there could be, or is, a direct association of both revenues and cost and which can be managed as either a profit center or line of business. In some cases, including any general service business, both the presale and aftersale services exist. In other cases, however, a combination of both product and service activities leads to the possibility of independent presales services (i.e., general customer services) as a general staff function, with postsale services being run as a separate profit or cost center. Pure product companies, for which presales service exists as a general staff function, have no need for full capability for aftersale service and support. In summary, in our discussion, analysis, and evaluation, our emphasis is on service businesses at and after the sale, as opposed to services before the sale as a staff function, unless such activities are tied into the general conduct of the service business.

SERVICE OPERATIONS IN DIFFERENT MARKET SEGMENTS

The basic concepts in service management, as described earlier, can be identified in a wide range of specific business markets and industries, including:

- Manufacturing using direct or indirect distribution channels
- Hospitals and healthcare
- Transportation and distribution
- Finance/insurance
- Banking
- Third- and fourth-party services providers
- Wholesale/retail
- Professional services

In the general market, as shown in Figure 2.1, three broad types of organizations (from a service perspective) exist:

- *Product manufacturers* have internal services to support their own plant and building operations, most also have external services to support products sold into the field, either directly or through indirect channels.
- *Traditional service businesses*, which include banking, healthcare, insurance, finance, transportation and distribution, and wholesale and retail operations, have internal service forces and also provide services to their customer base.
- *Third- and fourth-party service providers* comprise a new class of companies that do not manufacturer, sell, or own products or technologies but simply provide services as an independent (third or fourth) party.*

---

* These types of organizations offer a substitute for both the internal and external services provided by the first two classes of organizations. The term *third party* comes from contract law, which usually identifies the *first party* as the seller and the *second party* as the buyer of a product. Historically, third-party organizations moved into service by offering to provide service and support on an independent basis. In this terminology, a *fourth party* is an organization providing service to third parties.

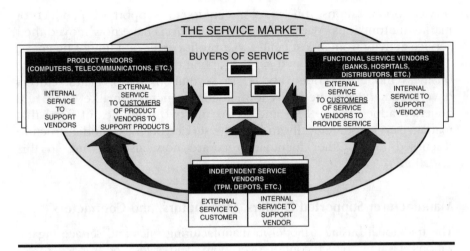

Figure 2.1   The overall service market.

Discussion of each of the industries or market segments from the perspective of a service business model is presented below.

Manufacturing Segment

Manufacturers, especially those operating in high-tech markets such as computers, office automation, and telecommunications, usually have their own external service organization or use wholesalers or retailers for sales and service. If a manufacturer uses direct sales channels and the product being sold requires services for design, engineering, installation, maintenance, and repair, this service requirement must be met. In such cases in which the manufacturer utilizes an indirect distribution channel through wholesalers, retailers, or contractors, the manufacturer's at and aftersale service requirement is limited (this approach is discussed later in this chapter).

In cases, where the buying customer's internal plant and building maintenance organizations are not capable of providing (or are not equipped to provide) services for the manufacturer's product or the manufacturer believes service is critically important to its customers and sees service as a competitive advantage, the manufacturer will build its own aftersale service organization. This was particularly true in the areas of data processing, advanced office automation (electronic copiers), telecommunications, and sophisticated medical and healthcare technology manufacturing. Organizations within those markets generally created service organizations run as cost centers in support of product or marketing functions. Many of these organizations have now moved their service activity from a cost center to a profit center or a line of business. These manufacturer-oriented service operations certainly fit the service business model described above. In several instances, manufacturers have used service strategically to maintain or increase market share and generate added value. IBM and Xerox are two examples of firms that manage service strategically and use the service business model structure discussed here. Other manufacturers are now also moving in this direction.

Manufacturer-Supported Dealers, Distributors, and Contractors

The traditional business model in manufacturing sales and service organizations assumes direct control over both field sales and service forces through local or regional field offices, in addition to central or national oversight, in order to provide market control. However, in product markets such as automobiles, office equipment, construction equipment, electrical distribution, lighting systems, material handling equipment, cable television, or satellite communications, more typical business models employ indirect channels through dealers, distributors, or contractors, with only general supervision and control in the field by the product manufacturer. This alternative service and sales structure is less expensive and involves a smaller investment than the direct model of manufacturing service described above. In this indirect model, the sales and service responsibilities are assigned to independent retail dealers, distributors, and contractors who take full responsibility for the sales and service of a manufacturer's product within their charter area of responsibility. Usually, this charter is defined geographically (by region) or by product mix or some combination of the two. Dealers and distributors can represent one manufacturer or several, particularly if the manufacturers' products are not directly competitive.

In this indirect channel sales and service field strategy, the manufacturer's responsibilities in the end-user market are primarily marketing and sales support and are directed toward influencing customers to purchase from that manufacturer's dealers and distributors. Some manufacturers also have their own direct sales to major national or international accounts.

In general, in these types of arrangements, the individual dealer or distributor operates its own sales and service organization and typically utilizes service as a mechanism for market penetration and market control and as a source of incremental revenues and profits. In fact, in some markets the profitability of the dealer's service business is significantly greater than the profitability of the dealer's product business. Some manufacturers prefer this indirect model because it significantly reduces front-end investment in distribution; it also reduces control and management of customer service and satisfaction in the field.

In this typical situation, the major manufacturer provides certain types of support to its retail dealer service network, including:

- *Warranty/credits.* The dealer usually supplies the warranty service and is credited by the manufacturer for the work done.
- *Parts and logistics support.* The manufacturer supplies parts to the dealer to support dealer service or for direct sale to end-users.
- *Training.* Manufacturer provides dealer training.
- *Technical assistance and support.* Such support by the manufacturer is particularly provided during new product introduction and roll-out.

Although some manufacturers attempt to create a standard service management system infrastructure or at least reporting mechanisms to coordinate dealer sales and service, others let their dealers make their own decisions about systems and infrastructure, particularly if vendors are available to step up and offer software and network-type infrastructure designed for specific dealer requirements.

In this service business environment that includes dealers, distributors, and contractors, it is of interest to look closely at the future direction of this indirect channel business model from the standpoint of service and support, taking into account:

- What the manufacturer should do to improve support to its retail dealer or distributor base without impacting the independent entrepreneurial spirit of the dealer organizations
- How individual dealers and contractors can achieve economies of scale or make use of advanced technology within the framework of their local financial structure and economic base

Areas of Potential Improvement in the Indirect Wholesale and Retail Services and Distribution Channels

In this regard, it is worthwhile to examine new technology and infrastructure development that could improve the efficiency of service operations at both the manufacturer and dealers level in the indirect channel business model:

- *Improving warranty, claims, processing, systems and technology.* For the last few years, vendors have started to develop warranty processing system software designed for use by both the manufacturer and its dealer base. The software provides warranty and claims processing capabilities on an application service provider (ASP) or service bureau basis; in effect, it offers the capability to outsource the entire warranty/claims process to achieve more timely and accurate performance.

■ *Service assignment, scheduling, and dispatch.* Most dealers and contractors lack advanced tools for handling service calls and for determining an optimum assignment and dispatch process that takes into account the availability of parts, levels of service commitments, needs of regional or national accounts, etc. Improved capabilities for scheduling and assignment at the dealer and contractor level, supported by the national manufacturer, could be very helpful.

■ *Parts/logistics improvements.* Extensive studies of many different indirect channel operations clearly show that logistics/parts support by the manufacturer to the dealers and contractors and to the dealer service forces in the field can be significantly improved. Very often a very long delay occurs between the time that the dealer service person in the field needs a part and when that part is finally delivered, simply because of the need to go through at least two bureaucratic/organization levels at both the dealer and manufacturer level. In addition, very little attempt has been made to optimize the full logistics pipeline control in a complex manufacturer/dealer operating structure. In addition, organizations traditionally operating as physical distribution specialists now provide full logistics service and support capability to the field level. By taking over the actual physical parts inventory, establishing repair depots, and utilizing extensive land and air transportation facilities, these organizations are able to minimize the cost of spare parts inventory in the full logistics pipeline and significantly decrease the time involved in delivery of parts required from the field.

■ *Field communications.* Significant new breakthroughs are also taking place in the area of field service communications on a wireless basis, with full global positioning service (GPS) and voice recognition.

The Impact of New Outsourcing Trends on Retail Dealers and Distributors

It is of interest to note that the indirect distribution channel, utilizing dealers, distributors, and contractors, has often been a business model of choice, especially where customers require a high degree of local sales support service. This retail distribution delivery model has been used especially where purchasers operate their own internal plant or building maintenance organizations and therefore do not require a high level of break-and-fix field service. However, a number of trends are beginning to change the character and level of field service and support that dealers and distributors have to provide. As indicated in Figure 2.2, key trends such as aging of the internal plant and building maintenance service organizations and increased integration and networking of systems are leading to more outsourcing of the internal plant and building maintenance forces.

What happens when these new trends require a much higher level of field service and support on the part of the retail dealers, distributors, and contractors? What action should be taken by both the parent original equipment manufacturer (OEM) and by the dealers, distributors, and contractors themselves in the face of these changes?

Original equipment manufacturers supporting indirect retail dealer, distribution, and contractor channels need to provide the following centralized capabilities to their dealers and distributors in order to improve overall field service efficiency. These include:

- Improved parts logistics, forecasting, planning, control, and distribution
- Establishment of a regional or national technical assistance centers
- Online real-time access to technical documentation, reliability, and configuration control data
- Rapid and efficient warranty processing

From the perspective of the individual retail dealers and distributors, improvements must be made in the following areas:

- Capabilities for call handling, diagnostics, and work force scheduling in order to improve the efficiency of allocation and scheduling of dealer labor personnel in the field
- Effectiveness of real-time communications to and from dealer or distributor field service personnel
- Central and dealer-level repair depot processing changing from job-shop to just-in-time sequencing

In summary, increased outsourcing of the traditional internal plant and building maintenance organizations is leading to greater dependence on service from retail dealers, distributors, and contractors. This dependence requires focus and cooperation by both the OEM and the dealers and distributors to handle the new service requirements being imposed in the field. This is especially true during the early stages of product launch and warranty coverage. The OEM must develop new product launches that include providing training for the field dealers and distributors for the new products, that supply the correct parts, and that allow for timely

Trend	Issues	Impact
Aging of internal plant and building maintenance forces	Average age is approaching 52. Skills are primarily mechanical and electromechanical, not electronic. Social costs (pension, medical, sick leave, etc.) are increasing.	Outsourcing of internal plant and building maintenance forces is increasing.
Technology becoming more sophisticated and computer controlled	Technology requires skills, training, and parts not in the hands of internal maintenance forces. Applications and functions are now software driven rather than hardware driven	New skills and diagnostic capabilities are required. Individual service engineers without real-time access to data and technical assistance are at a disadvantage.
Individual technologies becoming linked and networked as one integrated system	Service personnel need both network and integration experience and education, not generally in place with internal forces.	Network-linked diagnostic capabilities and configuration control have become increasingly important.
Individual manufacturers now using more common parts (microprocessors) Buyers no longer purchasing future spares	Decisions on what parts to stock and where they are needed require sophisticated systems and forecasting technology. Equipment owners no longer have parts on site.	Logistics and control of parts and full logistics pipeline are very important. Operations are parts forecasting driven.
Just-in-time manufacturing, for example, requires rapid response, measured in hours, not days	Rapid response to on-site plant and building maintenance still exists. Alternative service suppliers must be able to respond rapidly.	Outsourcers must invest in online real-time infrastructure and systems to provide just-in-time support.

Figure 2.2   Key trends affecting service market potential in the field.

processing of warranty coverage claims for reimbursement; otherwise, sales of the new product line will suffer. The lack of efficient OEM warranty processing of dealer claims can lead to serious problems between the dealers and the parent OEM, in addition to a failure to collect accurate mean time between failure (MTBF), mean time to repair (MTTR), and other reliability data.

Where is this happening and what are the options? Figure 2.3 shows the key market segments now being most affected by these important outsourcing trends (shown in Figure 2.2). In these particular segments and niches, the impact on dealers, distributors, and contractors is now growing, and manufacturers in these segments using the indirect distribution model must take immediate action, in conjunction with their dealers and distributors to step up to these new demands.

HEALTH CARE

Healthcare facilities, particularly hospitals, are clearly service organizations that are going through a major, almost revolutionary change in terms of the application and use of service management systems and technology. The reasons are varied but generally fall into three driving issues:

1. The switch in healthcare focus (at least in the United States) from cost reimbursement for services rendered to profit center management based on defined Diagnostic Related Groups (DRGs). Under this approach, healthcare facilities are given a comprehensive description of medical and healthcare procedures defined in terms of the diagnostic patterns defining the need for the procedures, descriptions of the procedures and processes themselves, and prices or reimbursements for the services provided. For example, different DRGs apply to the treatment of pneumonia and a broken leg. For any given DRG, the healthcare facility is compensated based upon the DRG procedures and payments. Facilities that can complete specific DRG processes under the DRG payment terms make a profit on those processes; if their costs for particular procedures are greater than the DRG payment terms for those procedures, they lose money. In essence, the DRG business model converted healthcare facilities from service cost centers to service profit centers, or lines of business.

2. The need to increase market density to increase economies of scale has, in turn, led healthcare facilities to broaden their outsourcing into the community. Many hospitals have moved from a single building, or even multiple buildings on the same campus, to region-wide healthcare services involving the combination of full health-

Market Segments	Important Niches	Immediate Trends	
		Internal Plant and Building Maintenance Force	Manufacturers and Dealers Immediate Trends
Industrial, commercial, and residential building owners and operators Banks Insurance and finance Wholesale/retail General office, etc.	Field, and central repair and depot support HVAC/electrical systems Voice/data/security networks Lighting Office equipment	Increased outsourcing of building maintenance forces Technology becoming more sophisticated	Some manufacturers going out of services Some dealers not equipped to handle rapid on-site services
Manufacturers	Process control and plant automation Robotics systems Material handling Other plant technology	Increased outsourcing of plant maintenance forces Technology becoming more sophisticated	Some manufacturers going out of services Some dealers not equipped to handle rapid on-site services
Hospices and health care	Medical technology Pacs technology Communications systems Building systems	Increased outsourcing of building maintenance forces Technology becoming more sophisticated Doctors offices and clinics, now owned by hospital	Some manufacturers going out of services Some dealers not equipped to handle rapid on-site services
Construction	Construction materials Construction tools and equipment	Support in field construction very haphazard and inefficient	Some manufacturers going out of services Some dealers not equipped to handle rapid on-site services

Transportation and distribution	Parts, subsystems for field and central (depot) repair for railroads and airlines, for example	Downsizing and outsourcing of service support	Some manufacturers going out of services Some dealers not equipped to handle rapid on-site services
Utilities (electric, gas, water, communication)	Field and central (depot) repair Logistics support	Downsizing and outsourcing due to deregulation and consolidation	Some manufacturers going out of services Some dealers not equipped to handle rapid on-site services
Government	Full logistics support Depot repair	Logistics and maintenance support shifting from internal responsibilities to outsourcing	Some manufacturers going out of services Some dealers not equipped to handle rapid on-site services
Printing and publishing/graphic arts	Prepress Production Image networks	Increased outsourcing of plant maintenance forces New technology	Some manufacturers going out of services Some dealers not equipped to handle rapid on-site services

Figure 2.3 Key trends in selected market segments creating new service opportunities.

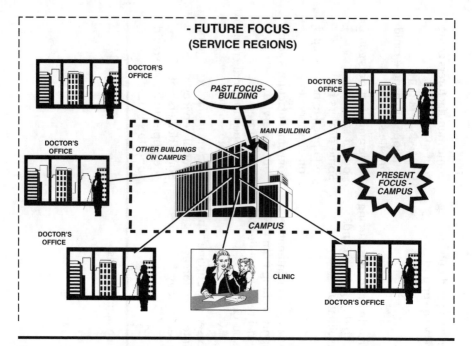

Figure 2.4 Emerging hospital service environment.

care service facilities (hospitals), separately located doctor's offices, and outpatient clinics (Figure 2.4).

3. New infrastructure and technology (particularly with respect to advanced diagnostic imaging systems), improved surgical suite technology, improved systems for patient record management, and advanced medically oriented telecommunications approaches have all led to an improvement in the management infrastructure of healthcare facilities.

These major trends combine to create a new service business model that must deal with two classes of customers:

1. Patients, potential patients, and past patients. The primary customer base of a healthcare facility is obviously its current and prospective patients and its primary orientation is to handle these customers rapidly and efficiently. The most significant costs of a healthcare facility relate to the use of its labor (e.g., doctors or nurses) and infrastructure (e.g., hospital beds or physical therapy facilities), and the DRG management approach provides incentive for the health-care facility to move patients through the system as rapidly as possible, penalizing the facility if too long a period of time is taken

in the application and use of these facilities and personnel to carry out a specific DRG process.

2. *Medical labor in terms of professionals and support staff.* The second customer group of healthcare facilities is the medical professionals and staff, who are supported by advanced technology that has been developed and installed in typical healthcare facilities and is generally designed to augment the medical professional or reduce or eliminate unnecessary activities. Diagnostic imaging technology, such as computed tomography (CT) and magnetic resonance imaging (MRI), significantly reduce the time required to process and read the images and they increase the accuracy of x-rays. New surgical technologies make operations less invasive and risky and reduce preparation or performance time.

In summary, healthcare facilities require a fully integrated service management approach and CRM infrastructure that provide both the patient and the medical professional and support staff with a full service approach.

TRANSPORTATION AND DISTRIBUTION

Another market segment that clearly falls into the category of service businesses consists of organizations focused on transportation and distribution. These are organizations that provide air, rail, truck, bus, and sea transportation services along with movement, stock piling, and exchange of passengers and freight. A simple review of many of the major companies in this market (including firms such as United Parcel Service; Federal Express; major railroads such as CSX and BNSF; and airlines such as United, American, or USAir) will reveal a general functional structure for all of the companies that is similar to the business models discussed in Chapter 1. The general trends found in the generic service organization include consolidation to achieve economies of scale, the use of advanced infrastructure to support the call management and logistics management processes, and increased use of data as a key resource to manage, control, and deliver services in response to changing random demands and are all very typical of the processes found in this segment.

ELECTRIC, GAS, AND COMMUNICATION UTILITIES

This segment is clearly a service in that these companies produce and distribute energy services or communication services to their customer bases. Traditionally, these businesses are run as a monopoly and managed through a regulatory process that sets prices as a function of cost reimbursement. The regulatory agencies involved have tended to focus on a requirement for efficiency in the production of these services, but less so in the distribution of the services. With full deregulation in the telecommunications utility business segment and new attempts at deregulation in the power (gas and electric) segment, the increased focus on profitability and full service management is rapidly converting the traditional ways of doing business to the new service business model described in Chapter 1. Electric, gas, and communication utilities are now focused strongly on the customer requirements, willingness to pay, array of services required, and competitive options, rather than on the analysis, evaluation, and data collection regarding internal costs required to satisfy public utility commission investigations. Here, too, we find increased focus on the efficient and effective management and deployment of service labor and materials/logistics managed through sophisticated call handling and logistics support infrastructure, as well as technology. We also see a significant increase in viewing data as a critical resource for forecasting future demand and managing both the supply and distribution processes.

THIRD- AND FOURTH-PARTY SERVICE PROVIDERS

A relatively new market segment that has entered the general marketplace includes organizations providing services as a separate line of business. Such companies are generally referred to as third-party (or fourth-party) providers, and they do not manufacture, sell, or distribute products but offer services. These organizations are generally in the business of providing field services to customers, depot repair, logistics, and transportation support services, or professional design and engineering or consulting services. These organization are being affected by two critical trends:

1. Economic benefits from outsourcing or subcontracting services that are not in the area of core competence of companies, including those organizations wishing to eliminate the high costs and low efficiencies associated with internal plant and building maintenance activities, as well as the cost and lack of performance associated with managing certain high-tech infrastructures, such as information technology networks or water treatment.

2. Interest on the part of product purchasers to move to an alternative to OEM managed and supported services. Because many OEMs in the computer, office automation, and telecommunication industries tended to view service of their technology as a highly profitable annuity, buyers of high technology found that the cost of aftersale service was continuing to rise. This increase led to a search on the part of the buyers interested in reducing these aftersales support costs to find alternative third-party providers.

Organizations providing third- and fourth-party services currently utilize the same business models and infrastructure described in the previous chapter.

FINANCE AND INSURANCE

In the financial and insurance sector, the service business model is less complex because the logistics is not a critical or important issue; however, this market requires extremely sophisticated call management capabilities and the ability to manage, coordinate, control, and access data. In the financial and insurance sector, the ability to respond rapidly and accurately to customer requirements for service and support is critical.

BANKING

Bank operations fit the service business model (described above) well. Both labor and material (cash) exist as resources, and the ability to manage and control data regarding the banking processes, portfolios, individual customer accounts, etc. is critical. Banks provide their services through their central and branch operations or through transactional systems, such as automated teller machines (ATMs) or online services. Here, again, time is critical, as is the ability to preserve the perception of a given level of service.

GENERAL WHOLESALE/RETAIL

One of the most complex and fragmented service sectors is the wholesale and retail field. Many wholesalers and retailers deal with products and, therefore, think in terms of product. However, in every case (except for a special few anomalies), wholesalers and retailers have the labor, logistics, and data components required to manage this process. The logistics covers the ability to provide the products which are sold.

We have already discussed the role of wholesalers and retailers in the indirect channel supporting high-tech and other product manufacturers. Many retailers such as Sears, Circuit City, Radio Shack, Wal-Mart, or Target offer services to their customers as part of their total value proposition. Restaurants such as McDonald's or Wendy's also fit within the general service business model in which customers arriving for food service are handled through a particular call process that utilizes labor, material (meat, bread, vegetables, etc.), and data on customer needs and requirements to deliver their service. Here, again, as in other markets, service time is critical and the perception of the ability to deliver the appropriate quality of service within a required time frame is strategically important to conducting business.

OTHER SERVICE BUSINESS SITUATIONS AND OPPORTUNITIES

The previous discussion has served to show that the service business model structure, as outlined in Chapter 1, has relevance in a broad array of different market segments. It has also been designed to show that the CRM infrastructure and systems technology concepts for service management transcend the product-oriented framework in which most of our management thinking is focused. In essence, the same functionality and systems technologies that work in a high-tech, capital-intensive service framework, such as the servicing and support of computers and office automation technology, can also be applied in low-tech situations, as well as in situations for which there is no tangible product, merely a customer. Thus, from the perspective of this new service management approach, the only real difference between the service business and support of a high-tech manufacturer or hospital or retail organization (see Figure 2.1) is the language and jargon used to describe the operation. In fact, service is not just another "product". However, the question arises as to whether or not the new service business model can be applied in less structured situations or under unusual market conditions. Some anecdotal illustrations of situations are discussed here to demonstrate the value of the new service model.

Locomotive Maintenance Service

The railroads, developed in the 1800s, came into their own as a major transportation service mechanism in the early 1900s as a result of technological innovations in locomotives and related control mechanisms, such as air brakes, and coupling systems. The locomotive was king in the railway service business; in fact, senior managers and executives tended to be promoted from the motive power management staff. In the early days, locomotives required a tremendous amount of service and support for maintenance and repairs, fueling, and servicing of locomotive components. This need for service continued during the transition from steam to diesel technology in the mid-1950s. Railroads generally bought their locomotives from outside vendors, such as General Motors, General Electric, or Siemens, just as they had bought their steam locomotives from Baldwin, Lima Hamilton, or Alco, if they were not built in their own locomotive erection shops.

While the locomotive manufacturer did provide some limited technology advisory services, these were provided for free or at low cost and were generally viewed as being in support of the locomotive product sale. At the end of the 1990s, as railroads merged and consolidated and management was taken over by financial- or marketing-oriented executives (as opposed to motive power experts), the railroads began to question why they continued to use so much labor, materials, and infrastructure in support of locomotive maintenance and support. The result of these inquiries was that the railroads began to turn to their manufacturing suppliers to determine whether they could offer such services as a separate line of business. For some manufacturers, this was a decided change in market conditions and situations, as their view traditionally was that service was generally a cost of and adjunct to the product sale of locomotives. Some manufacturers (including General Electric) began to recognize that service was an interesting and potentially profitable business on its own. In fact, the demand for locomotive servicing in the United States is more than twice as large as the demand for locomotive products. General Electric Transportation Systems (GETS) addressed this new service market by building a service-oriented infrastructure and focusing on the locomotive service and support needs of the railroad customers. General Motors' Electro-Motive Division (EMD) has also now moved in this direction.

In this case, as a result of changes in customer orientation and requirements, the major suppliers of locomotives have now moved into the third- and fourth-party service support of locomotives as a strategic service-based line of business. This is a real example of how customers' requirements can change and how the need for a particular service can effect a major change in the fortunes and roles of the product suppliers, creating new business opportunities or threats, depending upon one's point of view. In essence, new service opportunities are created when customers move away from servicing and supporting their own infrastructures and technologies or general support functions toward external means for doing the same through outsourcing. Product organizations selling to their customer base can also effect such a move toward outsourcing through proactive offers to take over more services. Failure to take advantage of this opportunity, either proactively or reactively, can significantly threaten the future of the product organization.

The Funeral Director Business

The business of funeral directors was for a very long time viewed within the context of classical product orientation, with a focus on the casket. In general, a potential customer seeking a funeral director would, after a short period of time, be taken to the "casket room" where a variety of caskets of varying levels of quality were displayed. The customer's ultimate choice of a casket (product) determined the level of quality of service the funeral director would provide. In essence, in the traditional funeral director business, the focus was on the sale of the casket as a product, with the associated services (embalming, transportation to the cemetery, etc.) being viewed as an adjunct to the product sale. However, with the growing popularity of cremation and the emergence of a new class of organizations selling either directly or through the Internet, caskets have become separated from funeral directors services, and the market has changed. The passing of laws that require funeral directors to provide services even when customers are able to provide their own caskets put a nail in the coffin of managing funerals from a product standpoint.

Funeral directors have been required to rethink their business in service terms and to place much more attention on the key functions involved in managing the service business. For example, many directors now offer a funeral contract in advance of death, a concept directly comparable to the perceived ability to provide a service, as discussed earlier. Some funeral directors focus on service requirements of specific segments. For example, the funeral service needs of a Jewish family are different from the requirements of a Catholic or Irish family. Here, again, the funeral directors business has switched from a product business orientation (i.e., selling the casket and associated services) to a service line of business focus.

Religious Institutions

Another example of application of the service business model is the management and direction of religious organizations. Ethnic and religious commitments of a traditional nature have changed; religion has become much more of a business. In some religions, the doctrine and the infrastructure are managed and directed directly by the church itself; in other religions, however, the church or synagogue is owned or run by the lay people as a non-profit business. The boards and executive directors of these organizations have begun to face some very severe problems associated with managing and directing the services offered and balancing the budget determined by revenues and costs. While on the surface it would appear that a primary role of churches and synagogues is the provision of religious services, the fact is that their "customers" require more than just religious services, including demands for education and training, social activities, and special occasions such as weddings, bar mitzvahs, or funerals. Many of the issues described for the general service model, such as the need to identify and appropriately schedule the services to be offered, require the need to manage both the perception and reality of the services as well as appropriate allocation of resources, which hold true for religious institutions.

SUMMARY

These anecdotal situations show that the basic service model concept and orientation can be useful in strategically managing a service business regardless of whether it is a manufacturer requiring service of its installed base, a retailer, a bank, an insurance company, a funeral director, a religious institution, or an organization that traditionally did not provide service as a business but whose customers now require new services. As shown in Figure 2.5 and in the discussion, just about all service businesses and service components of manufacturing organizations fit the basic model structure described in Chapter 1. Each is involved in managing a combination of labor, logistics, and data to create both the actual service and the ability to serve within a given time frame. In all of these service environments, time is critical and is a critical strategic element of the business process. The jargon and descriptions of basic processes and technologies will vary and the reasons for moving into viewing service as a profit center or line of business may differ, but the underlying models are the same.

To apply these concepts, we must first take the business at hand and restructure it in terms of a new service model, which means identifying the labor, material, and information resources required and, more importantly, identifying and describing both the actual service performance and production and the perceived ability to serve as engines of production. In doing so, we need to identify, understand, and develop the service requirements of the customer base in terms of the specific and explicit services required, the time frame in which the services are to be provided, and the parameters and mechanisms by which the customer measures service quality and satisfaction. This transition requires a quantitative and objective evaluation of both internal and external factors and operational environments. The next step would be to create a series of service portfolio scenarios that include pricing and delivery mechanisms that could meet customer requirements and to identify the service strategy and vision that offer the highest return on investment at minimum risk. The final strategy can then be implemented and taken to market through implementation of the appropriate executive direction and vision and systems infrastructure and technology, based upon customer relationship management, as well as real-time concepts, market and customer focus, and penetration that achieve maximum density.

Sector	Key Components			Critical Impact of Time	Existence of Two or More Optimization Objectives
	Labor	Material	Data		
Manufacturing with support services	Yes	Parts and supplies	Yes	Yes	Yes
Health care	Yes	Equipment	Yes	Yes	Yes
Wholesale/retail selling	Yes	Products sold	Yes	Yes	Yes
Manufacturing products		Clothes Food Other products			
Finance/insurance	Yes	No	Yes	Yes	Yes
Banking	Yes	Cash	Yes	Yes	Yes
Transportation	Yes	Vehicles	Yes	Yes	Yes
Professional services	Yes	No	Yes	Yes	Yes
Third- and fourth-party services	Yes	Yes	Yes	Yes	Yes

Figure 2.5 Service market segment analysis.

3

KEY SERVICE MANAGEMENT ELEMENTS

CONTENTS

As indicated in the previous two chapters, one can view the management of service as a line of business or as a profit center, generically (as described in Chapter 1) or specifically (as described in Chapter 2). Clearly, as in any other function such as marketing, manufacturing, or finance, the particular structure, character, and, most importantly, jargon and language will vary from market segment to market segment. As an example, a service person in a bank is called a teller; in a restaurant, a waiter; and in the high-tech field, a service engineer. They all, however, more or less follow the same general or generic model. The logistics focus (material) may also change from market to market. The high-tech field deals with parts; restaurants, food; and banks, cash. The basic processes and treatments are the same, though. Within this general framework, then, we now take a look at the major components of the service management structure that affect the overall performance efficiency and profitability of an organization, including:

- Service executives and management personnel (i.e., those people responsible for the overall direction and supervision of the enterprise)
- Technology and infrastructure utilized to manage the service labor and material using the available data regarding customers of the enterprise and the status of the service organization capabilities and deployment
- Market and customer base served in terms of its market density and volume

As indicated in Figure 3.1, the management direction that makes use of the infrastructure to manage the internal labor and material assets through which the customer base is served defines the overall management paradigm for a service enterprise. This strategic model (already described in Chapter 1) can be developed through benchmark measurement (internal assessment) and customer satisfaction measurement. Internal benchmarking measurement is described in Appendix A. Customer satisfaction processes are discussed in Part II.

This chapter discusses the first of these key elements, the executive and management structure itself, in terms of its roles, missions, requirements, and needs, and introduces the other two elements of infrastructure and marketing density, both of which are discussed in much more detail in Part II.

MANAGEMENT IN THE SERVICE ENTERPRISE

Extensive experience clearly shows that executive and senior management direction, vision, and general strategy are crucial to the success to any service organization. In essence, a business simply does not run itself. However, as discussed in Chapter 1, the basic business model, which is built upon the presumption of a product, is not rich or definitive enough to enable the typical executive or manager to deal with the complexities of a service business. More often, complaints from executives or managers are brought up in a product environment that service is too complex or does not fit the same business standards. Executives and managers moving

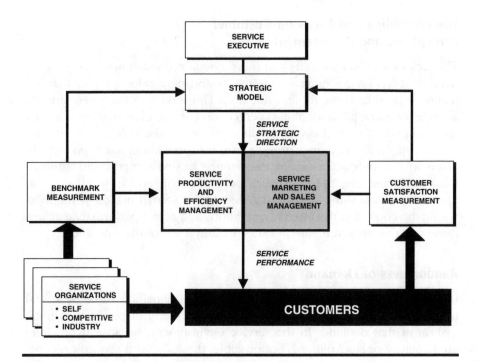

Figure 3.1   The service strategic direction process.

into the service environment are often called upon to "think out of the box" or to be "market centric". These broad descriptions are driven by the vague appreciation that managing and optimizing a service business are in certain ways different from doing the same for a product business. What, then, are the primary skills and capabilities that an executive or manager should have in order to address the issues and problems associated with managing a service business? At a minimum, a service executive or manager must understand and have experience in the following concepts.

Operating Environments in Which Lack of a Tangible Product Inventory Makes Time Sensitivity a Critical Element of Analysis and Management

A real difference in service vs. a product business lies in the critical importance of time, particularly time viewed from the perception of the buyer or market. In general, the markets of service businesses are very time sensitive in terms of such factors as the time of day and day of week coverage, response time, service completion time, guaranteed performance within a certain time, etc. The service executive must be very sensitive to time and time-related issues in their management process.

Understanding and Focus on Customer Perceptions and Requirements

The lack of a product means that the service executive must recognize the need to focus on customer requirements and perceptions, rather than the reality of product form, fit, and function. The service environment and the attitude or perception of the potential or current customer are, in fact, more important than the view of the service provision from the supplier standpoint. In essence, in a product business, maximum attention must be given to the product itself. In the service business, maximum attention must be focused on the customer's perception of service. In effect, management measures and data must reflect both external market perceptions within the context of the internal operations and actual performance against these external requirements in order to fully control the operation.

Randomness of Demand

In the product environment, the randomness of demand can be dealt with through building up an inventory or the stockpiling of products in anticipation of that demand. In the service environment, because maintaining an inventory or stockpiling is not possible, the successful service executive or manager must understand the theories of statistics and probability necessary to put into place procedures capable of meeting unanticipated or rapidly changing demand patterns. Doing so requires that service executives understand the importance of excess capacity in meeting customer requirements. In a product environment, the excess capacity situation must be minimized; however, in a service environment, excess capacity is the key to meeting the rapidly changing requirements of customers.

Market- and Market-Segment-Oriented Focus

Most product-oriented executives immediately accept the concept of market segmentation as a basis for differentiating products; however, for many, the idea of segmenting customers in a service environment is not as obvious. In fact, though, different service requirements are found in the various market segments and subsegments. The service requirements in banking, in which some banks are open 5 days a week, 8 hours a day, are quite a bit different from hospitals, in which the service is 7 days a week, 24 hours a day. An insurance company's ability to process claims rapidly can give it a competitive advantage over others who do not. A reasonably high correlation between meeting customer/market requirements for service time and customers willingness to pay has been observed (discussed further in Chapter 11). Those service organizations that more effectively meet the service time expectations and needs of specific customer segments and, in effect, charge a premium for the added value will be more profitable and well managed than those that do not.

Need for Strong Grounding in Marketing and Sales Management

Successful executives and managers in all business environments must understand and have some basic training in finance, administration, and marketing. Because many service organizations historically operated as cost centers or in support of a product or manufacturing business, it has generally been assumed that service managers did not require such interdisciplinary training. However, as service has moved to become a profit center or line of business, it is essential that the service executive manger become fully crossed trained. The need to understand marketing and selling is especially important in terms of the criticality of market density in managing service business. In summary, the successful service executive or manager will have an orientation in, and experience with, service-type businesses in which time and customer perceptions are critically important. These individuals should view service as a stand-alone business, with its own revenues, costs, and profit margins, as opposed to an adjunct to another business. Finally, the successful service executive or manager should understand at least the general concepts of marketing and sales and infrastructure design and technology.

Finding and Recruiting Service Managers and Executives

Unfortunately, at present, very few schools produce trained service executives and managers. Most undergraduate and graduate programs tend to focus on management within the context of a product business environment. Alternatively, service-oriented management courses and programs tend to deal with specific, anecdotal service business (e.g., banking, insurance, or retail). Therefore, the classically trained manager might not be fully educated in all the elements required to successfully manage and direct a service business. On the other hand, individuals with a well-defined business management or marketing management education are probably best equipped to deal with the subject. Obviously, formal management and marketing training coupled with experience in a service environment will help to produce an individual or individuals who can be successful in managing service as a business.

Managing and Recruiting Service Personnel

Moving away from a focus on senior service management and executives toward operational personnel in the service business environment, the supply of candidates is much greater. Many vocational and technical schools train personnel for service positions in fields such as technology, product maintenance and repair, banking, retail, insurance, or health care. Because of its high percentage of service-oriented activities, the military has also has been a traditional source of field service and support personnel. Finally, many organizations establish their own internal training and orientation programs in order to train newly hired service personnel in the specifics of their assigned service responsibilities. These service programs typically run between 2 and 4 weeks.

Use of Systems and Infrastructure in Managing the Service Enterprise

Having established a senior service executive and management structure, we can then turn to the design, construction, and implementation of the management systems infrastructure. This infrastructure will make use of customer relationship management (CRM) principles and technology but will have an increased level of focus on the specific functions, processes, and dynamic structures associated with managing the service enterprise. This design and structure are discussed further in Part II.

Marketing Density and Improvement to Achieve Economies of Scale

The final aspect of managing the service business is focusing on the served market. In both the retail and real estate business, three factors are most critical: location, location, location. This is another way of recognizing that the served market density is a critical key to success in service. If we can find a location that offers the maximum access to customers or can create a service portfolio and service focus that achieves the highest density customer base, we can, in turn, maximize our ability to achieve economies of scale and service. Density can be directly related to response time, travel time, and the ability to make maximum use of the logistics resources and material availability. Mechanisms to measure service requirements, needs, expectations, and perceptions and the model, structure, and dynamics required to increase customer base density are discussed in Part III.

II

CRM AND SMS
TECHNOLOGY

In Part I, we established that data and information are crucial resources in managing a service business. Through the use of infrastructure, systems, and technology, we can capture, organize, evaluate, forecast, and present results relative to customer demand in real time, as well as future requirements. In the service environment, this idea of a full, seamless, integrated approach to the management, coordination, control, and dissemination of data and information is known as Customer Relationship Management (CRM). Part II describes the general CRM infrastructure and technology, current and emerging state of the art, and functional concepts.

As we look to the design concepts, architecture, and application focus of CRM and supportive service management, we should consider those issues discussed in Part I dealing with the current fragmentation of service management processes. As we indicated, service businesses come in a wide variety of forms, ranging from banking services to healthcare services to servicing of high technology. All of these cases have service customers, and the service organization must offer both perceptions of the capability to serve and the actual service. Every service business requires personnel and service-related material.

However, as pointed out in Chapter 3, the terminology used differs. In banking, the service person is a teller and the material includes cash. In restaurants, the service person is a waiter or waitress and the material includes food and plates. In a high-tech service environment, the service person is a service engineer and the material includes parts. We offer a hypothesis that has been pragmatically tested, which, regardless of whether we are dealing with banking services, food services, or high-tech equipment services, the basic infrastructure and the strategic approach are the same. The differences are primarily found in the jargon and operating environment.

In our discussion of the infrastructure and technology required to manage service, we must deal with the issue of applying CRM and related real-time systems technology for service management while avoiding tedious and potentially overwhelming problems of describing the process and technology applications for each specific service business applications area. From a pragmatic standpoint, the fact is that most of the advanced development in systems technology and infrastructure in service management has taken place in the high-tech service environment dealing with computer service, office automation services, telecommunications services, and medical technology services. We have, therefore, elected to use the high-tech service management environment as the framework for discussing CRM technology. In essence, although we will be discussing the most sophisticated functional processes within the current state of the art, the basic concepts of call and logistics management, field communications, and database management will always apply.

In fact, we have found that it is extremely useful to approach the issues of design, development, and implementation of CRM technology and infrastructure from the standpoint of this most sophisticated concept, because it forces a serious consideration of the various optimization tools and techniques and process flows that could be applied, rather than viewing the service management process as it has emerged on an evolutionary basis in the individual service markets. Based on this approach, we have been able to jump into new and different kinds of service environments, such as drink dispenser service, service of patients in healthcare environments, or service management of paint-store customers, using the high-tech service model. In essence, the basic principles and functionality remain the same. In order to apply these concepts successfully, analysts must think in terms of basic service management functions and technology, rather than in terms of specific processes applied within the various market segments.

4

INFRASTRUCTURE AND FUNCTIONS OF CRM AND SMS TECHNOLOGY

CONTENTS

Thus far, we have described the general concept and models associated with service management. The technology for Customer Relationship Management (CRM) and the Service Management System (SMS) deals with the management direction and control of the interface between past, present, and potential future customers of the service organization. In basic terms, CRM and SMS are designed to provide a seamless interface between the service buyer and the service seller, providing for the coordination and control of the two key physical resources (labor and material) in the service business through the use of a third resource (data). CRM was orginally developed for a product business environment, whereas SMS is designed for a service business environment. In service, the concepts of SMS and CRM are the same.

This new technology and infrastructure have been created through the merger of CRM systems and concepts, which are driven by a focus on sales automation and control of the manufacturing and distribution processes, with SMS, which is driven by the requirement to manage the service process. In this discussion, we focus on the general design and structure of the service-oriented components of CRM, focusing on the functionality and technology required. While we discuss critical CRM technology concepts, such as sales force automation, data warehousing, and data mining, within a review of the current state of the art, we also provide much more focus on the service-driven functionality required and available.

Using the general concept of the required infrastructure and technology for service management within the framework of the general CRM concepts, we can provide an overview of the general functions that must be considered. Service management systems and technology are driven primarily by customer needs and requirements for service. These requirements are generally handled by central, regional, or local call-handling operations or functions, augmented by additional capabilities for technical assistance, call diagnostics, and screening. This process can resolve customers' service needs and requirements immediately by assigning and dispatching the necessary service engineers or service personnel, who will generally have access to the material necessary to meet the customers' service needs and requirements. An important subcomponent of this logistics support process is the fact that, in certain types of situations and as a direct result of servicing the customer, certain items and materials in the field that are no longer required but have value must be returned for processing or disposal, with the processing leading to potentially a return to the full logistics pipeline. This general concept, illustrated in Figure 4.1, creates the need for general functions associated with call management, call diagnostics, service personnel assignment and dispatch, logistics support, and general coordination of the overall service cycle. This basic model, which operates within the general framework of the CRM concept (as shown in Figure 4.2), in turn requires implementation of operating processes, systems, and technology to support specific key functions. These functions are described below.

DESCRIPTION OF KEY FUNCTIONS SUPPORTED BY INTEGRATED SMS/CRM

The structure of these functions will vary from one business situation to another, but they will exist at some level and will exist whether the establishment is a retail sales organization or a high-tech manufacturer of computers offering service to its customers.

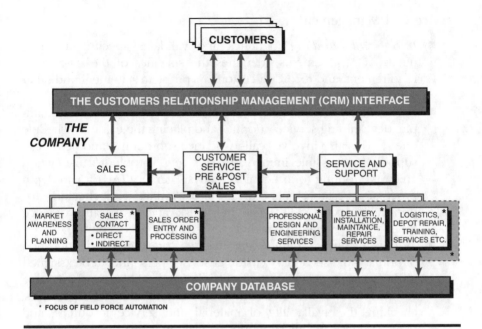

Figure 4.1 The general customer relations management concept.

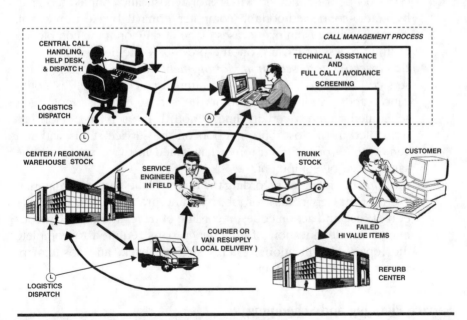

Figure 4.2 Primary functions in complex service operations.

Service Call Management

■ *Initial call handling* identifies and validates specific customer needs or requirements, identifies the specifics of the customer's requirement, and records a customer's problem statement and other special instructions.

■ *Processing of the customer's problem statement* includes, for example, determining service priorities and placing the call in a schedule queue. This also involves call-avoidance subroutines and help-desk support for possible immediate fixes (e.g., problem/cause/action analysis), routing to a technical analysis center (TAC) for in-depth processing, establishment of a call-back time, and checking for duplicate service calls. (The help-desk and TAC call-avoidance function is generally provided as a separate accessible function.)

■ *Making the service commitment* includes, for example, identification of primary and secondary customer service personnel to be assigned to the account; checking the availability and skill levels of available service technicians, mechanics, or customer service specialists; checking the availability of material and service resources; and paging service technicians prior to making a service commitment.

■ *Dispatching the service technician* to the customer or customer's site can be accomplished by telephone, by paging the service technician's beeper or handheld wireless or acoustically coupled terminal, by a radio-connected portable computer terminal, by electronic mail, etc. Dispatching is, in many cases, done during, or at the completion of, the process of closing out the previous customer's call.

■ *Call tracking and escalation management* includes updating of the service call status for any reason after dispatch, as well as notification and priority escalation if the service call has not been scheduled within a certain time period, if the service person has not called in to close out or report on the service status within a certain time, or if the customer has called in twice regarding the same piece of equipment.

■ *Call closeout* includes recording the time and the parts and materials used for the service task or job, updating problem codes, completion of case and action codes, recording of travel and miscellaneous expenses, identification of emergency parts required to complete the repair, identification of items shipped back, and a summary report of costs and expenses.

Service Planning and Scheduling

The typical service organization may also be involved in installing, maintaining, and supporting very complex equipment or equipment requiring installation or changes to physical structures, networks, etc. or simply preparing to install heating, ventilation, or air conditioning systems; therefore, project planning, preventive maintenance, and special task scheduling are necessary. These tasks include planning and scheduling capabilities for required installations and moves, adds, and changes, etc. The required functions include:

- *Project planning* requires the ability to define the resources required for a site location by type of project [predictive or preventative maintenance (PM), installation; moves, adds, changes (Mac); etc.], as well as identifying special installation tools and test equipment, recommended spare assemblies and parts, personnel resources required inside and outside the organization (subcontractors), contacts in other vendor organizations involved with the project, etc.
- *Maintenance scheduling* concerned with pre-planned work assignments to be reviewed against existing resources, schedules, current and future commitments, current and future budget allocations, etc. to ensure optimum deployment.

Logistics Management

Because material is an important component of the service delivery process, this functionality is generally required to provide basic logistics management and support and inventory control. The support should provide techniques for managing and controlling the complete service inventory and spare parts pipeline, from central and regional warehouses down to and including customer service representatives and the return repair cycle. Specific subfunctions include:

- *Inventory tracking and control* of the full logistics pipeline (from central warehouse to customer service representative level) keeps track of in-transit inventory and returned parts and equipment, in addition to providing borrowing control and repair/rehab stock control. Data are reported and tracked for effective and defective parts status by stockkeeping units (SKUs).
- *Customer spare parts order processing* includes online entry of orders, order pricing, order tracking and updating, allocation of inventory, automatic backordering as required, generation of picking documents, shipping papers and transportation documents (shipment optimization, way bills, and freight manifests), and recording data necessary for later billing and invoicing of the customer
- *Part management agreements* cover parts on customer sites or in special stocking locations and provide for the monitoring of used parts and their replenishment and ensuring revision compatibility with customer equipment.

- *Configuration management* keeps track of the installed base of customers and equipment being serviced, manufacturers of the equipment in the case of third-party maintenance, and any relocations of equipment in the field. Wherever it applies, this function will monitor revision of installed equipment and software used and will be updated whenever they are revised. (This subfunction should also be incorporated in the call handling and dispatch function to identify and verify parts and material requirements at customer sites.)
- *Inventory forecasting and planning* for all inventory stocking points allows better planning and forecasting of inventory and optimizes total inventory levels within the logistics pipeline.
- *Inventory replenishment* includes generation of material requisitions to the next higher inventory stocking level, identification of primary and secondary sources of supply for spare parts and consumables, generation of purchase orders to vendors or replenishment order to manufacturing facilities, quality control processing, and receipt processing to update inventory
- *Depot repair and scheduling rework/refurbishing operations* control schedules, tracks, and processes material through the depot rework facility.

Financial Control and Accounting

The key required basic functions include financial accounting and control and profit and loss analysis:

- *Invoicing and billing* are done for time and material service calls and for identification of maintenance contracts for which customer billing is due within 30, 60, or 90 days from the current date. Billing is the process of accumulating total cost and price data to enable the billing department to review, via online screen display or printed report, all data contained in the actual invoice. Invoicing is the actual generation of the customer's invoice and the recording of the customer's liability by creating an accounts receivable master file. The system should provide the capability to generate invoices or provide the data to a corporate financial and accounting system.
- *Cost allocation* of direct and indirect expenses is done to accurately reflect the profitability of the field service organization by customer, service area, service technician/mechanic, or other criteria, including (1) profit and revenues by product serviced, customer, or region; and (2) cost by type of service, product, or customer.

- *Customer credit checking* validates the customers' credit status for time and material and contract service calls.
- *Profit contribution analysis* determines profitability for the service organization in general and by specific type of service call, service area, service technician/mechanic, customer, equipment or product being maintained, maintenance contract, or any combination of these.

Database Management and Reporting

Critical to operations are the management and control of data and information describing customer relationships and structure. An integrated database management system that features a comprehensive, structured database to provide timely, accurate, and flexible information for reporting to all levels of the field service management and service organization structure is required.

Basic reports to be generated in the system include:

- Customer call processing analysis (response time analysis)
- Customer history (uptime analysis)
- Call-handling reports [e.g., calls per location, field service engineer (FSE), time to commit, response time]
- Scheduling service personnel load reports
- Standard reports:
  - Resources used vs. allocated
  - Contract profitability
  - Contract renewal
  - Installed configuration
  - Inventory status report by stocking locations
  - Purchase orders
  - Failure demand, such as reports for mean time between failure (MTBF) and mean time to repair or service (MTTR)
  - Labor distribution analysis (e.g., by product line or region)
  - Parts and material consumption analysis

The system usually provides the capability to generate new reports without having to write specific search and report routines.

Internal Systems Interfaces and Communication

The overall structure of the system is typically implemented on a standard, modular, executive-controlled basis, operating off a network or relational database management system (DBMS). Required system communications functions include:

■ *Field communications and support.* Service personnel could be equipped with portable laptop computers or wireless devices (e.g., PDAs) to communicate with the central system and to download and upload information for improved customer service and support. Elements of field communication and information exchange include:

■ *E-mail facility and bulletin board* — Such a facility allows posting of messages between the dispatch center and service personnel or from one service person to another. This is also a central facility to post and distribute service memos and recent problem solution information.

■ *Forms/reporting* — Service personnel should be able to download call or customer information, display it or print it locally in a structured format, enter their inputs, and transmit them back to the system. A representative list of reporting forms includes service call assignment, call information status and closeout, contract report, time and material report and billing input, service report, warranty report, and customer history report.

■ *Customer layout information and configuration data access.* The system should be capable of providing communications access and portraying graphic data with storage and editing capabilities. This capability would be used by service personnel to develop, record, and diagnose network topology, equipment location and layout, actual repair paths, parts information, etc. This facility can help inexperienced service personnel and call handling specialists to familiarize themselves quickly with customers' operational circumstances.

■ *WorldWide Web and global Internet access.* In certain cases, the system should be capable of connecting to the Internet and World-Wide Web for:

■ Customers requesting product, technical, and help assistance
■ Reporting general problems
■ Providing updates on new technology
■ Providing other communications to and from field engineers, logistics management, help-desk specialists, and other service and company representatives.

The full functional support system is outlined in Figure 4.3.

Integrated service management systems providing most of these functional capabilities are available and sold regionally or globally, with a significant number available in North America and Europe. The leading vendors in the United States and Europe are identified in Chapters 5 and 6. These systems will generally run on a wide variety of hardware

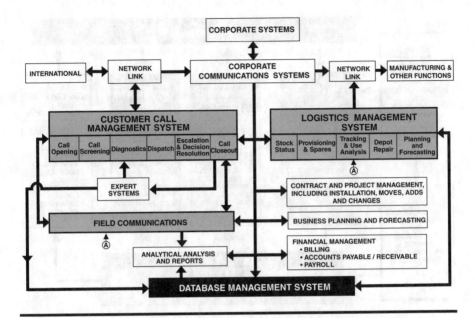

Figure 4.3 Overview of CRM/service management systems technology.

platforms. Many are written in fourth-generation languages (4GLs), such as Progress, Uniface, Oracle, and Dataflex.

NEW DEVELOPMENTS IN SERVICE MANAGEMENT SYSTEMS

A major new requirement in the service industry is the need for *optimization* of service operations. In general, most service organizations in the past have moved from a cost center to a contribution center or profit center or full strategic line of business (LOB) form of operation and have made the transition from a decentralized model to a centralized model. In this type of operation, the senior executives were primarily concerned about the development and implementation of a workable or viable solution that would allow them to meet the requirements for service of their customer base, as well as generate some level of profit contribution. However, as more and more of these organizations become charged with full responsibility for operating as a full strategic line of business, responsibilities of the senior service executive switched from the simple need for a viable business to becoming an optimal or optimized business. As a result, the focus is now on service organization management, particularly on the specific functions and technologies that fall within the general service management systems structure that can provide capabilities for optimization of the service business.

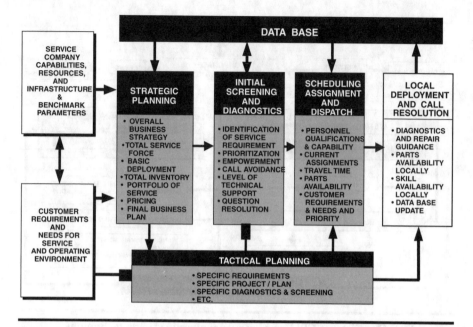

Figure 4.4 Overall service assignment, allocation, scheduling, and dispatch optimization process. (From Blumberg Associates, Inc., Fort Washington, PA. With permission.)

In order to understand these new requirements, it is important to examine the steps involved in optimization of service personnel operations, as shown in Figure 4.4. In essence, there are four major stages involved in service manpower optimization:

1. *Strategic and tactical planning.* The first step is to develop the appropriate business plans at the strategic level (general) and for specific customers or business areas (tactical), relative to the choice of the total number of service personnel and their deployment and the inventory and logistics support levels and their deployment, as well as the supporting infrastructure.

2. *Call management, diagnostics, and call avoidance.* The second area of optimization relates to the fact that a significant number of calls and requests for service can be handled more optimally through a centralized help desk or technical assistance center rather than through the more expensive and less cost-effective dispatch of a service person into the field, which involves travel to a field location. The capabilities for call screening diagnostics and call avoidance, therefore, become the second stage in the optimization process.

3. *Work force assignment and scheduling.* The third area of optimization occurs when a variety of alternatives are available for assignments, scheduling, and dispatch relative to a large number of field service engineers, with alternative logistics support capabilities and an array of customers with different priorities and different physical locations. Within this framework are a multitude of solutions that consider service cost; travel time; response and repair time; efficiency of service; engineer utilization; contract terms, conditions, and commitment; and service quality. Scheduling and assignment analysis in these cases can lead to optimized assignment and dispatch that takes into account all available information and intelligence.

4. *Field level call completion and close out.* The fourth and final stage in the optimization process relates to improvement in the ability of the service person assigned to identify, diagnose, and complete the assigned service task. In essence, the final stage in the optimization process relates to optimization of the actual completion of the assignment of the service person.

In essence, the new emphasis on optimization forces an increased focus on those functions and capabilities within service management systems that can support all of the four stages of optimization. It should be noted that these steps and stages apply for high-tech service, consumer services, etc. In other words, the basic processes are the same for a manufacturing service force, an insurance company, or a restaurant. The only differences are found in the semantics used to describe the process and the level of detail and precision required.

In general, new technology is now increasingly available to support each of the four stages:

1. *Computer models for strategic and tactical planning.* A significant development has taken place relative to the design and implementation of software for strategic and tactical planning. The BAI computer models have been designed to develop optimum solutions for strategic and tactical planning based upon input describing customer requirements for service at a given price, relative to options and alternatives available to the service organization for delivery.

2. *Systems for help-desk and technical assistance support.* The second major area of optimization relates to the ability to handle a large number of calls for service and deal with them in an optimum manner in a high-tech environment. For example, six types of service calls could come into a service organization, as shown in Figure 4.5. New software technology for this support process

TYPE	SERVICE	FOCUS	DRIVEN BY	TIMEFRAME	PROFILE
0	SYSTEMS DESIGN, SPECIFICATION & INTEGRATION	"PAPER STUDIES" & INVESTIGATION	• OVERALL CUSTOMER • SYSTEM ORGANIZATION	MONTHS	VARIES
1	INSTALLATION/ DELIVERY	• IMPLEMENTATION & INSTALLATION OF SYSTEM INCLUDING HARDWARE, SOFTWARE, & NETWORK COMPONENTS • INITIAL TRAINING	SYSTEM CONFIGURATION	DAYS	PROJECT
2	MAINTENANCE & REPAIRS	HARDWARE FAILURE SOFTWARE FAILURE COMBINATION HARDWARE & SOFTWARE FAILURE	USERS	DAYS	TIME PEAKS
3	INSTRUCTIONAL & "HOW TO"	• USER QUESTIONS • USER INEXPERIENCE • USER APPLICATION ISSUES	USERS	DAYS	ONE TIME PEAKS
4	NETWORK	NETWORK FAILURE	• USERS • NETWORK COMPONENTS	DAYS	TIME PEAKS
5	MOVES, ADDS, CHANGES, AND UPGRADES	SYSTEMS IMPROVEMENT & CHANGES	• OVERALL CUSTOMER • USERS	MONTHS	VARIES

Figure 4.5   Types of customer calls.

involves an increasing level of capability for identification, analysis, diagnostics, and evaluation, utilizing the step process shown in Figure 4.6. In essence, the general technology for help-desk and technical assistance can be utilized within the context of an overall

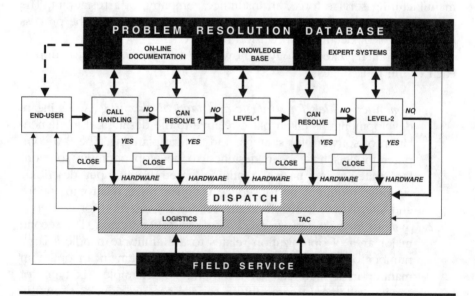

Figure 4.6   Call handling diagnostics process overview.

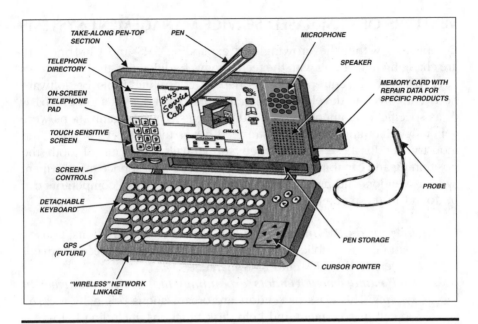

Figure 4.7   The field service terminal (PDA).

call management functionality to improve the efficiency and optimization of the call management process.

3. *Scheduling and assignment software.* A third major area of development relates to increasing availability of software specifically
designed to determine an optimal solution in terms of assignment
and scheduling of service engineers within the framework of an
authorized strategic or tactical plan.

4. *Direct support of the service person in the field.* The fourth and final
area of improvement relates to the ability of laptops and PDAs to
operate in conjunction with wireless networks to improve the
ability of service personnel to carry out their assignments. In
essence, laptops or PDAs offer not only significant improvement
in communications but also electronic-based manuals and test
processing augmentation to enable service personnel to solve on-
site service problems. New PDA laptop technology, illustrated in
Figure 4.7, is readily available.

In summary, the four functional areas and the specific technology identified to support those functions represent the cutting edge of the service
management systems and will be of increasing interest to managers trying
to select the "best in class" system and service technology support infrastructure to meet their needs.

VENDORS OF CRM-BASED SERVICE MANAGEMENT SYSTEMS

Competitors within the growing and expanding SMS and CRM industry are changing right along with the technology. Traditionally, the competitors have been small, entrepreneurial-oriented consulting firms or software houses involved in developing integrated SMS solutions on a generic basis or as specific assignments for individual clients. These organizations were generally small and financially strapped. Over the last 3 to 4 years, the industry vendor base has changed substantially in terms of both the positioning and capability of the initial integrated field service management systems vendors and new vendors. Today, five classes of competitors can be found in the market:

1. *Integrated CRM and SMS vendors.* Because of acquisitions, consolidation, and public offerings, these vendors have become major players in the CRM and SMS markets.
2. *Call management vendors expanding into service management systems.* This class of vendors are organizations originally focused on call management and help-desk functions, including help-desk and technical assistance center support. These organizations are moving into provision of integrated service management systems.
3. *Vendors with improved field communications technology support.* Another class of vendors coming into the market are those offering technological improvement or optimization solutions in the areas of PDA and laptop communications, improvements driven from the perspective of field service engineers rather than central service management systems.
4. *Software organizations with capabilities in specific functional areas.* A major class of vendors consists of those organizations that have built specialized or optimized functional solutions in such areas of service as support, logistics, scheduling, and assignment optimization.
5. *Systems integrators.* The final major category of vendors includes organizations willing to take full turn-key responsibility for design, specification, and development and implementation of customized solutions to meet the full advanced requirements for CRM and SMS.

In summary, the expanded base of vendors in the CRM and SMS market has changed substantially. In general, the fully integrated SMS vendors are now larger, financially stable, public or semi-public companies that have become significant players in the market through initial public offerings, acquisitions, or joint venturing. These organizations are all becoming more aggressive and are spending more marketing and systems development dollars due to the increasing market opportunities available, as the demand for advanced CRM and SMS systems increase.

5

MANAGING AND OPTIMIZING SERVICE USING CRM AND SMS

CONTENTS

The growing need for significant productivity and quality improvement in service most often takes the form of marginal (and sometimes very expensive) management systems infrastructure that makes use of computers, office automation technology, telecommunications, and other related electronic mechanisms to support the typical field service operation. However, extensive research into the mechanisms that influence service productivity and performance, coupled with a new understanding of service in terms of the customer's perception and the market environment, has led to a strategic identification of the key critical factors that help to manage and improve service productivity and performance and reduce or eliminate "pain" in service management.* These factors can play a greater role on improving service productivity and performance than the use of a computerized infrastructure alone, which, at best, can only be used to determine a reasonable or viable solution to the day-to-day challenges facing service organizations.

These organizations typically operate by employing functions and processes to receive and process calls for call handling, to assign and dispatch service personnel to satisfy the customer's request, to provide logistics and depot repair support, and, in general, to provide total management and control of the full-service process and relationship with the service customer. These organizations operate either in support of a

---

* The data and findings presented here are based on in-depth evaluations of the productivity and performance of over 250 small, medium, and large service organizations supporting a broad array of high-technology products in the United States, Europe, and the Far East (Asia/Pacific).

SERVICE VALUES & OBJECTIVES	KEY FACTORS
DIRECTLY INFLUENCING SALES AND ADDING VALUE	• SERVICE IS MOST CRITICAL TO THE CUSTOMER IN FINAL SELECTION DECISION • SERVICE ADDS VALUE
GENERATING REVENUE AND PROFITS DIRECTLY	• CUSTOMERS ARE WILLING TO PAY FOR SERVICE DIRECTLY • CUSTOMER'S WILLINGNESS TO PAY IS BASED ON VALUE IN USE - NOT COST
PROVIDING MARKET CONTROL	• SERVICE CUSTOMERS TEND TO STAY WITH PROVIDER ONCE SATISFIED • PERCEIVED SATISFACTION LEVELS GENERATE SUBSTANTIAL LOYALTY

Figure 5.1   Strategic service values/objectives.

product business (such as an equipment manufacturer or product dealer) or in the role of independent (third-party and multivendor equipment) service provider. Some organizations operate in both roles. The overall general values and objectives of these organizations (as shown in Figure 5.1) are to:

- Provide added value to products
- Generate revenues and profits directly from service
- Provide market control

The emphasis in these objectives is a function of the role of the service organizations, as either an adjunct providing support to a product business or as a stand-alone service provider.

GENERAL STRATEGIC OPTIMIZATION TO SOLVE THE "PAIN" PROBLEMS OF SERVICE EXECUTIVES

As indicated above, service optimization requires a very serious consideration of goals, objectives, and trade-offs within the service business environment. To move forward, we must start with the primary "pain" problems encountered by service executives. These tend to deal with the issues of:

- *Balancing resources* to maximize both customer satisfaction and profitability in a rapidly changing market environment
- *Controlling in both the long term and in real time* the allocation and scheduling of individual resources
- *Dealing with both perceptions and reality*
- *Operating under business rules and models* designed for a product environment, which do not appear to fully "fit" the service business, dynamics and structure

Figure 5.2 shows a list of both general and specific "pains" faced by service executives and managers and links these pains to symptoms, solutions, mechanisms, and specific technologies. In broad terms, these solutions to the service manager's "pains" are related to:

- General system infrastructure development and implementation to obtain accurate data in real time and link it to specific models and calculations
- Benchmarking of internal operations vs. competition and market research into customer satisfaction, requirements, and needs to achieve strategic direction
- Density of customer service base

Strategic Systems Infrastructure Design

As indicated in Chapter 1, data are a critical resource in service management. Full optimization requires that the proper data are available, accurate, and in real time. With the correct data, calculations, and models, it is possible to optimize the allocation of labor (people) and material (parts) to meet changing customer requirements. The basic system infrastructure that has emerged is the full-service management system described in Figure 5.3. This system can be implemented on a standalone basis or as part of a fully integrated customer relationship management (CRM)/enterprise resource planning (ERP) system solution. The two key elements of this service management system (SMS) infrastructure are:

1. Call management and control
2. Logistics management and control

These functions are discussed in detail later, including the state-of-the-art sources of support for specific optimization.

Importance of Density in Service Optimization

A most critical general tool for service optimization is based on density of the customer base. Extensive studies (by Blumberg Associates, Inc.)

have shown that density is the single most important factor driving service productivity and efficiency. For example, comparing servicing 1000 units randomly distributed around the country to servicing the same 1000 units in one building, the ability to obtain, manage, and deliver service for one building with high density is much greater than for the low-density situation. This has been clearly demonstrated in studies of the impact of density on profitability, in which different levels of density (Figure 5.4) produce significantly different levels of profitability (Figure 5.5), and systems infrastructures have an increasing effect on service profitability.

In essence, increasing installed base density through either critical selection of customer base geography or expansion into multivendor equipment service (MVES) to build increased density can generate higher levels of economies of scale. Increasing density creates more options for scheduling and logistics assignments, as opposed to decreased density, which limits scheduling and assignment alternatives. This means that a company servicing computers can gain productivity by servicing other computer and information technology at the same customer site. With the dramatic increase in the use of microprocessors in office automation, communications networks, plant automation, building automation, etc., the opportunities for increased density through expansion of services offered through MVES is high.

The broad issues of symptoms, infrastructures, benchmarking, customer satisfaction measurement, and density are the initial building blocks leading to service optimization; however, we must also understand how optimization is determined. This chapter demonstrates that various mixes of systems, infrastructures, policies, procedures, technology, measurement systems, etc. can lead to approaches that can produce optimum strategies (Figure 5.6), but how is the optimum determined? In the product business model, where bottom-line profits are the preliminary objectives, the process is fairly straightforward. By identifying alternative strategies it is possible to determine the optimal direction (as mentioned in Figure 5.6). In the service environment, though, several objective functions can be identified that typically include:

- Profitability/productivity
- Customer satisfaction
- Market control

Determining an optimum solution or strategy when two or more objectives exist is difficult. As shown in Figure 5.6, it generally involves setting values for each objective, using a weighting scheme, and finding a midpoint strategy that maximizes each objective equally or as a function of the weighting scheme.

"Pain" Point/Problem	Symptom	Potential Solutions	Solution Mechanism or Technology
Inability to manage or control service business on day-to-day basis	Attempt to run as a product business on a decentralized basis Little or no accuracy on timely data	Development of service business model Recognize importance of data	Service strategy CRM/FSMS with infrastructure
Labor costs too high and service personnel ineffectively deployed	Service personnel overworked Service personnel underworked	Full call management Call handling, tracking, and control system	Call manager system
Logistics and inventory costs too high or inefficiently used	Constantly buying new parts Parts not at right place at right time	Full logistics management system	Logistics management system
Lack of real-time control over field people and parts	Customer dissatisfaction Slowness in response to customer requirements in field	Provide field-level automation on ongoing basis	Wireless, integrated PDA with GSM, GPS, and voice recognition

Specific customer or customer segments not satisfied with services	No compliance of portfolio with different delivery levels at different prices First-come, first-served processes	Advanced market research Advanced pricing Call diagnostics	Market evaluation and research Pricing models Call diagnostics and evaluation
Field service not optimized	Low profitability or customer satisfaction Long response time	Online, real-time call diagnostics and scheduling of service forces	Call diagnostic systems Work force management and scheduling systems
Logistics not optimized	Low profitability or customer satisfaction	Online, real-time control of logistics pipeline down to field engineer trunk and back	Service logistics control and scheduling system Service parts optimization system
Inability to control and manage business strategically	Low margins Low customer satisfaction Low revenue growth Morale issues	Increase density through MVES Manage trade often strategically and tactically Use optimization	Strategic planning CRM/SMS Optimizing technology Move into MVES and TPM services

Figure 5.2 Major service "pain" points and related solutions.

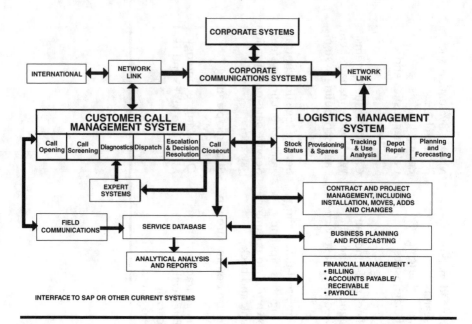

Figure 5.3 Overview of service management systems technology.

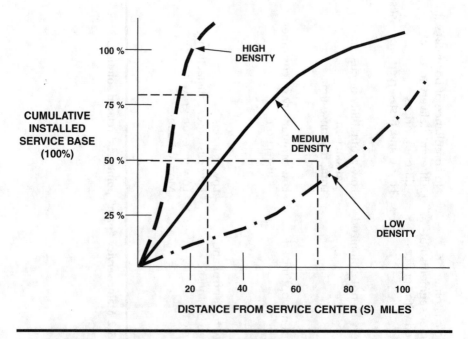

Figure 5.4 Types of installed base density. (From Blumberg Associates, Inc., Fort Washington, PA. With permission.)

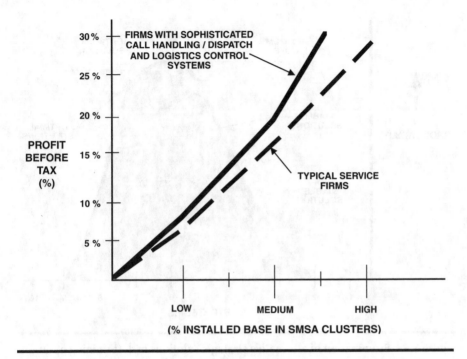

Figure 5.5 Impact of density on service profitability.

As shown in Figure 5.7, one basic strategy usually does not optimize all parameters. Thus, in general, a mixed strategy is required. In this case, the final optimum solution must be based on both risk and return on investment and recognition of the array of strategic and tactical opportunities for changing the strategic results. For example, as indicated above, changing density through changing revenues, can change productivity and profitability, just as systems, technology, infrastructure, and procedures can also change productivity. Changing the service portfolio (in terms of, for example, committed response time, repair time, time of day or day of week coverage) and prices in general and through segmentation can also affect profitability.

Benchmarking and Customer Satisfaction/Market Research

Optimization-based service strategies can be developed by two parallel mechanisms:

- Market research and measuring customer satisfaction can be used to determine service needs and requirements, capability to meet requirements, gaps in service, perception of the firm vs. competition, willingness to pay, and new and emerging requirements.

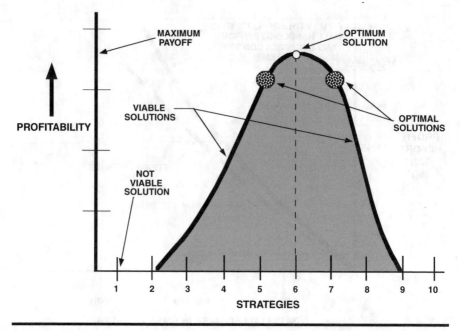

Figure 5.6   Examination of alternative strategic solutions in determining optimum on a single parameter. (From Blumberg Associates, Inc., Fort Washington, PA. With permission.)

■ Benchmarking provides the capability to measure internal performance against industry averages for specific parameters. The key
issues in benchmarking are to determine the correct parameters to

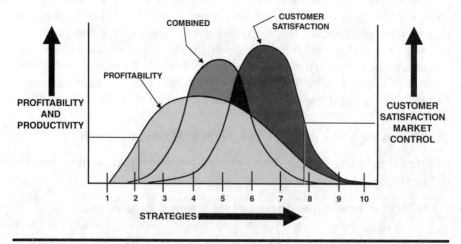

**Figure 5.7   Alternative strategic options in a service environment involving mul-
tiple parameters.**

(MEAN)

PARAMETER MEASUREMENT	BEST PRACTICE COMPANY*	TYPICAL FIRM	PERCENT IMPROVEMENT
REVENUE PER FIELD ENGINEER	$254 K	$ 178K	43%
PRETAX PROFIT PER FIELD ENGINEER (FE)	41%	18%	128%
CALLS PER FE PER DAY	6.6	2.4	175%
PERCENT OF CALLS AVOIDED BY FE	36%	21%	71%
PERCENT OF CALLS RESOLVED REMOTELY BY SUPPORT CENTER	40%	28%	43%
FE UTILIZATION**	86%	55%	56%
DIRECT COST PER CALL	$ 143	$ 208	45%

* Based on Cross Representative Sample Evaluation of Firms in IT/Telecomm/Medical with 250 or more Fes
** Without travel

Figure 5.8   Key operating benchmark associated with field service optimization.

measure and then determine the actual metrics through either limited single-shot surveys or in-depth research. Some consultants provide benchmarking data, in general, and by size and type of service organization.

Both benchmarking and customer satisfaction/market research studies are available through consultants and professional associations.

General benchmark studies carried out by BAI comparing industry averages to the best in class for both service personnel and logistics benchmarks (shown in Figures 5.8 and 5.9) demonstrate the significant potential for improvement/optimization through a comparison of general industry averages to the best performers. To be useful, the data must specifically compare directly compatible firms using externally developed benchmarks, as opposed to internal data.

Ultimately, the final optimized strategy must take all of these issues into consideration. The next chapter outlines the general impact on productivity and efficiency of changing major functions, including call management, logistics, management and optimization systems, and technology, as well as general operating policy and practices, as the starting point for developing a fully developed overall service optimized program.

(MEAN)

PARAMETER MEASUREMENT	BEST PRACTICE COMPANY*	TYPICAL FIRM	PERCENT IMPROVEMENT
TOTAL CALLS PE R REPAIR COMPLETION	1.1	1.4	21%
% OR CALLS "BROKEN" DUE TO LACK OF PARTS	14%	26%	46%
FIELD FILL RATE	92%	52%	77%
RESUPPLY RATE IN DAYS	180	300	40%
REPAIR TURNAROUND (IN DAYS)	3.2	5.8	45%
FIELD DEAD ON ARRIVAL (DOA)	1%	2%	50%
TRANSPORTATION COSTS AS A PERCENT OF TOTAL COSTS	8%	11%	27%
LOGISTICS OPERATING COSTS AT A % OF TOTAL COSTS	10%	13%	23%

* Based on Cross Representative Sample Evaluation of Firms in IT/Telecomm/Medical with 250 or more Fes

Figure 5.9 Key operating parameters associated with service logistics parts planning and forecasting.

STRATEGIES AND TACTICS FOR OPTIMIZING PRODUCTIVITY OF THE FIELD SERVICE STAFF

Assuming that steps have been taken to improve density (or the option to improve density does not exist), the next area of immediate focus should be on improvement in productivity and efficiency of the field service work force. Because the costs for a service organization, including travel and per diem, typically run between 50 and 65% of service revenue, the payoff relative to improving service staff productivity can be quite high. Several steps can be taken to improve field service engineer productivity.

Introducing a Managed Approach and Discipline to Call-Handling Assignment and Dispatch, Call Tracking, and Call Close Out

Many service organizations approach call handling as if it was merely a process of message storage and forwarding (i.e., passing messages from customers about service needs to an assigned service person). However, evidence suggests that significant improvements in productivity and efficiency of the field service force can be achieved by (1) converting the call-handling and dispatch process into a managed approach to taking calls;

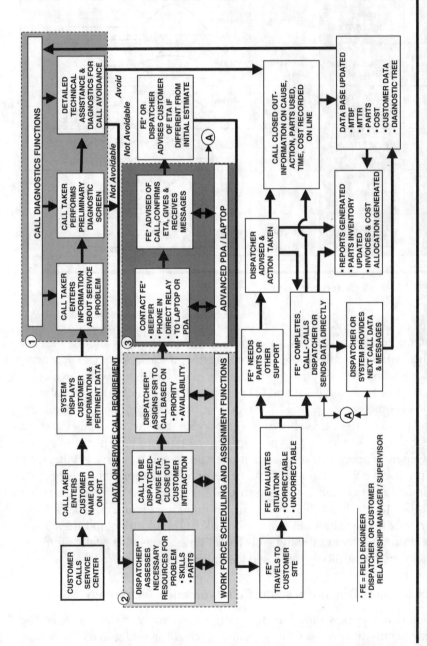

Figure 5.10 Overview of recommended call management, call handling, and diagnostic, assignment scheduling and dispatch, tracking, and call close-out process.

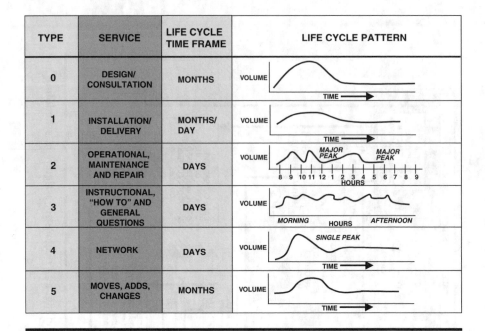

TYPE	SERVICE	LIFE CYCLE TIME FRAME	LIFE CYCLE PATTERN
0	DESIGN/ CONSULTATION	MONTHS	
1	INSTALLATION/ DELIVERY	MONTHS/ DAY	
2	OPERATIONAL, MAINTENANCE AND REPAIR	DAYS	
3	INSTRUCTIONAL, "HOW TO" AND GENERAL QUESTIONS	DAYS	
4	NETWORK	DAYS	
5	MOVES, ADDS, CHANGES	MONTHS	

Figure 5.11   Call patterns by type.

(2) introducing analysis and evaluation of the call requirements in real time to determine the possibility of avoiding an on-site call all together by utilizing remote diagnostics; (3) optimizing the on-site dispatch, assignment, and scheduling process using intelligence and customer data developed from the diagnostic analysis; and (4) controlling the call close-out database.

The recommended processing sequence for call handling, assignment, dispatch, and close-out, as shown in Figure 5.10, starts with normal handling of the incoming service call. Typical call arrival patterns are shown in Figure 5.11. General experience dictates that centralized call handling is inherently more productive than regional, local, or decentralized approaches, especially if 24-hour call coverage is to be provided, as it can make use of changing time zones to level out the service arrival rate (see Figures 5.12 and 5.13). Call arrivals in any one time zone will peak in the morning and then again in the afternoon; by combining calls for all time zones, the peaks fill in the gaps and creates a more stable service call arrival rate.

Use of Remote Diagnostics and Call Avoidance Technology

The first major opportunity for improving productivity in the call-handling process occurs in terms of the specific process for preliminary screening and in-depth diagnostic analysis and call avoidance. The purpose of this initial screening and in-depth diagnostic analysis is to:

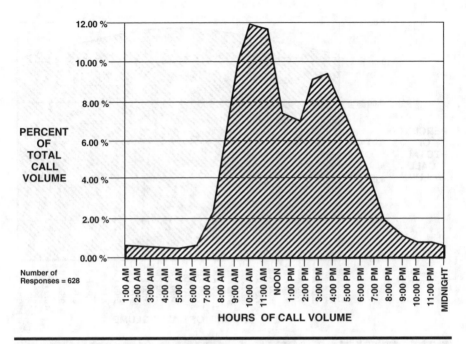

Figure 5.12   General pattern of service call handling and "help desk" call volume by hour (in percent) in single region (based on general experience). (From Blumberg Associates, Inc., Fort Washington, PA, and Help Desk Institute, Colorado Springs, CO, 2000. With permission.)

- *Identify* the service call requirement and ensure that the call is passed to the individual or organization most capable of meeting the service need; this will be determined by the nature of the call.
- *Evaluate* the call to determine whether or not an on-site service engineer is required (i.e., call avoidance).
- *Determine*, through on-the-line diagnostics utilizing historical information on the problem–symptom–cause–corrective action procedure, if the user can be instructed to correct the service problem directly without on-site dispatch of a service engineer or if the problem can be solved by sending parts, software, or consumable supplies.
- *Identify* the formal service requirement and intelligence about the service call for dispatch and assign a specific service engineer who is the optimum choice in terms of having specific skill levels and the necessary parts, based on the diagnostic process and taking into consideration the need for other services at the same or nearby site (e.g., preventative and predictive maintenance or installation).

This process is described in Figure 5.14.

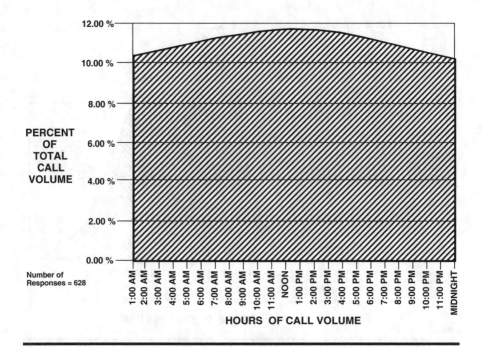

Figure 5.13 **General pattern of service and help desk call volume by hour (in percent) for global system (based on general experience). (From Blumberg Associates, Inc., Fort Washington, PA. With permission.**

Optimization of ETA Scheduling and Work Force Management

The second stage in the call management process where productivity can be improved relates to providing the customer with an accurate estimated time of arrival (ETA), taking into account the customer's service requirements, willingness to pay, and guaranteed service level, as well as the availability of service engineers, skill levels, parts availability, and travel time. Experience indicates that the ETA estimate is very critical to both customer satisfaction levels and perceptions of service quality and capability. Customers typically pay very close attention to the ETA commitment and expect it to be met, particularly if they are paying a premium for a service-level agreement (SLA). If the estimated time of arrival is provided in an off-hand manner and the service person arrives after the time of commitment, the customer's perception of service quality will drop substantially. On the other hand, if the service engineer arrives much more rapidly than the committed ETA, the customer will be unable to assess this level of improvement. If you hire a taxi, for instance, and the driver arrives 30 minutes earlier than scheduled, you might understandably feel rushed and even annoyed by the waiting driver. It is, therefore, just as

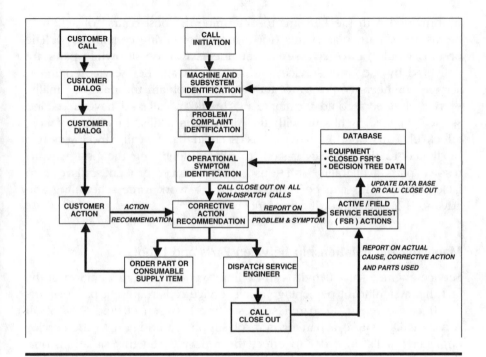

Figure 5.14 Remote diagnostic (decision support) process flow in help desk/technical assistance center (TAC) application.

important to avoid arriving too early as it is to avoid arriving too late. An ETA estimate that provides for just-in-time arrival is the most optimum with respect to maximizing both customer satisfaction and minimizing service call costs.

Achieving this objective requires the use of advanced fine-tuned work force scheduling and assignment using force management and scheduling systems that take into account currently available service personnel, current and future service requirements (emergency requests, preventive and predictive maintenance, installations, etc.), critical travel time, service contract commitments, parts availability, and skills in order to determine the optimal allocation of service engineer (and parts) to customer requirements, taking into account customer priorities as established by willingness to pay and contract terms, SLAs, and scope of the service contract. Advanced or best-in-class workforce scheduling systems are available from such companies as ServicePower, ClickSoftware, CGS, and Telcordia.

Once an optimized assignment schedule has been determined, the next major step in improving the call-handling management process relates to the ability to resolve actions online on an optimum basis using the best available information. The call-handling process and system should be provided with mechanisms to determine the best course of action to be taken for particular events (for example, requiring certain parts). The options would be to have service engineers wait on-site while parts are delivered by a courier service, mobile van, or another service engineer; service engineers could go to another site to obtain the part; or, finally, service engineers could terminate or "break" a call and have a second service engineer sent out with the right parts, skills. In order to most effectively carry out this analysis, it is essential that the call-handling system be linked to the logistics system to allow identifying the best way to resolve parts availability situations and to reduce "broken" calls due to lack of parts. This can be achieved through work force scheduling and advanced logistics coordination and control.

Managing the Relationship between Parts and Labor

Service engineer productivity can be improved through recognition of the fact that a significant percentage of all service calls require a part or parts to effect the repair. Research suggests that between 60 and 75% of all service calls require a part or item of supply, in addition to the service engineer's skills, in order to effect the repair. Given this situation, productivity can be improved by determining optimum stock levels to be assigned directly to the service professional to be stored either in a parts caddie or in the service person's vehicle. This stock could be augmented by alternative methods for resupply in the field, including same-day courier service, mobile vans, or same-day couriers dispatched by radio or wireless technology to the service person's location. Improving stock availability can reduce the extremely inefficient occurrence of a "broken" call in which the service personnel must leave the site to travel back to the service center for parts and return at a later time with the appropriate parts. This logistics support process is discussed in more detail in the next section.

Improved Productivity Through Improved Field Communications

Service personnel productivity can be improved by providing better direct, real-time, reliable communications between central call-handling and logistics support systems and the service person in the field. Historically, it was relatively easy for a service person to communicate by simply picking up a telephone at the customer's site; however, with the trend toward private PBX service and call lockout and security protection it is increasingly difficult to use just any telephone, particularly if a long-distance call is involved. New technologies that allow direct, real-time communications between the central service offices and the local or field service person include wireless beepers, pagers, FM radio, or cellular radio. In any case,

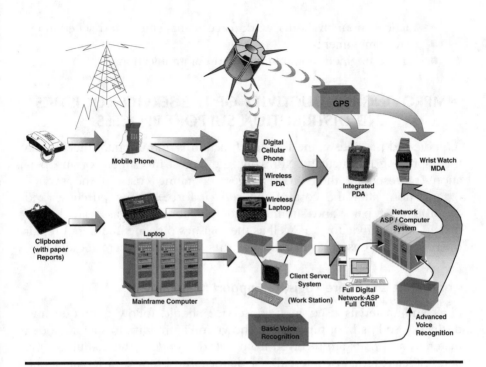

Figure 5.15   Evolution of field force automation.

the service person is provided with a portable, handheld data terminal that may also include onboard computer capability, in order to receive calls, close out calls, request parts, or receive technical assistance. These devices also improve service force productivity. Centralized call handling is inherently more productive than regional, local, or decentralized approaches, especially if 24-hour call coverage is to be provided, and is being used to provide test data or recommended repair and diagnostic sequencing. The development and evolution of advanced PDAs or laptops, wrist PDAs with full voice recognition, and global positioning systems (GPS) are shown in Figure 5.15. Communications to and from field service personnel was originally by wire, but today advanced wireless technology can be employed to enhance productivity.

Summary

In summary, the key mechanisms for optimizing the service labor force are:

- Strategic Assessment and allocation of manpower and resources
- Call opening
- Call diagnostics and avoidance

- Tactical (hour by hour) work force management and scheduling
- ETA commitment
- Service engineer commitment and communications

IMPROVING PRODUCTIVITY OF THE SERVICE LOGISTICS AND DISTRIBUTION SUPPORT PROCESS

As indicated previously, the logistics function is an important mechanism for improving productivity. Normally, the largest investment of an operation (representing the second largest operating costs in the service organization, after the cost of the service force) is the purchase and acquisition of parts and subunits and the labor costs associated with managing that inventory, as well as the logistics pipeline and depot repair operations that ensure availability of parts when and where required.

Controlling the Entire Logistics Support "Pipeline"

Parts and materials used in field service should follow a unique and distinct closed path, or pipeline, as shown in Figure 5.16. In such a model, materials and parts are received from outside vendors, the manufacturing line (either external or internal), or depot refurbishing and repair operations. They are then stored in a central warehouse. Material is shipped from the warehouse to regional or local storage locations and finally placed into the hands of service personnel or delivered to customer sites.

As the service personnel engage in maintenance, repair, installation, and preventive and predictive maintenance activities, they "pull" parts and subassemblies from whole units or equipment that they believe have failed. These parts are returned to a regional or central depot for repair and retrofit, refurbishment, or disposal. This inventory, once refurbished and qualified, then flows back to either the central or local/regional warehouses. Thus, as indicated in Figure 5.16, one can envision total service logistics to be an overall pipeline flowing down to the field and returning to a central location through the depot refurbishing process and the "reverse logistics" process.

In examining this service logistics pipeline, it is important to recognize a number of critical parameters or factors affecting productivity:

- Nearly 50% of the value of the inventory is normally found below the manned national or regional/local depots, usually flowing to the service personnel by way of the service personnel's trunk or "boot" stocks or kits or by flowing back to the local or regional storage locations or to the repair depots. Parts and subassemblies may also be maintained by service personnel at local sites, in

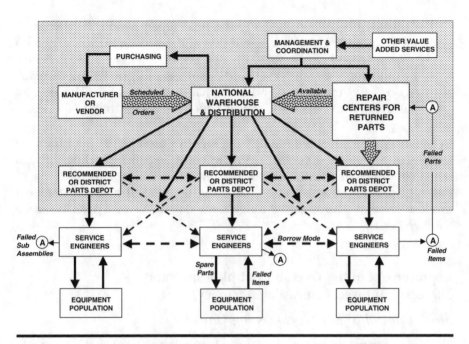

Figure 5.16   Service logistics pipeline flow.

lockers, or at home. Thus, it is absolutely essential to introduce mechanisms for direct control of the inventory at the field service engineer level. This is best done through the call-handling and dispatch process at call close-out, during which a requirement should exist for the service personnel to report on parts used and the parts, subassemblies, and whole units returned, as well as new parts received, to compute the optimum "fill rate" at each storage location, including trunk stock.

■ Experience indicates that approximately 80% of the value of the service pipeline is returned through the reverse logistics and depot repair operations annually; a very significant portion of the total logistics pipeline flows through the return or reverse logistics loop to the depot refurbishing operations. This clearly suggests that it is much more efficient to make use of the return cycle, including optimized scheduling and sequencing of the depot itself, as the primary mechanism for refilling the pipeline, rather than to make use of external purchases.

■ A portion of the returns to central or regional repair depots are actually good parts and units. Service personnel have tended to adopt a pull-and-replace philosophy to maintain and repair equipment in the field — for example, pulling a circuit board or subassembly when initiating the field repair action. If, after such a replacement, the unit is still down, the service person may then pull a second circuit board or subassembly. In general, such results would imply that the first board or subassembly pulled was actually good, and experience indicates that approximately 30 to 40% of all returns to depot are actually good units (no trouble found).

In summary, a major step in improving logistics productivity is to formally establish computerized control over the entire logistics pipeline through direct control of the central and field manned inventories, through use of the call close-out information on parts use to control the service engineer trunk stocks and returns, and through same-day delivery of parts to reduce "broken" calls.

Improvement in the Overall Control of Inventory Through Improved Forecasting Accuracy

Stock Control of Key Stockkeeping Units

Typically, a service organization controls possibly 20,000 to 40,000 stockkeeping units (SKUs), of which approximately 10% (i.e., 2000 to 4000) are active. In addition, the most critical SKUs used in day-to-day maintenance and repair actions are typically only 10% of the active items, in the range of 200 to 400. Thus, the primary focus of inventory control should be on the active and most critical items and transactions concerning the storage, movement, and receipt of the active SKUs, in terms of both effective and defective stocks. This involves online updating of the inventory status at each location, including field personnel use.

Use of Advanced Forecasting

Advanced forecasting methodology should be used to anticipate future inventory demands. This involves initially segmenting SKUs into various classes or groups. In general, experience suggests that the cumulative stock demands will vary as a function of stage in the product life cycle. For example, demand will be considerably higher and nonlinear in terms of SKUs used in support of a product in the phase-in stage. Similarly, demand would also be nonlinear but decreasing in the event of a product phase-out. Thus, the first step in improving the accuracy of forecasting is to segment the SKUs by status of the products they support (i.e., roll-in, roll-out, or normal operation) and then use a cumulative model fit to a standard linear or logistics curve expressing the general status of the product to SKU level demand.

Same-Day Delivery

Reducing the time for parts delivery can substantially increase the return on investment for a given inventory; as delivery time is improved, the number of days of inventory required to achieve a given fill rate decreases rapidly.

Bar Coding and Other Methods for Identifying and Improving Accuracy of Inventory Counts

Typically, in many organizations, the transposition of SKU numbers or misreading of these numbers can lead to significant variation between the inventory levels and status as reported and actual physical counts made. These types of errors can be significantly reduced by introducing a bar code on each SKU and utilizing scanning devices at stockrooms and repair depots and in the field to report actual SKU information and data on received and shipped parts and such assembles, as well as determining the number of good vs. failed units on hand. PDAs can be very useful in support of this task.

Improved Just-in-Time Scheduling and Control of Depot Repair Operations

As indicated earlier, one of the most efficient mechanisms for refilling the logistics pipeline is to significantly speed up the schedule and assignment of work within the repair and refurbishing operations as part of reverse logistics. Typically, returned stocks are selected by individual depot bench technicians, who move the parts to their own benches and subject them to the appropriate diagnostics and testing to complete repairs. This material is then either immediately sent out directly to the field or goes through a limited quality assurance process (sometimes by the same bench technician). The problem with this approach is that advanced technologies for diagnostics and initial quality assurance testing are not employed. Much more important is the fact that in this approach the depot works on an inefficient job-shop basis with no prioritization or scheduling of work flow.

A more efficient approach is to operate the depot on a just-in-time basis, which would involve, first of all, doing a quality assurance check at the time of receipt of parts to be able to identify and return to the field those units that are good or for which no trouble was found (NTF). Defective units (after passing through the quality assurance test) would then be put into the work-in-process inventory. As parts are demanded by the logistics pipeline, depot personnel first pull the appropriate SKU from the work-in-process inventory and pass it through a preliminary diagnostic screen utilizing artificial intelligence mechanisms. This diagnostic screen determines the specific work stations through which the SKU must proceed in order to achieve a total fix. Conveyor systems can be used to move the parts to the individual work stations or bench technicians. By sequencing assignment and scheduling of parts retrofit and repair on a just-in-time basis, the individual workbenches are staffed by the service technicians skilled in a particular type of repair. Upon completion of the repair process, the unit is then sent through quality assurance and placed back in the operation pipeline. Thus, by shifting the depot rework and repair operations from a job-shop approach to a just-in-time, optimally scheduled and controlled operation utilizing basic production principles and by centralizing the operation, the efficiency of the entire logistics pipeline can be improved.

IMPROVING PRODUCTIVITY OF MOBILE FORCE WORKERS

Over the past few years, a great deal of attention has been paid to significantly improving the productivity and efficiency of mobile work forces. This interest has been driven by the growing recognition that simple manual and clerical processes for static assignments of service engineers to specific tasks on both a planned and emergency basis result in very low levels of efficiency and utilization. In addition, it is clear that providing field personnel with more local support and intelligence will improve their operating effectiveness.

It has been shown that productivity and efficiency of call utilization can be improved by 20 to 30% or more through careful and precise examination of the skill sets available from field service personnel; their education and training; their assignments, travel times, and distances; and parts availability. The ability to achieve this level of improvement is brought about by combining two new technological developments:

- Development of advanced optimizing algorithms for workforce assignment and scheduling
- Development of advanced wireless technology to allow real-time communications to and from the central core management dispatch and assignment operation to service personnel in the field

The development of these technologies, plus the addition of expanding capabilities for precise geographic positioning and real-time reporting for field personnel, is leading a number of organizations to seriously consider implementing advanced field-force-oriented communications and automation systems and technology for both centralized and remote (field personnel) support. This is particularly true in the information technology, utility, and telecommunications markets. Specifically, in the telecommunications market, where scheduling of two or more resources to achieve a given task is a continuing occurrence, the need for the use of this technology is very high. This type of complex assignment and scheduling and improved support to personnel in the field, found in many application areas, can now be handled by means of these new field force/work force automation systems.

Technology Developments in Mobile Work Force Operations

Up until recently, the choices and options for improving communications to and from field personnel and mobile workers were limited to PDAs and laptops, with the ability to download and upload upon connection to a wired outlet. The alternative was to make use of specifically designed, field-force-oriented communication units with full wireless capability from firms such as Telxon/Symbol, MDSI, or Viryanet. These specialized units were based to some extent on the original development of the concept by Motorola and IBM, were marketed under the name Ardis (now Motient), and offered both specialized digital communications services and terminals. While this special-purpose technology was helpful, it came at some expense for both the special digital communications service and for the designed terminals.

New technology options,* however, significantly affect the cost effectiveness of mobile force automation:

- Expanded full wireless capabilities for standard lower cost laptops and PDAs
- New software and devices designed to direct deployed equipment in the field to a central facility for monitoring and diagnostics
- Advanced voice recognition technology for field use that results in the creation of user-friendly portable units with inputs provided by the human voice rather than keying data in
- Global positioning, which allows field engineers to determine and report on their actual position with a high degree of accuracy
- Very high-density memory cards and chips, which make available electronic repair manuals or wiring diagrams that can be updated in the field
- Advanced centralized work force management software integrated with field communications, which are now being developed to provide central workforce assignment, scheduling, and dispatch and direct real-time communications with the field force; vendors include Telcordia and Wishbone

---

* This new technology was discusssed previously.

GENERAL APPROACHES TO SERVICE MANAGEMENT

In addition, we can look to changes in policy and procedural processes, as outlined below.

General Approach to Reducing Service Costs in the Service Organization

Our studies show that a number of management approaches can be used to control or reduce the cost of services. These include:

- *Standardization.* The establishment of standard, well-defined service modules or portfolios can lead to reduced cost through the ability to control the human element in service delivery. McDonald's has used this approach in its service strategy.
- *Alternative delivery systems.* Service organization investment and involvement in service management and control can be reduced by using alternative delivery systems. In essence, customers become more involved in the service delivery process. Electronic banking, including banking by telephone and the use of ATMs, is an example of this service strategy.
- *Market segmentation and focus on high- and low-price or price-sensitive and -insensitive service markets.* Significant service sub-market segments are price insensitive, but price-sensitive service market segments also exist. Generally, price-sensitive customers will do more for themselves, including performing more self-maintenance and delivery functions, that might normally be done by external service vendors at added cost. Ikea, the furniture distributor, is an example of service directed toward the low-priced customer base.
- *Efficient use of a network and virtual office technology to deliver service.* Quite often, service can be delivered by some type of centralized network structure. Changing or simplifying this network through either improved service segmentation and focus or expansion of functions and service options can be used to reduce overall service costs and improve service delivery time and efficiency.
- *Changing service response and completion times.* A final tactic that could be utilized to reduce costs or increase margins is to change or lengthen the service time response and delivery characteristics. In essence, some customers simply are willing to wait longer than others to reduce costs; others require a rapid response and are willing to pay a premium for such service.

General Approach to Improving Service Value to the Customer/Market

In addition to cost reduction, management strategies can be utilized to improve service values and associated revenues, thus also improving efficiency and bottom-line profitability, through increased density and economics of scale. Our studies show that a number of mechanisms are available for improving service values to the customer:

- *Combining standardized service elements on a customized basis.* By creating a combination of standard service elements with a menu, it is possible to produce a perceived customized package of higher service quality and value that allows an emphasis on value-in-use of services to price-elastic customers.*
- *Proactive identifications of high service value-in-use requirements by specific customer segments.* Such identification can also be used to maximize profit margins. Processing of information from customer service activities and market research surveys can be utilized to pinpoint these new opportunities.
- *Improved management of service delivery and demand through price segmentation.* A combination of pricing and scheduling can be used to shift customer demands over time to achieve highest values to the customer without incurring additional costs. The combination of technology and short-term, part-time, or subcontract employees can also be used to shift the capability to meet changing demand requirements.
- *Strict and enforced service quality control standards.* A most important factor in maintaining or improving perceived value to the customer is to increase the customer's confidence that service will be performed in accordance with strict market-oriented standards.
- *Fixed contract price vs. time-and-materials pricing.* Many services are provided on a time-and-materials basis. Establishing a fixed price for a service contract over a specified time improves the customer's confidence that the service will be provided within budget. For example, in a fixed-price contract, a surcharge or premium can be added (by the service vendor) to reduce or eliminate the risk to the customer of a budget overrun.
- *Increased customer involvement.* A focus on customer involvement can be utilized to increase value, if it is justifiable in terms of the

---

* A full discussion on value-in-use and value-in-use pricing is found in Chapter 11.

customer's value in use or perception of service quality improvement. This is particularly true when experience with the typical customer generally suggests that increased customer involvement should result in price reduction.

General Mechanisms for Improving and Optimizing Service Productivity

It is important to recognize that the overall service productivity and efficiency can be improved or changed in response to changing requirements of the market. Productivity in service can be improved through three broad mechanisms:

1. *Functional substitution through improved infrastructure delivery.* A major area of productivity improvement involves the use of functional or system infrastructure support alternatives to labor-intensive service.
2. *Improved network and technology support.* Support mechanisms and systems can be provided to service personnel to improve their ability to carry out service more efficiently or effectively or in less time through remote support.
3. *Use of technological breakthroughs.* New services can be created or existing services can be significantly enhanced through major technological breakthroughs such as wireless communications, just-in-time repair technology, and a wired/wireless virtual office infrastructure.

Service density can be proactively improved by:

■ Expanding services offered to existing clients (e.g., moving into third-party and multivendor equipment service as a full line of business)
■ Move to full site service
■ Servicing vertical market segments, such as banks and hospitals, which are normally found in dense metropolitan areas
■ Offering discounts or incentives for service contracts in specific high-density areas

A general cross-sectional comparison of the performance of over 100 service organizations showed that significant improvements in productivity and efficiency through basic or average (viable) solutions can more than double the productivity (Figure 5.17).

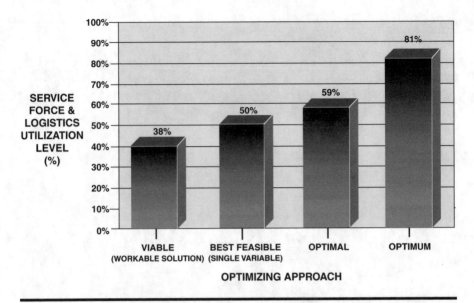

Figure 5.17 Impact of optimization techniques on utilization/productivity. (From Blumberg Associates, Inc., Fort Washington, PA. With permission.)

6

STATE-OF-THE-ART CRM
AND SMS TECHNOLOGY

CONTENTS

The previous chapters in Part II have dealt with the general design, structure, and functionality of customer relationship management (CRM) and service management systems (SMSs) and their applicability to managing and optimizing service business operations. Certainly no technology is stagnant, and the CRM/SMS infrastructure is no exception. Continuous improvements in technology, design, and implementation are a result of pressure to extend the functional capabilities of CRM/SMS to cover service management as well as product management and the critical attention now being paid by CRM users to achieving maximum payoffs and returns on investment. Functional areas where new technology is being developed and applied include:

- *Call diagnostics and call avoidance.* New technologies are necessary for analyzing and evaluating calls for service and the development of models, tools, and techniques to determine the optimum approach to meeting service demands given customer requirements for service, willingness to pay, criticality, etc. The new emerging call diagnostics mechanisms are very much state of the art.
- *Work force management, scheduling, and optimization.* The second major area of technological development relates to improving the scheduling, assignment, and dispatch of service personnel (and parts) to meet the requirements of customers based upon receipt of calls and call diagnostics. Advanced technology for work force management and scheduling is also on the cutting edge of new developments.
- *Logistics management and forecasting.* Full optimization of logistics support processes requires control of the physical inventory and transportation and distribution between inventory stocking points, the field, and returns to the depot for repair. Optimization also requires the capability to accurately and efficiently forecast requirements and demands and support the processes of call diagnostics (to determine specific parts requirements) and work force scheduling to ensure that the correct service personnel are dispatched and that they have the necessary parts, subassemblies, and materials. Significant new breakthroughs are being made in this field.
- *Database warehousing, management, and mining.* One of the most important contributions of CRM has been drawing attention to the critical importance and value of creating a fully integrated and seamless database to warehouse, store, coordinate, and retrieve all relevant data concerning customers and the development of new tools and technologies to make use of that database on a real-time or long-term basis. New developments in call diagnostics and call management, workforce scheduling, dispatch results, and

logistics management, as discussed above, create new and additional datafields for use in improving the data warehousing and mining processes. Important new technological breakthroughs in data mining and warehousing are being made.

Finally, in examining the state of the art, we must also recognize improvements that have been taking place in the general process of design and selection of advanced CRM/SMS systems to meet current, emerging, and future requirements of the service organization. This process of design, development, vendor selection, and implementation also represents improvements in the general state of the art for application and implementation of these new systems. The remainder of this chapter discusses each of these technologies and their current status.

CALL DIAGNOSTICS AND CALL AVOIDANCE

Over the last decade, the development, application, and use of advanced diagnostics and artificial intelligence technology for field service have increased. Research carried out in the early 1980s, in fact, showed that service problem diagnostics could eliminate between 30 and 35% of all on-site field service calls and in-depth diagnostic evaluation could significantly reduce the number of "broken" field service calls through more intelligent dispatch and assignment of both parts and service personnel.* Since the time of this research, a great deal of work has been carried out to further develop and apply advanced diagnostics technology in the field service industry.

It is of value, therefore, to examine the current state of the art and experience in the application and use of problem diagnostics and resolution technology in the health equipment field service industry, as well as to explore both the successes and failures of artificial intelligence and advanced remote diagnostics and decision support methodology in service.

An Overview of the General State-of-the-Art in Remote Diagnostics

The role of artificial intelligence (AI) and remote diagnostics in the service environment is usually part of the overall call managing process and is based on the strategic use of information and data acquisition methods to identify, isolate, analyze, and ultimately diagnose and evaluate a fault within a unit of equipment or system. The goal is to improve the efficient allocation and timeliness of service-oriented resources and to raise the

---

* See Blumberg, D.F., Strategies for the use of diagnostics technology in improving field service productivity, *FSMS Journal*, Spring, 1984.

productivity of the service force and uptime of equipment through efficient use and deployment of service personnel and parts. Improving performance in the service function relies on having the most efficient technology to identify, isolate, predict, or repair faults or potential faults. This requires a service organization of such sophistication as to fully exploit the available and potential benefits of current diagnostic maintenance practices.

In general, service productivity can be improved in four ways:

1. Anticipation of potential future failures through predictive and preventive maintenance to initiate fieldwork that avoids emergency, unanticipated failures
2. Reduction or elimination of actual, on-site service calls through more efficient problem and fault diagnosis in response to emergency call requests and prior to emergency call dispatches
3. Use of improved fault diagnosis to optimize performance of site-dispatched calls by identifying the required craft and skill levels and parts
4. Reduction of on-site repair time through more rapid isolation of the actual problem

The underlying issue is the acquisition and use of information to diagnose and refine the service call decision as part of the call-handling process, prior to actually initiating the on-site service visit. The data acquisition methods used and by what means that information is manipulated and presented represent the technological focus of artificial intelligence and remote diagnostics in service today. Within this context, the maintainability of the database is the most critical issue in terms of utilizing diagnostic knowledge bases; as knowledge bases become more complex due to inclusion of ongoing subsequent data, maintainability of the systems becomes a key factor. Knowledge bases must be constructed to ensure reliable diagnostic information within the limits of a maintenance system.

An example of how a detailed knowledge base can be transformed proportional to the value of support in maintainability can be shown in terms of:

■ Breakdown/emergency repair
■ Preventive maintenance
■ Predictive maintenance

In the traditional practice of breakdown and emergency repair (Figure 6.1), information used to diagnose the equipment or system fault is usually obtained after the fact. Costs associated with breakdown and emergency

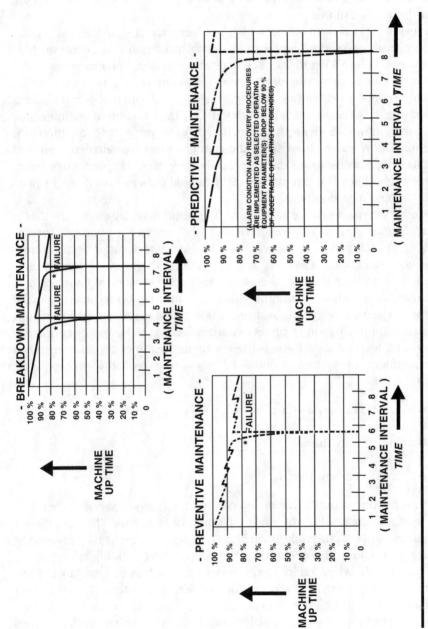

Figure 6.1   Illustrative examples of maintenance and repair practices on equipment uptime.

repair include unanticipated production losses and the related costs of idle production inventory, wasted and inefficiently allocated craft and manpower, and downtime and damage of associated machinery resulting from the initial failure.

Preventive maintenance, in which maintenance is scheduled at regular time intervals, provides significant levels of protection from catastrophic equipment failure (Figure 6.1); however, such maintenance may incur higher than necessary costs due to parts replacement, overhauls, etc. when the equipment is operating well within desired operating parameters. Manpower costs may also be inflated by the preventive maintenance approach. Information used in the design of a preventive maintenance schedule is typically taken from the manufacturer's original design and maintenance specifications data; optimally, however, the preventive maintenance schedules is tempered by the personal experience of the responsible maintenance engineer.

Predictive maintenance is (Figure 6.1) condition triggered. By that it is meant that service is provided when the operating condition of the equipment is shown to be deteriorating to the point of catastrophic failure. Condition-monitoring methods are dependent upon the criticality and function of the equipment, the ability to apply sensors to monitor and communicate conditions, and the volume of information required to make competent service decisions and predictions. The primary tool for acquiring accurate information in predictive maintenance is the use of condition-monitoring technology to assess the operating health of a particular piece of equipment or system. Condition monitoring typically utilizes such measures as:

- Vibration analysis (fast Fourier spectrum analysis)
- Temperature
- Fluid flow/volume
- Pressure
- Electric current fluctuation

Preventive and predictive maintenance may provide service when it is not required, increasing the costs of equipment service. The condition-monitoring approach, while incurring costs to implement the monitoring apparatus, could optimize the usage of service by providing maintenance and repair only when critically necessary to maintain the integrity of the equipment. In general, preventive and predictive maintenance works best for mechanical and electromechanical equipment that tends to fail gradually; demand repair works best for equipment that either works or does not work (i.e., electronics technology).

The use of remote diagnostic tools and practices is becoming commonplace within the full service call process architecture. The most common diagnostics mechanism is the technical assistance center (TAC), which typically has a staff of experts complemented with technical documentation and possibly access to diagnostic-based systems. The TAC provides end-users with initial call handling and implements any call avoidance routing (talking the end-user through the solution, sending a user-replaceable part, or, when required, beginning the service call escalation procedures).

The overall call management system with remote diagnostic capabilities typically contains:

- One or more help desks or call management centers
- Technical assistance centers linked to the help desk
- Local area networks (LANs) connecting individual workstations at both the help desk/call center and TAC

In developing an integrated approach to call management and TAC systems, five general functional modules are necessary:

1. *Configuration management module*, which is required for overall network control as it provides the ability to identify and locate hardware/software components
2. *Troubleshooting module*, which provides the ability to examine information from the LANs, PC controllers, and other devices through the use of integrated diagnostics
3. *Problem tracking and trend analysis module*, which provides the ability to track all supporting activities and responses by configuration, in addition to identifying long-term trends in problem or service calls
4. *Software control module*, which provides the ability to support the process for loading new programs, controlling system enhancements, and enforcing software version control
5. *Shared peripheral resources module*, for improving and reporting on multiple use or sharing of certain devices (such as displays or printing)

When examining the typical customer configuration and need for service and the business environment in which the service operates, one can observe a variety of calls arriving as a function of the stage and life cycle of the support system, the extent and sophistication of the system, the size of the deployment, and the education, training, and sophistication of the user group.

As discussed earlier,* the general classes of customer service calls fall into the following categories:

---

* See Chapter 4, Figure 4.5.

- *Type 0 — System Design, Specification, and Integration Requests.* These calls tend to be related to new or emerging requirements and are often random in nature and typical of the calls that occur during the very early stages of a system development project.
- *Type 1 — Installation.* These calls represent both system-specific and general customer requests and occur at the point of installation after system approval, design, and integration. These calls often relate to scheduling of the implementation, installation, initial training, and concerns over workability.
- *Type 2 — Maintenance and Repair Service Requests.* Typical customer calls in this category involve requirements for maintenance and repair services due to hardware failure, software failure, or a combination of hardware and software failure. These calls are not only very critical but tend to be the calls that are perceived by most service organizations as the primary type of service call request. However, the pattern of call arrivals for type 2 calls is quite different from the call patterns for other types of calls, and the mechanisms for response are also different.
- *Type 3 — Instructional and How-To Customer Calls.* A new class of customer requirements emerges due to increasing sophistication of systems, systems being used in real time by non-technical personnel, and initial instruction at the point of installation being inadequate. Such calls involve user questions regarding application and use of the equipment, user inexperience, or lack of user understanding of a specific or general application. These calls tend to be critical in terms of the overall service delivery process to the user, but it is important to avoid confusing type 3 calls with type 2 calls because the mechanisms, delivery approaches, and optimum handling mechanisms are quite different. In addition, many service organizations tend to see type 3 calls as being noncritical or, even worse, as not their responsibility. However, from the user perspective, these calls are just as important and critical as type 2 calls.
- *Type 4 — Network Calls.* This class of customer calls occurs as a result of the increasing deployment of sophisticated local and wide area networks. These calls relate to failure of the network as a whole or elements of the network. Because general users, particularly in a physically distributed mode, remote from other users, are unable to determine that the cause of their mutual problems may be a network type failure, rather than a failure or problem in their own units, these calls are also often perceived as type 2 or type 3 by customers. In addition, the service organization can easily misinterpret these as type 2 calls unless some particular technical screening and network-oriented evaluation process is put into

place. In essence, the failure of either a local or wide area network can generate a very large number of type 2 calls by individual users. An appropriate problem-resolution and self-organizing data system can relatively easily discern whether this rapid series of arriving calls is in fact network related and flag such calls. Such identification of network failure avoids further work trying to fix an individual box that is failing to operate and directs attention instead toward a network failure. The service organization system must be able to recognize network-related problems and focus on a network fix if it is to avoid being overwhelmed by misleading type 2 or 3 calls from individual users.

■ Type 5 — Moves, Adds, Changes (MACs) and Field Improvements. These calls are usually generated as a result of changes in system environments or user needs; in that sense, they tend to be very similar to type 0 calls. Alternatively, they could be self-directed by the service organization itself monitoring all calls, as a result of pattern or statistical analyses and evaluations of the demands associated with type 2, 3, or 4 calls that indicate a need for a field engineering changes or modifications in hardware, software, or network structure in the field to reduce or eliminate certain types of problems in the future.

In general, the character of the total demand pattern of these calls is well defined.

Remote Diagnostics State-of-the-Art

Work in the field of advanced remote diagnostics and artificial intelligence in the field service industry initially tended to focus on the use of expert-oriented decision techniques based upon either rule or heuristic expert models and processes. Within the last few years, this array of technology has been extended to include self-organizing systems and processes, as well as application of new intelligent data storage and retrieval approaches (see Figure 6.2).

Specific mechanisms within the area of remote diagnostic advisory systems include:

■ *General fault* models show all the ways a device can fail and the causal linking among the failures. Information about applicable tests and repairs is attached to each fault situation. This approach has been shown to be not very useful for repair diagnostics for new products and technologies.

■ Troubleshooting models are usually augmented fault models that follow the pattern of the general fault model but also describe

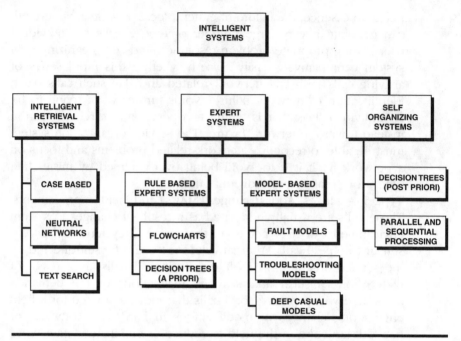

Figure 6.2 Overview of types of data and intelligent diagnostic systems used in help desk/technical assistance center (TAC) remote diagnostics.

how the fault diagnostics strategy should be modified under certain conditions. In general, troubleshooting models add "if–then" logic to the standard fault model to support repair analysis.

■ *Deep causal* models actually describe how the unit under repair is structured and assembled. The knowledge base describes how the device is put together, how it works, what the relationships are, and how likely each piece is to fail and generates a troubleshooting strategy based on these relationships. These models are most often used when the equipment being diagnosed is very new or highly complex or when little or no effective troubleshooting strategy currently exists.

In addition to model-based expert systems are rule-based expert systems, which involve flow charts or procedural rules that can be used to diagnose a repair situation or the use of decision-tree technology. The decision-tree concept (Figure 6.3) is based upon the use of a tree-like structure that can illustrate the relationships among machines or products, complaints, symptoms, causes, and ultimately corrective action recommendations. This type of analysis can be carried out before any type of repair action is completed by reliability and maintainability engineers, who con-

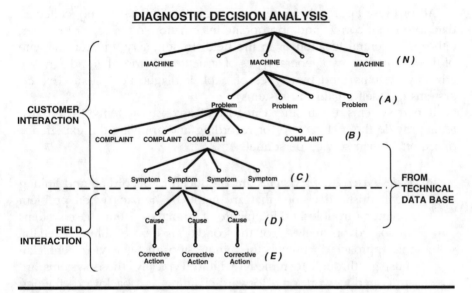

Figure 6.3 Basic diagnostic decision analysis tree structure used in the call handling process. (From Blumberg Associates, Inc., Fort Washington, PA. With permission.)

struct the tree and branch relationships without actual experience in the particular repair. Alternatively, a call-handling, dispatch, and call close-out process could be established that makes use of the same decision-tree structure after the fact. This is easily done by linking information obtained from the arriving calls for service (e.g., identification of product or machine-related complaints) to a specific close-out call relating the cause to the symptom and the ultimate corrective action that resulted in a fix or repair.

Decision trees can be built before repair actions are taken through reliability analysis or reverse engineering analysis; in this case, they are used within the context of a rule-based expert system. Or, decision trees can be built into the call-handling process that are based upon completed and closed out call data within the context of a self-organizing approach. Recent new developments in the design and application of self-organizing systems have also focused on parallel and sequential processing, utilizing a combination of logic, hypertext, and parallel processing to achieve the same solution as utilized in the after-the-fact decision tree described above.

Another major application of technology to the field diagnostics is making use of newly developed intelligent (data) retrieval systems. These approaches attempt to use high-speed computer technology to search existing files for case-based situations that are similar in nature to the diagnostics being executed or to make use of neural networks or very high-speed hypertext searches.

All of these approaches attempt to make use of historically collected data to present correct and appropriate information to the repair provider, either in a central location or in the field. In summary, the current state of the art involves two general types of structures (retrieval and diagnostic advisory systems) and two types of explicit diagnostic systems (expert systems and self-organizing systems).

Expert systems are another category of advisory systems. Expert systems provide the architecture for recording and applying the experience of expert human service personnel:

- *Rules-based expert systems* are produced by recording and linking the heuristic decisions that are made by humans when problem solving or troubleshooting failure of a unit or system; these systems are based on analyses of the conditions before failure. Literally, this approach documents the minute steps that a service technician must go through to remedy a fault. Typically, these systems are structured to work on a forward-chaining or a backward-chaining logic, depending upon the specific situation for which the system was designed.
- *Model-based expert systems* are also developed on an *a priori* basis from a database of the calculated or anticipated failure structure and behavior of the system or unit. This format makes the model-based approach better suited for the fault analysis of new equipment with which service personnel may not be familiar. Methods to add historical information as it is developed are desirable in a model-based expert system.

Within this diagnostic state of the art, the basic process model for call resolution and fault diagnostics and isolation, as shown in Figure 6.4, follows these procedural steps:

1. Gather and collect information to determine the symptoms and situations in which the problem appears.
2. Form a hypothesis, selecting a fault that is most likely to have caused the observed symptoms.
3. Select a goal or set of goals to resolve a particular call derived from the hypothesis previously developed. This step usually takes the form of determining whether element x is faulty by artfully selecting a specific part out of all the parts to blame, making the process much more manageable and leading to a faster resolution, assuming the initial choice (or guess) is correct.
4. Determine which action would most efficiently achieve the selected goals; the action might be a diagnostic one (observing certain values

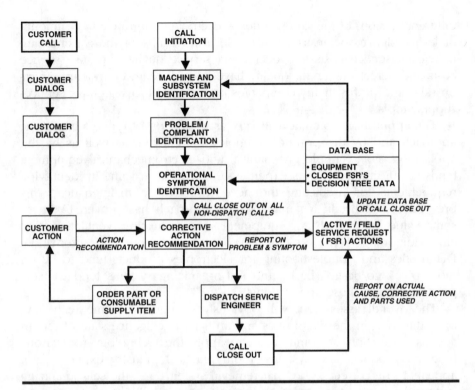

Figure 6.4 Remote diagnostic (decision support) process flow in help desk/technical assistance center (TAC) application.

or indicators), it might be testing, or it might be a type of repair or maintenance, such as calibration, cleaning, or replacement of a part.

5. Perform the action recommended and observe its results. For example, if the action taken was repair of the faulty unit, the observation step will usually require repair verification or retesting the equipment that failed to see if the repair action was effective.

6. Analyze whether or not the results of the action confirm the hypothesis. If they do, then the problem can be isolated and resolved; otherwise, the hypothesis must be refined and the process repeated.

This fault isolation process requires extensive knowledge of the serviced equipment; service personnel obtain such knowledge from formal training, on-the-job training, accumulated experience, and equipment manuals.

Several trends, however, make it difficult for service personnel to obtain and preserve all the knowledge required to perform their jobs most efficiently; one such trend is the rising complexity of modern equipment. Another is the number of different types of equipment to be serviced: different manufacturers, different models from the same manufacturer, different versions of the same model — each one requiring a large amount of knowledge to be instantly available. The results of these trends are increasing service costs and decreasing service quality; because service costs and perceived service quality have immediate and important effects on sales and profits, many companies have decided to search for service-support tools.

The application potential will vary as a function of type of diagnostic approach and by the product technology employed, as well as by the application. For example, mechanical and electromechanical equipment tends to fail gradually, thus expert systems can have value in identifying requirements for predicting the need for advance maintenance. This preventive and predictive maintenance approach has proven to be of some value, particularly for equipment such as heating, ventilation, and air conditioning (HVAC), medical technology, and building automation. Diagnostics and troubleshooting for electronics products tend to be on more of a "go/no-go" basis, and self-organizing systems tend to have greater value in these applications.

The overall assessment will obviously change over time with new breakthroughs in the diagnostics and artificial intelligence state of the art and as a function of commitment to apply the technology for various types of products and systems. From practical industry experience, it appears to be correct to say that retrieval systems and the self-organizing systems have a role in service and that the applicability of the technology will vary as a function of type of product (electronic, electromechanical, or mechanical) and the stage of product use (e.g., new product roll-out, mature product, product being phased back into service).

Current Overview of Diagnostics Technology in Field Service

Extensive developments in the area of remote diagnostics technology (and artificial intelligence) to improve service-based troubleshooting and repair capabilities, both centrally (for call and help-desk diagnostics, call avoidance and TAC support) and in the field, have resulted in a variety of new products available off the shelf to support diagnostics and repair decision-making in field service. Fully integrated help-desk and TAC systems are also available, on a stand-alone basis or as part of an integrated field service management system program.

Cost Benefit and Impact of Remote Diagnostics

Full quantifiable measurement of remote diagnostics cost benefits has yet to be demonstrated. It is clear, however, that diagnostics technology does have some measurable impact. Our own comprehensive study of the

Cost Justification Basis	Technology			
	Computers and Office Automation (%)	Telecom- munications (%)	Medical Electronics (%)	Building and Plant Automation (%)
Gain general competitive edge	55	35	50	64
Capture and retain some expertise/knowledge	41	45	48	55
Improved telephone troubleshooting	35	42	28	31
Improved call avoidance	31	43	21	34
Reduced training time and costs	21	18	14	21
Reduced mean time to diagnose and repair in the field	37	28	19	34
Reduced "broken" calls due to parts/ technical skills	31	21	22	20
Other (increased revenue, justification of added product value/price)	11	10	12	10

Figure 6.5   Specific cost savings, benefits, and justification used for diagnostics projects. (From Blumberg Associates, Inc., Study of Diagnostic Market, Fort Washington, PA, 1994. With permission.)

primary benefits and impacts of service diagnostics revealed a wide array of benefits, as indicated in Figure 6.5. These benefits can be measured both in terms of their impact on the service provider as viewed from the perspective of the field service organization itself, as well as from the perspective of the customer.

A survey of well over 100 service providers indicated that service diagnostics can reduce the training time and reduce or eliminate the effort required to collect and analyze repair and maintenance data. Diagnostics can also help the service organization directly by improving the allocation of both personnel and parts resources to reduce costs. In a survey of over

250 customers, diagnostics technology was found to provide a way to deliver better service and greater product differentiation to the customer, from the perspective of both the service providers and the customers. Additional direct benefits include reduction in the overall mean time to repair and a reduction in the number of "broken" calls due to a lack of availability of on-site parts or skills. Finally, both the service providers and the customers have observed that service diagnostics can be used to improve the ability to deliver service in remote or inaccessible areas.

The primary direct benefit of diagnostics, as shown in Figure 6.6, was in the creation of a competitive advantage and a reduction in mean time to repair and the number of "broken" calls. This result was most directly measured in terms of the reduction in the total elapsed time for repair for complex calls, which typically are about 20% of the total number of calls carried out by service organizations in the markets of computers, building and plant automation, and medical electronics. Where measured, diagnostics also tended to increase the uptime and the mean time between hard failures. Finally, the survey of service organizations suggested that the best delivery mechanisms were via laptop or portable devices through deployment directly to field service personnel. As shown here, evaluating the impact of diagnostics technology in field service, as of this time, is still based mostly on "soft" issues, although there are clearly some specific situations and instances where the savings have been substantial.

In summary, remote diagnostics technology has been shown to have a direct cost benefits impact on:

- The service and support organization
- The service user

The impact is by far the greatest on the service and support organization. The primary impacts observed in these studies included:

- Creation of a competitive advantage and reduction of direct competitive threat by Independent Service Organizations (ISOs) or third-party maintainers
- Reduction in mean time to repair
- Reduction in field diagnostics and troubleshooting time
- Improvement in dispatch assignment and allocation
- Reduction in number of "broken" calls due to lack of parts
- Improvement in the ability to detect a need for field changes or field modifications
- Better control and allocation of high-value critical parts inventory

The effect on the service organization varies primarily as a function of the implementation approach taken. If the technology is based on

Benefits	Effects	Beneficiary	
		Service Provider	Customer
Reduce the training time and skill levels of maintenance personnel.	Reduce labor costs per maintenance person.	X	—
Reduce or eliminate effort required to analyze data.	Reduce personnel requirements.	X	—
Reduce or eliminate effort required to collect data.	Reduce personnel requirements.	X	—
Reduce elapsed time required to assess and diagnose problem(reduce mean time to repair, MTTR).	Reduce personnel requirements. Improve uptime.	X	X
Improve predictability of failure in order to initiate preventive maintenance prior to emergency failure (increase mean time between failure, MTBF).	Reduce personnel requirements. Improve uptime.	X	—
Improve response time of service call or call avoidance probability.	Improve customer satisfaction and customer retention.	X	X
Improve craft and resource allocation.	Reduce personnel and parts inventory costs.	X	—
Reduce "broken" calls due to lack of parts/skills.	Reduce personnel costs and MTTR.	X	X
Provide greater service and product differentiation.	Improve potential to gain new markets and position in currently served markets.	X	—
Improve ability to deliver service in remote or inaccessible areas.	Reduce personnel and parts inventory costs.	X	X

Figure 6.6 Primary benefits and impacts of service diagnostics in equipment service. (From Blumberg Associates, Inc., survey of 100 service organizations and 200 customers of service firms using diagnostics technology, Fort Washington, PA, June, 2000. With permission.)

internal development, research and development (R&D) are usually maintained and carried out by the corporate R&D organization, with liaison support into the service organization. If the technology is purchased, the development and application are usually controlled and coordinated by the manager of information systems (MIS) or the service organization. In either case, maintenance of the database and diagnostics algorithms must be maintained by the service organization, typically by the technical and logistics support department.

Service problem diagnostics applied to central call management help desks and the optimal assignment and dispatch of personnel for on-site calls clearly indicate the potential of online remote diagnostics technology to improve service force productivity and efficiency, thus making more effective use of service resources (people and parts). A survey of current and planned future expenditures for diagnostics used in field service clearly indicated that the overall service diagnostics market is sizable, around $2.6 billion in 2000. This expenditure and growth will primarily continue to occur in the electronics arena, but substantial development and application investments are occurring in both electromechanical and mechanical areas. The pace of investment may fall off as the service industry shifts from development and experimental research initially to the application and roll-out of standard off-the-shelf technology.

WORKFORCE SCHEDULING
AND ASSIGNMENT

Workforce assignment and scheduling have also received a great deal of attention. The random pattern of arrival of service requests, the need to maintain both the perception and reality of service capability, and the need to optimize service level productivity complicate the process. In earlier days, scheduling was usually accomplished utilizing simple first-come/first-served queues on map boards. The map boards displayed the service call requests, and managers attempted to solve the allocation and scheduling problems by using their knowledge of travel times, skill sets of the service personnel, availability of material, etc. The new technology combines queuing theory, linear programming, simulation, and other optimization methods to develop solutions that best meet the most service requirements at the least cost.

One example of this approach is the so-called "traveling salesman" problem, in which a salesman must travel from point to point, making sales calls, taking into account travel time and sales time at each site. The issue is to determine the optimum routing to meeting all the requirements at minimum cost. Software designed to solve the traveling salesman problem can be applied to workforce scheduling.

A number of software packages for vendors, such as ServicePower, ClickSoft, Wishbone, among others, specifically focus on determining optimized workforce scheduling. This process can be improved by combining the ability of remote diagnostics functions to identify the service issues and problems with optimum workforce scheduling to ensure that the appropriate service person is optimally assigned to the proper service problem.

Logistics Management and Forecasting Technology

The very significant changes that have been taking place in the high-tech service industry over the last 10 to 15 years have led to dramatic improvements in the strategic management, control, and direction of logistics support and spare parts control. In order to understand and make use of these improvements, it is essential to see, in a broader perspective, the almost revolutionary changes that have taken place in the typical field and logistics support service organization. In general, from the 1950s through the 1980s, almost all equipment manufacturing (particularly in the area of high-tech data processing), office automation, telecommunications, process control and building and plant automation, medical electronics, and related industries operated field service (including the provision of installation, maintenance, and repair) as a cost center. Typically, these service organizations were highly decentralized, focusing primarily on the issues of getting the service personnel to the sites to support installation tasks or, in the event of failures observed by customers, to repair the equipment. Service management, as it existed, was primarily concerned with the supervisory questions associated with field control of service personnel, with a heavy emphasis placed on general customer satisfaction along with adherence to the agreed-to budget or cost allocation. In this context, logistics and physical distribution support generally came from the factory manufacturing function. Parts were usually obtained from the manufacturing inventory or, in crisis situations, directly from the production line. This highly decentralized, fragmented cost center approach to service has changed dramatically and will continue to do so.

Service is now being managed typically as a profit center or independent line of business, as opposed to a cost center; it is generally run centrally with its own physical distribution, logistics support, parts management, and control functions. In the modern service organization, service calls from customers are not viewed as automatic on-site dispatches but rather as the basis for determining what actions are to be taken to resolve the customers' problems in the most timely and cost effective manner possible. In-depth technical analysis, remote diagnostics, and call avoidance mechanisms are now being increasingly used as an on-line part of the call-handling process in an to attempt to eliminate altogether the need for physical on-site dispatch (through advising customers to take their own corrective actions or through the dispatch of parts, supplies, corrective software, etc.) In cases for which actual on-site calls are required even after such call avoidance diagnostics, analysis as part of the call-handling process can provide specific accurate recommendations to service personnel in regard to which parts should be taken with them on their service calls, thus reducing the percentage of "broken" calls or calls in which the service effort must be halted until a subsequent time when parts and the necessary technical assistance are available.

In summary, as shown in Figure 6.7, substantial changes are taking place with respect to the management, direction, and control of the full logistics pipeline. While much is being currently done in the area of improvements in call handling and dispatch, systems automation, and service marketing, it is in the area of service spare parts and logistics management and control where some of the most innovative and productive improvements have been made.

Service operations usually require a combination of service personnel, skills, and parts in order to complete the process of installation, maintenance, and repair in the field. Depending upon the product technology involved, 50 to 70% of all service calls on average require a part or parts to complete a repair. As a result of this important requirement for parts in the field, stockpiles of parts tend to proliferate, often being found in the trunks of service personnel's cars, on sites, and, in some cases, squirreled away in service personnel's homes or lockers.

As indicated in Figure 6.7, an analysis of the general flow of parts and materials within the typical field service organization clearly shows a process that can be described in terms of an integrated closed-loop pipeline. Materials flow into the logistics pipeline, ordinarily from the internal manufacturing line or from outside purchases, and are initially stored at some central warehouse or depot. The parts and materials then flow down through regional or local depots or stock centers to the service personnel who use them in their day to day operations. In general, and particularly for electronics and electromechanical equipment, a very high percentage of the parts in terms of total investment (close to 80%) represent high-value items or subassemblies that are repairable. These units are usually pulled and, as part of the repair process, replaced with good parts and sent back to a local or central depot for refurbishment or repair. Ultimately, at the completion of the logistics process, the parts are then sent back to the central or regional depot for reuse.

Given both the general structure and the above parameters of the logistics and distribution pipeline, it is very important to recognize that

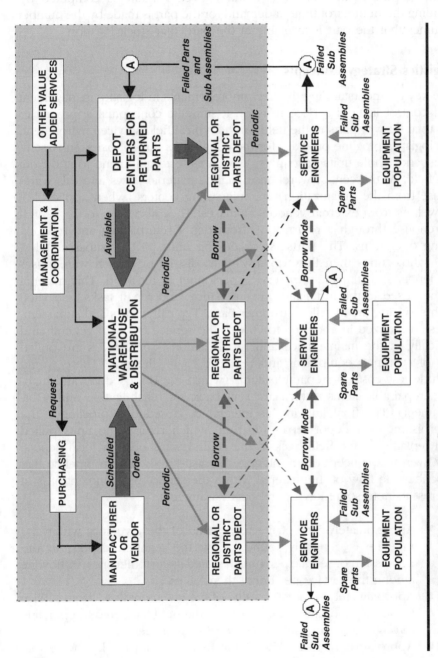

Figure 6.7   Service logistics pipeline flow.

perhaps the most important element of the pipeline is ensuring an optimum fill rate at the service personnel level. Fill rate is computed by dividing the number of times a demand for the part is made by the number of times that the part is available at the particular stock location.

Logistics Strategy Concepts

The key to understanding the new improvements in logistics management and control in field service rests on a strategic conceptual approach to the total flow of parts in the field. In the typical field service environment, the logistics pipeline provides for the continuous flow of parts, subassemblies, and whole units or loaners, as well as test equipment, to and from the field. At the central warehouse facility, material flows into this warehouse from the organization's manufacturing centers (when applicable), as well as from external vendor purchases. They also flow to the central warehouse through a return loop from depot refurbishing and rehabilitating operations. The parts (stockkeeping units, SKUs), subassemblies, and whole units then flow downward to district or branch warehouses or depots and ultimately to service personnel in the field. This material is then used in the installation, maintenance, and repair tasks associated with servicing the installed customer base. Typically, parts and subassemblies are utilized in about 65 to 70% of the service tasks. In general, and typically in the maintenance and repair actions, some SKUs are pulled out of customer equipment and replaced to fix the unit. These would include low-cost or irreparable items (which are disposed of) and high-cost, repairable items (which are sent back for rehabilitation and refurbishment). The final link in this integrated, closed-loop pipeline is the refurbishment or depot repair function, which returns the units pulled and replaced in the field back to the central warehouse or local depots.

Given this concept of an integrated logistics closed-loop pipeline that describes the flow of the material within the service environment, it is of interest to note some key operational parameters:

- Approximately 50% of the total value of the inventory within the pipeline is generally found below the manned depots, in the possession of service personnel, stored at customer sites, or flowing among the service personnel themselves.
- Approximately 80% of the value of the inventory flows from service personnel and the installed base in the field back into the pipeline through the refurbishing and rehabilitation depots.
- Approximately 30 to 35% of the material returned by the service personnel from the field to the refurbishing depot are, in fact, good units. This particular parameter is increasing as more and more

service personnel tend to use a pull-and-replace strategy as part of their diagnostic test activities in emergency maintenance and repair.

These improvements in logistics can best be done through reporting of parts used at the time of call close-out in the field as they occur in real-time.

Other organizations fail to recognize the vital importance of the refurbishment/rehabilitation and repair return loop. In point of fact, through utilizing a just-in-time approach to field depot repair, it is actually possible to significantly reduce the total logistics inventory investment. Finally, many logistics organizations are still utilizing inventory control systems and processes developed from the manufacturing environment. They fail to recognize the much more complex parts demand patterns that exist in the service environment due to the existence of a return cycle and long-run product life cycles, which can affect demand patterns over time. In the manufacturing inventory, demand patterns can be forecast using production requirements forecasting and materials requirements planning (MRP). In addition, the parts used in the manufacturing process do not, in effect, actually return. In the production environment, the logistics inventory flows only outward to the customer. The tremendous complexities produced by the return loop cycle in the typical field service inventory generally invalidate the normal inventory forecast models and mechanisms used in the manufacturing environment for inventory control.

Strategic Factors Affecting the Efficiency and Productivity of the Logistics Pipeline Management and Control

For logistics managers, it is vitally important to recognize several key factors that influence the ability to manage and control the parts pipeline and optimize the service personnel fill rate with minimum investment and logistics operations costs. These factors include:

- *Installed base density impact.* The density of the installed base has a significant impact on the bottom-line profitability of the service operation. The key factor is that higher density makes it easier to stock, control, and deliver spare parts and to avoid "broken" calls. Density also, of course, influences service personnel travel time and, therefore, response time. Thus, the denser the base of equipment served, the easier becomes the job of determining how much and at what locations the parts inventory should be allocated. Again, as the level of circuitboard integration rises, parts replacement at the board level, rather than repair at the component level on site, becomes more efficient. As increases in the cost of carrying inventory in the field become significant, the density becomes a more important factor in profitable performance. When parts are a significant element of cost, an increase in the number of customers without retaining or improving density levels can result in less profit, rather than more. Unfortunately, the installed base density is typically not under the control of the logistics manager, but rather the product managers or, in the case of third-party maintenance or independent service organizations, service marketing managers. In point of fact, the introduction of third-party maintenance service in a product-based service organization can provide a mechanism to significantly improve installed base densities and therefore improve the effectiveness of logistics management and control.

■ *Key inventory control mechanisms.* A most important factor affecting the efficiency of the logistics management is the level and specificity of control of the pipeline. Parts can be controlled at the individual SKU level or in kits, or through a combination of parts and kit control for a specific product. Both kit control and SKU control have value in logistics management, but it is critical to understand where kiting strategies work and do not work. Kits are best employed in situations involving very limited installed base density or during product roll-in or roll-out. Kits are not effective as SKU control during the general mid-term life cycle of a product, particularly if the densities are reasonably high. Generally, service organizations should be using a combination of parts and SKU control down to and including the service personnel level.

■ *Efficient use of depot refurbishment/rehabilitation.* Another mechanism that can be used to fine-tune the performance of the logistics pipeline is the detailed scheduling and control of refurbishing and rehabilitating depot operations. By introducing a quality assurance check at the arrival of subassemblies from the field and tracking those subassemblies back to the service personnel who initiated the field pull and replacement, it is possible to identify those service personnel who are, in essence, utilizing the SKU pipeline as a test and diagnostic mechanism. Such data could be utilized to retrain service personnel in the field to improve the effective use of service personnel trunk stock, as well as to introduce more formal diagnostic procedures at the field level. Perhaps most important is the concept of detailed scheduling of resupply to the field through very rapid turnaround of the depot repair operation. Some service organizations, such as Texas Instruments, have utilized artificial intelligence mechanisms in their depot refurbishing lines to improve the ability to refurbish or repair any type of circuit board (from Texas Instruments or other manufacturer), as well as to reduce the amount of time required to diagnose and ultimately repair the board or unit. By using artificial-intelligence-based diagnostics and automated conveyer systems to move the diagnosed SKU to the appropriate work stations for refurbishment and repair (R&R), it is possible to bring the total elapsed time from initiation of a scheduled request for a SKU or board repair from a holding inventory to shipment to within approximately 2 hours. With this type of elapsed R&R time, a significant percentage of all service requests can be filled from the R&R depot, rather than from central stocks or placed on back-order for manufacturing or external vendor shipments.

In summary, a number of mechanisms can be utilized to bring about significant improvements in the efficiency and effectiveness of the logistics pipeline, including changing the installed base density through focused, proactive, third-party maintenance selling; improving SKU control down to the service personnel field level; improving forecasting mechanisms and systems; and improving the efficiency and turn-around time of depot refurbishing and rehabilitation operations.

Advanced Forecasting Mechanisms for Logistics Management and Control

Of the various tools and techniques available to the logistics manager, one of the most important, and yet least understood, is the use of advanced forecasting to determine stock demand. Typically, most field service logistics organizations utilize simple linear or exponential smoothing forecasting models based upon inventory control systems developed in the manufacturing environment. Unfortunately, such simplistic techniques do not account for the more complex demand patterns found in a field service environment. In broad terms, parts demand is primarily affected by the multiple effect of both the product life cycle and the installed base density. Once a product has been rolled in and before phase out, and assuming a very large density of base, it is relatively simple to forecast demand using standard statistical models.

Control Mechanisms within the Logistics Pipeline

Given the general structure within the logistics pipeline, it is quite clear that certain control "pressure points" can be used to optimize the pipeline and fill-rate efficiency. Clearly, the fact that 50% of the logistics inventory is below the manned stock levels indicates the need for highly accurate and dynamic reports on parts usage at the time of call close-out at the service personnel level. This can be best done through the introduction of formal reporting on parts use through an online call handling and dispatch system. The most important control mechanism for managing the logistics pipeline relates to the forecasting of future parts demand. Forecasting in many organizations is much more an art than a science, driven largely by the lack of availability of accurate field data on parts demand and the lack of training of logistics specialists in forecasting technology. The service management team must understand the critical importance of optimizing the logistics pipeline to achieve overall service profitability. This is the first step in recognizing the vital need for improving forecasting accuracy and capability in logistics management and control.

Factors Affecting Forecasting Mechanisms in Field Service Logistics Management

Although forecasting is of critical importance in optimizing the field personnel trunk stock fill rate, as well as fill rates at each of the stocking levels within the logistics pipeline, most logistics managers tend to use very simplistic techniques such as simple averaging and straight-line extrapolation. The application of effective forecasting must begin with recognition of the key factors that drive parts and SKU demand. The SKU mix and parts configuration of a given product are, of course, dependent upon the product design and structure and its level of modularity. Some equipment can include, in one module or subassembly, components that might reflect hundreds of SKUs in another design. The actual demand patterns for SKUs will be affected by:

1. Mean time between failure (MTBF) of the individual SKU
2. Life cycle of the parent product
3. Speed of resupply for the next higher stocking level

From the standpoint of the logistics manager, the one factor that can be most directly affected by logistics organization is the speed of resupply. The MTBF is, of course, a function of the equipment design. The life cycle is usually determined by the marketing organization.

From the forecasting standpoint, recognizing the effect of what the stage or phase of the product life cycle has on individual part or SKU demand is also important. In essence, when products are in an early roll-in stage, one might find a relatively high demand rate caused by burn-in and initial acceptance testing. However, after this initial stage has passed, stabilization of the product, engineering changes, and other factors tend to reduce the failure rate and it becomes stable over a relatively long period of time. As the product begins to mature or wear out as a function of use, failure rates begin to creep up. Finally, as the product is pulled back and is no longer supported, the demand will vary over time dramatically as a function of product life cycle, installed base equipment configuration, and basic logistics management strategy of the service organization.

Forecasting Methods in Logistics Control

Critical to effective control of the logistics pipeline is the use of accurate forecasting mechanisms that can provide (1) the basis for setting the stock levels to be maintained at the manned central and regional depots as well as the service personnel trunk stocks, and (2) the ability to adjust these stock levels in terms of both minimums and maximums over time as the product life cycles that drive the parts demands change. The first step in developing an effective forecasting approach is to recognize that data must be collected on an accurate basis, driven by the use of parts at the time of repair, rather than on the basis of requests or issuances. It is essential to determine the actual MTBF by SKU in order to develop demand estimates. The use of data relating to issuing of parts tends to reflect the tendency of service personnel to stockpile or hoard parts. It may not be directly related to the product life cycle driving the demand, the MTBF of a particular SKU, or the effects of the actual logistics management strategy employed.

Given that accurate data can be developed on demand (MTBF) by SKU, the next major step, prior to actual forecasting, is to recognize that the data can be analyzed on the basis of either demand in unit time or cumulative demand. The problem of looking at demand patterns in unit or sequential time is that the demands can be masked or affected by changes in product life cycle demand. The general characteristic cumulative demand curve profile is significantly different than the average demand over time. In essence, converting the unit time demands to cumulative demand not only smoothes out the demand patterns but provides a framework for analytical consideration of the effects of the product life cycle on parts demand.

Given the demand data and consideration of product life cycle stages, generally six types of analytical forecasting methods can be used in logistics control:

1. *Simple averaging.* The typical approach used by many logistics managers is the use of simple averaging, which involves computing the average of all past demand data in order to produce a future demand forecast.
2. *Moving average.* The moving average method selects data from the last few time periods and provides somewhat more accurate results that reflect recent changes and trends.

3. *Weighted moving average.* The weighted moving average method places different weights on the historical data for different time periods. This approach is generally an improvement on either the simple moving average or the basic averaging technique, but it does require the introduction of judgments for the weighting mechanisms.

4. *Exponential smoothing.* The exponential smoothing method is a variation of the weighted moving average that utilizes an exponential weighting curve to develop the weighting mechanism. Thus, the weights are applied systematically, eliminating the need for judgmental views. The exponential smoothing method is probably the most widely used among sophisticated logistics managers.

5. *Holt's method.* Holt's method is a more sophisticated variation of the exponential smoothing forecasting approach in that it adds additional factors or historical trend mechanisms. In general, Holt's method will improve on exponential smoothing forecasting accuracy if the general changes in demand are gradual.

6. *Bayesian inference.* The most powerful of the analytical forecasting methods is the use of Bayesian inference. This provides the ability to adjust forecasting methodology and techniques based upon the probability of state change of individual SKUs. Bayesian inference is particularly valid for the typical case of an electronics environment with slow-moving parts for which the demands are spiked or the changes are not gradual.

In addition to the use of an integrated logistics pipeline approach to total management of the logistics inventory that includes (1) control over parts used by the service personnel at the trunk stock level through parts reporting at the time of call close-out, and (2) application of advanced analytical forecasting, other sophisticated tools and techniques can be used to control the logistics management pipeline. These new approaches are based upon improvements in technology through rapid deployment of parts. Until recently it was presumed that the most efficient way to manage parts was to stockpile them at the point of use; however, significant improvements in distribution have led to the recognition that parts could be stored centrally or regionally, with a lower inventory level at the trunk stock level and relying upon the use of rapid transportation mechanisms, and still achieve a high trunk stock fill rate. Same-day courier services, such as Sonic Air, or next-day express services, such as Federal Express or United Parcel Service, can provide the necessary transportation mechanisms.

An even more sophisticated approach is the use of a roving van based in each major metropolitan area that can be dispatched to the individual service personnel during the day as a result of arriving customer calls for assistance. Under this concept, each call is initially analyzed through a problem diagnostics and call avoidance mechanism in order to identify the required parts for the individual service call. Computerized systems are then used to determine whether or not the parts are available in the trunk stock of the service personnel assigned. If the stock is not available, the van (usually stocked at the 99.5% level or better) is then dispatched to provide the service personnel with the necessary parts. Use of a roving van with higher stock levels, combined with a mid-range investment in trunk stocks, can generate an extremely high inventory fill-rate capability at the service personnel level, without imposing unacceptably high investment requirements in stock. In essence, the roving van, in conjunction with trunk stock levels at a lower service personnel inventory fill rate (say, 50 to 60%) can produce a significantly higher fill rate at the trunk stock level without incurring the normal cost of distribution and deployment of individual parts stock to each individual service person's trunk stock.

New tools and techniques are being implemented by sophisticated service organizations to significantly improve the efficiency and effectiveness of logistics management and control. Advanced forecasting methods and techniques are being combined with these new tools and technology for rapid delivery and deployment of central, regional, or local stocks to field service personnel and are producing significant improvements in the profitability of field service operations.

It is very clear that the strategic approach utilized in logistics management and control has a significant effect on both operational productivity and efficiency of a field service organization, as well as its bottom-line profitability. Improvement of the fill rate at the service personnel trunk level can significantly reduce the number of "broken" calls and overall average repair times on site. At the same time, logistics strategies that make use of modern technology for integrated management and control based on forecasting and depot R&R generally generate a higher number of asset and spares "turns"* and higher field fill rates then alternative strategic approaches. It is recommended that all service organizations begin to examine and evaluate their existing logistics strategies in light of these concepts.

DATA MINING AND WAREHOUSING

Much of the CRM literature cites the need to include data mining and data warehousing as part of the overall CRM functionality and infrastructure. Over the last several years, the array of technology and software for data mining and data warehousing has grown enormously; however, most

---

* Defined as multiple use of same inventory in the same year.

of the applications (with respect to the data mining and warehousing functions) tend to focus on the value of collecting, collating, and restructuring presales and marketing data on the premise that a full understanding of all the customer interactions for the company can be extremely useful in pinpointing and accurately estimating new customer requirements.

While the above is certainly true, the fact of the matter is a real need exists for data mining and warehousing in the aftersale service part of the CRM infrastructure. Once products are sold and installed, an extremely interesting and highly valuable dataset begins to emerge. For even basic products, information about the sale and initial warranty information are generated by the customer filling out and returning a warranty card. If the product has been sold with a maintenance and service contract, this information is also very useful. Particularly for high-tech products, additional information can be obtained pertaining to installation, service requests for preventative maintenance, predictive maintenance, or emergency failures, and even, in some cases, requests for moves, adds, and changes in configuration or location.

In point of fact, the service personnel in most firms tend to have the greatest knowledge about current and emerging customer requirements. In essence, while the sales and marketing staff are most involved with the customer before the sale, it is the service personnel whose involvement continues well after the sale. The most experienced marketing and sales personnel, particularly in the high-tech areas of information technology, office automation and copiers, telecommunications, and medical technology, all recognize that the service personnel (particularly if they are experienced) are far and away the best source of information about customers' organizational structure, current experience, and future product needs and requirements. Even though this information has great strategic value, it is often ignored and overlooked by the typical marketing and sales staffs when developing CRM specifications for data warehousing and mining.

To illustrate the critical value of data warehousing and mining in aftersales service, consider a simple process. In each individual case in which a service request is made, the first step is recording the service problem or complaint at the time that the call is received centrally, in addition to any information resulting from further conversation between the handling center and the customer. Once the service call is assigned to a service person in the field, the next step is to track the call, ultimately reporting the final cause of the problem as identified and the final corrective action initiated. This could include, for example, information regarding specific failures, the need for software or hardware updates, or use of service parts, as well as information on mean time between failure, mean time between repair, or service call costs (see Figure 6.8).

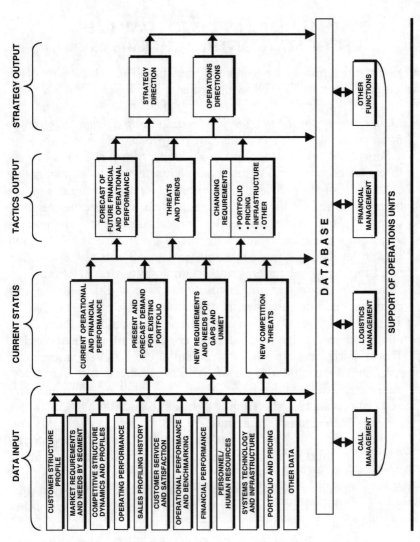

Figure 6.8 General structure of data base for CRM/SMS for service.

If this information is carefully collected and recorded on an online, real-time basis using a direct connection between the service personnel in the field and the central call-handling facility (on a wired or wireless basis), it is possible to build a diagnostic decision tree linking product problems and symptoms to causes and corrective actions.

SYSTEMS DESIGN STEPS TO MAXIMIZE USE OF STATE-OF-THE-ART CRM/SMS

Ensuring that the appropriate system design has been chosen involves serious consideration of the following issues:

1. *Identifying opportunities for productivity and efficiency improvement in the service force.* This can best be accomplished through a benchmark assessment and evaluation of current levels of performance compared to industry standards, as well as a quantitative evaluation of current levels of customer satisfaction and support being provided in the field as measured against customer requirements. To the extent that either or both customer requirements and competitive imperatives are driving response times beyond current levels of performance and operational cost reductions, the need for improved systems and technology can be justified.

2. *State-of-the-art review and evaluation.* Given the development of requirements, the next step is to examine the current state of the art in both service workforce management assignment and scheduling systems and advanced field communications technologies. This should provide a clear assessment of costs, development time, risks, and availability of vendors. This type of state-of-the-art information is available from consultants, as well as from industry associations such as the Helpdesk Institute and the Association for Services Management International (AFSMI).

3. *Development of a formal specification and request for proposal (RFP).* This third step establishes a functional specification defining functional needs and requirements; organizational, operational, and system interfaces; and deployment considerations. This should be sent to a short list of vendors developed during the state-of-the-art review and evaluation (see previous step).

4. *Analysis and evaluation of response and offers based upon full proposals and formal show-and-tell demonstrations.* It is critically important to understand the capabilities of vendors and observe their demonstrations and performance against well-defined scenarios. Steps for vendor selection are outlined below. The scenario should test flexibility of applications to respond to customer requirements,

the level of automation built into the decision logic, ability to conduct rapid real-time calculations of load data, ease of interfacing with existing systems, effectiveness of the computational algorithms, etc.

5. *Management development and implementation process.* The final step is to appoint the appropriate program manager to ensure full and successful implementation of systems and technologies, as well as their efficient deployment and roll-out into the field.

Vendor Selection Steps

In selecting a vendor, it is important to consider the following capabilities:

- *In-depth technical experience.* It is essential that vendors possess extensive experience in the design, development, and implementation of workforce management systems and wireless communication systems in similar geographic areas and with reasonably close structural consistency to your organization. Their level of experience should be verified through direct reference checks.
- *In-depth experience in similar applications.* Vendor organizations with specific experience in your applications area and with knowledge of your specific business environment will be much more qualified to provide you with optimum solutions. At least three references should be obtained.
- *Complete solution.* Quite often buyers of field force management systems are tantalized by the hype and "gee whiz" nature of such offers. It is important to recognize that the full return on investment and anticipated improvements in efficiency will only come through a completely integrated solution. It clearly is not enough to have the mobile communications or the field assignment software set up separately. This is not to suggest that selected vendors must have all the technology within their own portfolios, but it is critically important that a single vendor is selected to take full responsibility for the development and implementation of the complete solution.
- *Financial stability.* Over the last 10 years, vendors offering advances in field force automation and communications have come into the market and then quickly exited. Financial stability and staying power are extremely vital elements in the selection of any vendor to ensure that the vendor will be around to develop and implement the solution, as well as provide continuing maintenance and support after installation.
- *Fast turnaround.* New technologies can have a significant impact on any field service operation. It is therefore very important that vendors be able to offer and clearly demonstrate an ability to provide solutions and full implementation and roll-out. Full systems

deployments should not take more than 6 to 9 months from start to finish after full design approval. Additionally, actual cutover time from an old system to a new one should be kept to an absolute minimum (1 to 2 months).

■ *Business flexibility.* An important factor leading to success in projects of this type is the ability of vendors to be flexible in their interactions with the buyer. Every company is different, and the differences may very well be directly related to specific competitive advantages. It is therefore important that vendors be capable of adjusting to these differences and requirements. At the same time, vendors must not be *so* flexible that they produce unique, customized solutions that are so unusual they cannot easily be maintained or supported, they lack the ability to interface with existing enterprise systems and platforms, and they are not easily scaleable.

■ *Architectural structure with well-designed interfaces.* An important factor in vendor selection is that vendors should be able to offer appropriate architectures for standard wireless gateways that allow for growth and expansion over a minimum 5-year period. Vendor's platforms that feature full compatibility with network and data standards are preferred.

■ *National or global coverage.* Because mobile forces are usually deployed over large areas, vendors must have the ability to provide the assets and resources necessary to support the system where and when required.

■ *Full maintenance and support.* It is obviously not enough simply to have the capability for the design, development, and installation of an integrated and seamless system. It is also critically important to be able to maintain and support that system on a real-time, 24-hour basis. Very careful review and evaluation should be made of a vendor's service strategy and infrastructure to ensure that they are fully responsive to the user's needs and requirements.

■ *Initial and full life cycle price.* Finally, price is a critical, but not the only, consideration. Vendors quote both licensing fees (many on a "per seat" basis) and consulting fees. It is important to look at both costs, as well as after-installation maintenance costs and continuing communications costs, to determine full life cycle price.

SUMMARY

The process of and approach to designing, developing, and implementing an integrated CRM/SMS involves a number of new technology features and options and requires a series of carefully orchestrated and planned steps. The actual vendor selection process also involves careful consideration and evaluation of the major issues as outlined above.

7

USING E-COMMERCE TO SELL, MANAGE, AND DELIVER SERVICE

CONTENTS

The previous chapters of Part II have discussed the functionality design structure dynamics and state of the art of customer relationship management (CRM)/service management system (SMS) integration and the applicability of such systems in the management of service businesses. Clearly, communications are a critically important element of the service management organization with respect to two classes of participants:

1. *Customers of the service organization* who need to communicate with and receive information from the service organization
2. *Members in the service organization*, (e.g., service or logistics support personnel) who need to be able to communicate with other participants in the process and to the customers

We have already discussed the general communications technologies that are being developed and implemented for field use involving wire and wireless laptops, PDAs, cellphones, etc. These technologies are definitely improving the ability to provide purpose-designed systems to improve the efficiency and effectiveness of mobile and field service personnel; however, this is not the only area of improvement possible. The general concept and technology of e-commerce, which is supported by the Internet on a national and global basis, is also important in improving the ability to efficiently manage, control, coordinate, and deliver services on a profitable basis.

Many service organizations in the transportation and distribution fields now use the Internet as a direct link to provide customer service before, during, and after the sale and to coordinate and control this service and support. E-commerce and Internet technologies are used to provide online real-time access to the availability of transportation and distribution and to supply price quotes, not only changing the entire service process associated with booking transportation space, but to some extent eliminating the need for certain retail brokers of such service (e.g., travel agents) by directly linking customers to providers through the Internet. Also, the reaction time for a response to requests for service and logistics has also been shortened and the process made more efficient. The primary value of the Internet lies in its ability to provide an efficient and cost-effective link between customers and service participants to centralized systems to further improve the seamless interface between all participants and the CRM/SMS database.

In addition, other key approaches that need to be considered in developing a CRM/SMS solution using the Internet include:

- *Consideration of application service provider (ASP) alternatives to a stand-alone SMS.* Until recently, the lack of reliable and efficient real-time data communications made it imperative for a service organization to install, manage, and deliver its CRM/SMS via its own internal computer and data network operations. The rise of global Internet and e-commerce technology has led to mechanisms for providing such functional capabilities on a virtual basis. This is essentially the ASP model, in which all or most of the functionality described previously can be provided over the Internet to individual service organizations. This can result in significantly reducing the time and cost to implement new CRM/SMS technology.
- *Warranty support.* Another functional area that can be supported by either a stand-alone or Internet-based delivery system is technology for warranty support and coordination. New software and communications networks designed to support the warranty and return process have now been developed and are available for use and deployment.

The general approach to the management and coordination of field service operations and general customer service and support has been evolving rapidly due to three major trends:

1. A switch in service management strategy from cost center to profit center as a strategic line of business
2. The increasing demands of the service customers for more rapid, responsive, and a broader range of service and support over a wider time frame (24 hours), with greater regional, national, and international coverage and control
3. Advances in the technologies of computers, network communications, the Internet, and service management systems software

Our discussion will focus on the third trend, which deals with new technology, systems, and concepts for managing field forces efficiently, effectively, and responsively.

In the early days of computing, it was generally recognized that the high cost of computer mainframes might inhibit system development and application in smaller organizations. A concept that emerged to overcome this economic barrier was service bureaus. By relying upon service bureaus, computer users did not have to make major investments in computer plant and equipment or in computer operating and support staff. They could simply share time on service bureau computers with other users, paying for that service and support on an as-used basis. While conceptually this approach made economic sense on paper, it was inadequate for applications and functions that required very rapid or real-time support. A major problem was the lack of very high-speed, reliable, secure, data communications technology and networks. In fact, time-shared service bureaus did become successful for batch-type applications, such as payroll processing, that did not require real-time digital communications. Also, in the last several years, with the advent of the Internet, extremely high-speed data transfer, new broadband communications utilizing fiberoptic and satellite technology, and T1 linkages, the entire issue of time sharing has now been reopened and reinvented.

With the advent of the Internet and its growth and deployment have come a number of advances in the way business networks and applications are constructed and used. This technology has led the way to an Internet approach to business applications where applications are delivered to users through browsers, and management of the applications is done centrally on a real-time, online basis, with the technology being shared by several users to reduce costs. This has broken down the traditionally high investment barriers requiring service applications to be purchased by, and physically located on, a single corporate system. A recent survey showed that over 70% of the 500 largest companies in the world have moved to an Internet approach to deploying business applications.

In summary, then, the combination of the Internet, coupled with system-to-system or hub–spoke communications, has opened up a new vista for advanced service management systems on a virtual or time-shared basis through the concept of an application service provider (ASP). ASP firms provide the operating framework by which three individual capabilities, involving field service and customer service systems software, wired and wireless technology, and the Internet, are brought together to provide new integrated service features, functions, and capabilities. With respect to field service management coordination and control, the ASP concept offers very powerful values with an extremely high level of cost effectiveness and return on investment. The ASP provides the ability to:

- Reduce or essentially eliminate the need for significant front-end investment in hardware and software
- Reduce the cost of development and installation and the time associated with this process
- Provide an expanded array of basic and value-added services and functionality rapidly
- Improve communication abilities between customers and central headquarters and between central headquarters and field service engineers, utilizing a combination of wired and wireless communications technology

The field force ASP can offer all service organizations (small, medium, and large) essentially an immediate fix with little or no up-front investment. The application can be implemented incrementally (by geographic area or region), nationally, or internationally. The combination of online real-time communications, computational capabilities, and firewall security protection provides an extremely flexible and reliable structure that enables a broad variety of service business models to be implemented. The primary advantage of the ASP is, of course, a significant reduction in front-end investment. The ASP functionality can also be updated over time, following the state of the art, with the cost of updating being shared by all users. This avoids the added expense of upgrade investment usually found in the stand-alone system. Thus, the ASP solution converts the typical front-end investment and added upgrade costs into a flatter, pay-as-you-go cost.

New ASPs for field force and CRM service providers are offered by Industry and Financial Systems (IFS), Siemens Information and Communications, and FieldCentrix, among others. Some of the standard service management system vendors, such as PDSC, are also planning to announce new ASP services. All service organizations should look to ASP solutions as very real, cost-effective options for developing and improving their system infrastructure.

MANAGING WARRANTY SERVICE USING STAND-ALONE OR INTERNET-BASED SYSTEMS

The role of warranty and post-warranty support service is neither well understood nor well managed in most industrial and commercial firms. The reasons for this are complex, but they primarily relate to the inability to fully understand the strategic value of warranties and the requirements for the appropriate infrastructure to manage and, in fact, optimize warranty and post-warranty support service. It is also important to understand the critical importance of perceptions (from the points of view of both the purchaser and the seller) in successfully managing the warranty and post-warranty process.

Starting with perceptions, we should recognize that (in the minds of buyers) the warranty is a guarantee of performance, in general, and of the form, fit, and function for products and services, in particular. It is intended to be an insurance policy offered to the buyer by the seller ensuring that the purchased goods or services will be consistent with the marketing or sales offer made. This guarantee, or insurance, could be broadly implemented in terms of two mechanisms:

1. *Payment of compensation.* Financial compensation represents one mechanism for warranty support. In essence, an amount is paid to the buyer in the event of the failure of the product or service to perform or meet the sales commitment. This is often tied in consumer products to the product return or reverse logistics process. This approach is used for small appliances and inexpensive consumer goods (e.g., clothing, cosmetics, household cleaners, or food), with a warranty typically stating, "Return for full (or partial) refund in the event of dissatisfaction." This approach is also applied to small returnable goods in which excess wear or partial failure can be physically determined (such as the case of a return warranty on tires being based upon the date of purchase and observed tread wear). This warranty mechanism is also used between manufactures and wholesalers and wholesales and retailers for the return of unpurchased goods (e.g., books, clothing, or pharmaceuticals), with the initial buyer being compensated or credited for returns, with the returned goods being sold in a secondary market.

2. *Remedial or repair service.* The second mechanism for satisfying the warranty commitment is to provide the appropriate services either in the field or at some defined depot repair location to fix or remediate the deficiency or problem in the products or services sold. As in the case of the payment mechanism, this process will also involve some reverse logistics. It also requires a combination of proactive and reactive response either to effect a fix or repair rapidly or to prevent the performance failure from occurring at all. This is obviously the more complex and sophisticated guarantee, because it is intended to leave the buyer with full satisfaction with the product, rather than a simple cash payment.

In essence, a significant difference exists between the warranty strategy involving repayment on a partial or full basis or exchange in which the warranty acts very much as a simple insurance policy vs. the more sophisticated service-supported warranty process, in which the selling organization commits to making the repair or fix within a given time frame. Both approaches must be managed and involve a reverse logistics component. However, only one, the service warranty support, requires the seller or the seller's dealer to set up and operate a complete service organization and infrastructure (Figure 7.1).

MANAGING THE STRATEGIC VALUE OF THE WARRANTY PROCESS

Looking at this general business model for warranty support, we must also recognize that, in both warranty and (in the case of service support) post-warranty performance, the process, if appropriately managed, can have strategic value. Actual experience in the retail field, such as consumer electronics, for example, shows that warranties can be extremely profitable. Circuit City and Sears have found that buyers tend not to make as much use of service warranty guarantees as they might be entitled to for the following reasons:

- The unit purchased simply did not fail within the warranty or extended warranty time frame.
- The buyer forgot that a warranty applied.
- The buyer moved to a new geographic region, in which the warranty service was not available.
- The purchased unit was sold to a third party or is no longer used.

Experience also indicates that, especially in well-planned warranty offers based on accurate failure forecasting, that actual warranty service

| Warranty Guarantee | Required Structure | | Organization | | | |
	Policy Procedures	Infrastructure and Systems	Field	Reverse Logistics	Depot	Business Model
Payment in cash for failure	Payment for loss of use of replacement of equivalent product/ services	Management structure Reverse logistics	No	Yes	Yes	Insurance
Payment in services	Service level commitment	Full service management system Call handling Logistics	Yes	Yes	Yes	Service line of business

Figure 7.1 Warranty strategies.

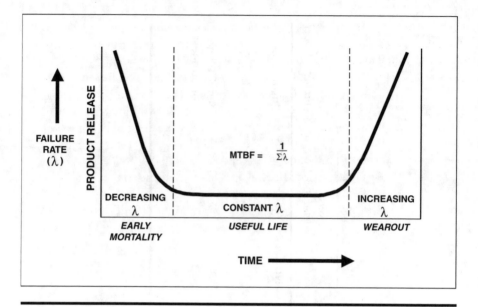

Figure 7.2 Typical failure rate as a function of time.

is used a lot less than was planned for in initial product cost allocations. This could make the profitability of warranties and post-warranties quite high. One can immediately see the result of this simply by going to any large consumer electronics or appliance (refrigerators, washing machines, air conditioning, etc.) retailer. In these organizations, when the product sale is complicated, additional warranty coverage is immediately offered to the customer because of the high margin associated with the warranty. On the other hand, poorly planned warranties can lead to both profit margin erosion and loss of market share. Thus, a warranty system that can track and identify failure rates of the entire unit, subassembly, or stockkeeping unit (SKU) levels and can then proactively respond either by allocating parts properly or by making engineering changes in the field or manufacturing changes to increase the profitability of the warranty or extended warranty function.

The key component in this evaluation and planning is that, in general, product failures are not constant over time. As shown in Figure 7.2, failures tend to be high in the early burn-in stage during initial use of the product (typically, part or all of the warranty period), but then they stabilize, particularly if engineering changes and retrofits and changes in parts reliability have been made in the field or product line based upon earlier mean time between failure (MTBF) experience. Finally, as the product begins to mature and age, or is not fully supported, failure rates again begin to arise. This idealized pattern depends upon the critical assumption that the initial warranty-use period is monitored closely for failure down to the SKU level, subassembly level, and whole-unit level, with linkages between the individual SKU components and the overall system being identified. If this monitoring is carried out on a continuous, real-time, comprehensive basis, the observed failure rates can be significantly limited or reduced due to being able to identify failure rate trends early in the game and take corrective action at the manufacturing level, at the initial purchase, at installation, or through preventative and predictive maintenance in the field.

Such monitoring is perhaps the most important element of the warranty management process. Warranty systems and infrastructures should be designed and implemented such that they provide continuous tracking of MTBF (at the assembly, subassembly, and SKU levels), in addition to identifying linkages between the part, assembly, and subassembly level failures. These failures should also be linked to problems and symptoms as reported by users. This information is best collected starting in the warranty process. Such data can be of great value if accurately collected and reported on a real-time basis and then analyzed and evaluated to identify failure rates and trends, making use of advanced forecasting models and purchasing models (such as expediential forecasts, the Weibull distribution, or logistics simulations). Other related technology can minimize failures in the field through preventative and predictive maintenance, thus producing a much more profitable picture.

The design of the warranty and post-warranty offer must take into account:

- Value of warranty to buyers
- Specific allocation of warranty-generated revenues (out of the total product price) to avoid excess profits being attributed to the product or underfunding warranty support buyouts and offers (i.e., the warranty process should be tracked and evaluated as a separate profit center)
- Setting appropriate extended warranty prices — too high implies poor reliability, too low could lead to losses; extended warranty pricing should be based on market research on customer service perceptions, value, and willingness to pay
- Value of engineering changes or part and subassembly replacement or upgrade in order to improve reliability in the field (covered by the warranty charges)
- Need for predictive or preventive maintenance, paid out of warranty charges, to reduce high-cost emergency repair

IMPORTANCE OF PERCEPTIONS IN MANAGING WARRANTY AND POST-WARRANTY SERVICE

Another issue of critical importance in successfully managing the warranty process is recognizing the very real differences in perception (and reality) on the part of buyers vs. sellers (Figure 7.3). Sellers want to make the warranty guarantee as precise and specific as possible and at the same time do not wish to suggest that the reliability or quality of this product or service is at risk. The warranty specifications are thus usually written in extremely fine print and constructed utilizing legalistic phrases. Sellers' policies and systems also tend to be focused on analysis and evaluation of submitted warranty claims and requests to limit exposure.

Buyers, on the other hand, perceive the warranty as a real guarantee of quality, reliability, and service support in the event of a problem. Warranties are generally viewed as a security blanket, and the buying customer assumes that a warranty provides an extremely high level of commitment to service and support. Customers generally do not read the fine print and in all probability do not understand, or are not aware of, the *caveat emptor* ("let the buyer beware") framework in which the warranty is often quoted. Specifically, however, if buyers receive the service and support they require during the warranty period (or if they never require it), their brand loyalty most likely increases; thus, full service warranty support can lead to improved brand value and greater market share.

Once we can recognize this very real and critical difference between buyer and seller perceptions, we can also begin to understand the strategic

Warranty Commitment	Perception Basis	
	Seller Perception	Buyer (Customer) Perception
Payment for failures	Set aside revenue to cover warranty payments Reverse logistics system in place to authorize return payments	Clear return policy, procedures, and infrastructure Timely response from seller
Services to fix failures	Establish and maintain full-service optimization Establish and maintain service management infrastructure	Clear definition of support services, response time, special costs, etc. Ability to provide service seamlessly

Figure 7.3 Differences between buyer and seller perceptions and realities under alternative warranty services.

implications of those differences. A buyer's perception of the value of a warranty depends not upon future events but upon a series of past events and previous personal experience, the experience of peers, and general market and industry experience, including common knowledge. IBM's very high commitment to warranty and post-warranty support added significant value to the IBM brand name, leading to higher market share and the ability to maintain high prices in the presence of competition.

On the other hand, most sellers tend to view the warranty commitment as part of the sales process without seeing the added strategic value of the warranty service associated with the sale. They see customer complaints, particularly about product or service quality, performance, response, etc., as necessary evils or as being a problem of trying to appease a certain class of difficult-to-satisfy customers. This perception is made even more difficult as manufacturing organizations report on their own output quality, resulting in cases in which the product quality (represented by MTBF) as measured by the manufacturing organization can seriously differ from the observed MTBF as reported by the customer. This is made worse when the service organization fails to respond to a service call rapidly or takes no preventive or predictive maintenance activity.

In addition, customers' perceptions tend to be holistic, dealing with the entire interface between the customer, the product, and the manufacturer; the manufacturer, however, deals with these problems in terms of explicit and specific events or factors, an approach that can often put the manufacturer at odds with the customer. For example, operator error due to not following a particular instruction may cause a copying machine to malfunction and be viewed by the buyer as unreliable, even though the machine was not at fault. The product seller, however, most likely would view this malfunction as a failure on the part of the customer to train the user personnel properly. Anybody with experience in product support knows that most user organizations tend to perceive product failure as being the cause of any problems encountered, as opposed to any improper actions by their personnel. It is, therefore, important to measure performance and reliability from the buyer's side.

MANAGING WARRANTY AND POST-WARRANTY SUPPORT IN A DEALER ENVIRONMENT

The question of managing warranty and post-warranty service and support is made even more complex when indirect channels or dealers and distributors are involved (Figure 7.4). In the case of the direct distribution model, all of the above issues can be dealt with centrally and strategically. However, in the presence of dealers and distributors, the problem is made

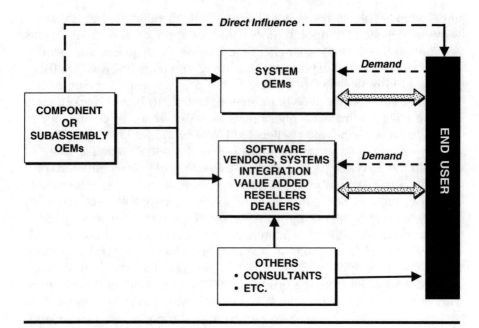

Figure 7.4 Sales and service using indirect channels.

much more complex in terms of the question of what or who takes responsibility for the strategy as opposed to the tactical issues of who pays for what.

Most indirect distribution strategies assume that the dealers and distributors have responsibility for both sales and service. In general, the manufacturer establishes the product form, fit, function, and price. In many cases, a manufacturer's "suggested" price can be modified by the dealers or distributors as a function of their specialized or additional cost of sales and service. Because responsibility for the product warranty is generally assumed by the manufacturers, they establish the warranty policies and processes. In cases when the dealer is required to carry out warranty services on the part of the manufacturer, the dealer or distributor is reimbursed by the manufacturer based upon some type of claims processing system or procedures.

A key question at this point is whether or not the manufacturer views the warranty and post-warranty support as one integrated process or separates the overall service into two components: service under warranty, which is paid for by the manufacturer, and service out of warranty, which is covered by the dealer. As indicated above, the warranty process, if properly managed, can provide great insight into failure and repair characteristics and can be useful in determining optimum service parts logistics allocation, provisioning, and sparing. Management teams assuming control for just the warranty period as opposed to coverage for full warranty and post-warranty service can lead to suboptimization.

Another more important issue is whether the participants (the manufacturer and the dealers) view the warranty process as a zero-sum game, in which the original equipment manufacturer (OEM) and the dealer are at odds, or as a win–win/lose–lose situation, in which both organizations can either win or lose depending upon their synergistic relationship.

Actual experience suggests that the zero-sum gain view is still prevalent, even though it can be clearly pointed out that both the warranty and post-warranty pricing and service portfolios are interactively affected. In addition, engineering changes and changes in manufacturing processes or purchased parts to improve field reliability can directly affect profit margins after warranty.

Resolution of this issue must also give specific weight to recent trends in the general market for outsourcing. In many markets, the traditional internal plant and building maintenance service organizations have been eliminated through outsourcing. This reduces the ability of the buyer (for many types of technologies and products) to turn to the existing internal service force to effect minor repairs or to act rapidly. The trend is clearly to depend more and more on the manufacturer or the dealer distributor (in the indirect channel model) for a full array of services. Thus, a very critical effect of the general outsourcing trend, particularly for companies utilizing an indirect distribution channel, is the significant increase in the amount of field service that the dealer or distributor must provide.

If the manufacturer, in these circumstances, continues to see the process as a zero-sum game, it is quite clear that a major conflict could arise between the manufacturer and its dealers relative to dealer profitability and level of service provided. In essence, the impact of outsourcing requires manufacturers to pay much more serious attention to dealer service in regard to extended warranties or after warranties are no longer in effect, including but not limited to ensuring efficient service parts resupply. Outsourcing also requires much more elaborate and sophisticated analysis and evaluation of the entire warranty process, including the policies, procedures, and infrastructure, in order to ensure optimization of both the manufacturer and dealer or distributor warranty support.

The bottom line is that management of the warranty and post-warranty process requires:

- Clear understanding of the requirements for, and the degree of customer's interest in, both the form and type of the warranty repayment vs. corrective services

- ■ Understanding the importance of the full service guarantee as opposed to the reimbursement guarantee to the buyer group and individual segments
- ■ Understanding the long-term strategic value of the full service warranty commitment

The use of the full service approach in the warranty commitment process and guarantee must be related to overall long-term higher perceived reliability and quality and increased revenues and profits. Because the service organizations can directly identify, measure, and correct failures in the field if the appropriate infrastructure and systems are in place to control the problem–symptom–cause–corrective action process in the call opening, tracking, and close-out procedures and in the reverse logistics process, they can build a strong and accurate database to increase mean times between failure and reliability through optimizing purchase of stocking materials, recommending engineering changes and modifications that could result in extending the product mean time between failure, and identifying other changes and modifications such as onboard diagnostics to significantly improve mean time to repair.

It is essential to recognize the strategic value of warranty and post-warranty service in terms of generating revenues and profits from service performance. In essence, the initial warranty coverage if properly managed, marketed, and priced, could provide a starting point for the sale of a longer term extended warranty or after-warranty service and support, at a substantial profit. Because so much of the warranty and post-warranty process requires on-line interaction between many participants (the customers, the retailer and/or others in the distribution channel, the service provider, etc.), e-commerce technology is especially well suited to general support of the process.

III

MARKETING AND SELLING SERVICE

Thus far, we have approached the issues of marketing and selling from a service perspective. While some of the ideas contained in these next chapters may also apply to product businesses, they specifically focus on the service market and mechanisms to increase service customer base density through an objective, logical, and full analysis of customer service requirements (both at present and in the future). Appropriate survey and measurement mechanisms can reveal the customers' current levels of satisfaction, customer perceptions of your firm vs. competitors, the appropriate service portfolio and pricing to attract more customers, or a need for more extended services or service performance improvement. The continuous goal of providing service quality and customer satisfaction to meet current and unmet service needs and requirements or gaps is crucial to maximizing service-based density.

These service customer metrics and parameters, when tied and related to internal performance benchmark measures and historical demand patterns, can be efficiently collected, collated, analyzed, and evaluated in customer relationship management (CRM) databases, which provide information and the platforms necessary for using the information to create new service strategies or update and fine-tune existing ones.

The primary reasons for focusing on marketing and selling service goes back to the importance of density in service management. We must continually look toward the customer base, including current customers, future customers, and past customers, to see how well their service requirements are met and to identify service gaps and competitive threats. The reason is strategic. The more satisfied the existing customers are with more services, the higher the service-based density can be. The reasons for marketing and selling are to create the optimum service base.

In developing the marketing and sales plan, and in measuring service customer satisfaction and unmet gaps, one more important issue must be considered. In a product environment, these types of issues are and should be focused on the product form, fit, and function; however, for service, the focus must be on a customer's total needs for service.

It is essential to recognize, as discussed previously, that service is largely perceived; perception can be as important as, if not more important than, reality. Therefore, our marketing and selling, process, and measurement mechanisms must go beyond the box and focus on customers' total needs for service, rather than a specific service. For example, a plumber looking only at the service needs of a plumbing system will ignore or miss the building owner's total needs for service and support of his entire operating environment, including heating, ventilation, and air conditioning (HVAC), security systems, fire protection systems, etc. Looking at the service needs of customers through their eyes (or perceptions), rather than the seller's, leads to successful identification of the full array of unmet gaps and requirements and new service portfolio elements that can lead to increasing service-based density.

8

MEASURING AND EVALUATING SERVICE QUALITY

CONTENTS

As companies recognize the need for achieving quality service and optimizing customer satisfaction, they begin to focus more on both the process and mechanisms for improving them. Unfortunately, service quality is often viewed in general and fuzzy terms and as being equivalent to keeping the customer satisfied. Many service organizations have made limited attempts to educate employees regarding the need for improved customer focus and sensitivity as a means for improving satisfaction. This general orientation tends to treat service as an afterthought and makes a general appeal akin to "motherhood and apple pie". Such an approach usually does not work in practice. Many employees view customer needs negatively, as something that creates more work for them. In addition, employees not involved directly in sales rarely get to see customers, much less measure their reactions and needs.

The greatest problem may be that employees view customer service requirements as being dumb, stupid, or inconsistent. They do not understand customers' perceptions and points of view. In essence, employees understand the practices and nuances of their own company's service but fail to understand why customers do not. Employee training helps but is by no means the only way to achieve and maintain service quality.

It is not practical to leave the responsibility for meeting customer satisfaction up to employees on an *ad hoc*, informal basis. It is necessary to set up structured systems, procedures, and disciplines to define service quality and to track performance. The payoff is high to the firms that do so. Our market research and other studies show that perceived service quality and consistency of customer service satisfaction have much to do with customers staying with existing vendors or switching to new ones.

Market studies, carried out for almost every product line, show that customers use perceived satisfaction levels as a *critical factor* in deciding to buy product or service from one vendor or another. The potential buyer of a high-tech product, for example, generally uses a *two-step approach* to choose a vendor.

- *Step 1 — Determination of purchase limits.* The first step usually involves potential buyers defining the form, fit, and function of the product (or services) required, based on their needs and objectives. They establish the general budget boundaries at both the high and low levels. They define the minimum they are willing to pay for a particular product or service and also establish a general upper limit as the maximum beyond which they will not go. They will then search for the vendor that will satisfy their needs. This search will identify at least two or three potential vendors, although in the initial growth stages of a product life cycle the buyer may find only a single vendor.
- *Step 2 — Final vendor selection.* When buyers have identified potential vendors, they then evaluate and compare vendors who generally fit the specifications established in step 1. Buyers will

usually pick as the final vendor the one they think offers the highest quality service. This analysis usually involves some trade-offs on reliability and maintainability. Reliability alone will not guarantee selection because users are usually aware that no possibility of an infinite mean time between failure exists. Buyers recognize that products will fail at some point, at which time service response and repair quality will be critical. Finally, the positive perceived image of customer service satisfaction and quality will generally lead to positive vendor selection.

An understanding of this critical two-step process is key to understanding why organizations such as IBM, which offered a high-priced product and pursued a "second-in" or follower approach to product features and capabilities, continued to dominate its markets. In general, IBM was often selected because it was perceived to offer the highest levels of customer satisfaction. If the product purchased did not work for any reason, IBM service would make it right. In effect, IBM's service store was perceived as being expanded to meet each customers needs. When IBM's service became more rigid and bureaucratic, with less focus on full service, and the product technology changed, IBM lost that premier service position.

KEY MEASURES OF CUSTOMER SATISFACTION

How do you best measure, control, and deliver customer satisfaction on a professionally managed basis? This question leads immediately to the issue of what measures and limits of customer satisfaction and service quality are most important. Market surveys over the last 20 years have questioned customers about factors they use in evaluating service quality and responsiveness. It is clear that service response and delivery time (time-based parameters) are consistently used by customers to measure their satisfaction. For every type of product or service, customers have a specific opinion regarding how long they are willing to wait for service, how long the service should take, or some other time measure.

These studies have also identified an important phenomenon. When customers are surveyed, about 80% will have a fairly precise view of how long they are willing to wait for service. Time thus becomes a critical factor in determining customer satisfaction. A customer satisfaction index can be developed, as shown in Figure 8.1, that is directly related to the perceived ability of the service organization to achieve a certain level of response and repair time (note that this is the *perceived*, rather than the *actual*, time). Customers are extremely sensitive to situations in which their service needs are not being met during a critical period and the service organization has apparently failed to respond. Thus, the customers'

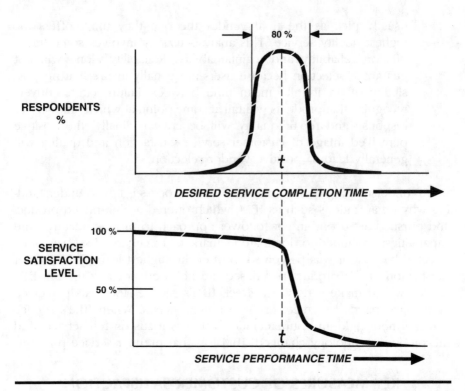

Figure 8.1 Relationship of desired service completion time to customer satisfaction levels.

views of service performance are biased. They view service quality within the framework of the nonlinear step function of the index. They are relatively insensitive to the provision of too rapid service, but they are highly sensitive to the lack of service when time requirements are critical.

Most service managers tend to think of the customer satisfaction index as linear and positively directed. They believe that decreasing service performance time should lead directly to a linear increase in satisfaction. In reality, once the service response and repair time limits are met, an increased level of responsiveness does not "buy" an increased level of satisfaction.

The level of satisfaction is primarily perceived. It can be highly influenced by the service management practices of a given organization. For example, if an organization estimates an arrival time when a customer calls and then fails to meet that requirement, the customer views service as being of low quality even though the actual response time may meet his requirements. This suggests that it might be a good thing to provide an estimated arrival time when the customer initially calls, but our studies clearly show that the customer very much desires being given an estimated time of service arrival. The total closure time is also important to the customer, not just the time of arrival on the site or the start of service. Customer perceptions are invariably related to the total elapsed time between the initial request and completion of the service task.

CUSTOMER SATISFACTION AND WILLINGNESS TO PAY

Service executives often become confused because customer satisfaction does not necessarily correlate to willingness to pay. They presume that customers are not willing to pay more for more satisfaction. In fact, a high correlation exists between willingness to pay and satisfaction. The typical service manager, however, often fails to understand the underlying factors and characteristics of that satisfaction. BAI studies show there are at least three, possibly four, types of customers:

1. *Price-sensitive customers.* Government agencies and educational institutions are particularly sensitive because of their procurement policies; price is the primary issue, regardless of quality.
2. *Price–quality customers.* Much of the marketplace makes a balanced trade-off between price and quality.
3. *Time-sensitive customers.* This class is extremely sensitive to time and is relatively price insensitive; service quality alone is important.

The highly price-sensitive and time-sensitive customers do not react in the same way. BAI studies suggest that the price–quality segment (which balances service quality against price) accounts for about 50% of the market. An average 35 to 40% of the user market is very time sensitive, and the rest of the market (10 to 15%) is highly price sensitive.

A fourth class of customers has an unusual attitude on service price. These are the less sophisticated buyers for whom price becomes a direct indicator of quality. Customers in this class tend to use price as a direct measure for quality and are willing to pay a *higher* price because they believe this will lead to greater satisfaction and better service.

MECHANISMS FOR MEASURING AND SURVEYING CUSTOMER SATISFACTION AND SERVICE QUALITY

The experienced service manager should pay much attention to measuring customer satisfaction. Because the level of customer satisfaction is both nonlinear and generally a perceived factor, it is critical to measure it on a regular basis (at least annually), using some form of market research.

Customer Satisfaction Survey Mechanisms	General Description	Advantages	Disadvantages
In-depth personal interviews	1- to 2-hour one-on-one interviews with users, using structured or unstructured questions	Ability to obtain detailed information	Expensive Time consuming Difficult to schedule
Focus groups	2- to 3-hour sessions with 6 to 12 peers in each group	Ability to obtain consensus Ability to see the effect of other perceptions	Difficult to administer and control Could be biased by one participant
Full telephone survey	30- to 45-minute interview using structured questionnaire based on telephone	Ability to obtain unbiased results Ability to control	Somewhat expensive Not easy to compare complex alternatives
Full mail survey	30- to 45-minute structured questionnaire sent out and returned on a random basis	Ability to obtain unbiased results Ability to obtain quantitative data on complex alternatives	Expensive Sample response not controlled
Telemarketing/ call handling	3- to 5-minute initial call screen, usually used with call handling	Ease of administering to existing base	Does not test non-client base
Mail-in cards	Card given to customers by service region at call close	Inexpensive	Does not test non-client base

Figure 8.2 Alternative survey mechanisms.

Proactive Survey Mechanisms

The survey mechanisms shown in Figure 8.2 involve a mixture of direct personal interviewing, mail and phone surveys, and focus groups. Each offers advantages and disadvantages. A quantitative, structured mail or phone survey, conducted on a random, statistically valid basis, is the most effective way to measure satisfaction. The service organization can introduce a direct measure of undesirable bias if it fails to recognize that customers respond differently to surveys if they have a preconceived or particular view of its purpose. Believing that a survey is to be used as a mechanism to raise prices or change service response or repair terms may bias their responses. They may believe a more critical or negative response will lead to improved service, or they may fear that a more critical response will lead to a worsening of service. Similarly, they may think a positive response will lead to either a worsening of service or a further improvement of it. So, it is critical that the survey be masked as much as possible with respect to the initiating service organization. If the organization must identify itself, the first instructions should be explicit about the survey's purpose. Anonymity must also be guaranteed from an operational standpoint. If the service personnel in the field can directly influence or change a service response, the survey results cannot accurately measure satisfaction. Most people dislike criticizing an individual directly, so it is unlikely that respondents will be totally accurate in their answers if they believe the service personnel supporting his facility will see the results.

Types of Survey Approaches

Firms use several types of survey approaches to measure satisfaction. Larger organizations use some type of internally generated questionnaire to be distributed either quarterly, semiannually, or annually on a sample of their customers. Such surveys are highly qualitative and subjective. They are developed in terms of the company's own view of the service factors of importance. A second approach elicits responses from generalized, multiclient surveys. A third involves industry-publication-sponsored "beauty contest" responses from readers. A fourth involves blind, or confidential, surveys that measure specific service issues and performance on a quantitative basis. Each of the four offers advantages and disadvantages. The strengths and weaknesses of each type follow:

- *Internal surveys.* The primary problem with internal surveys is that they introduce bias. Research shows that a survey questionnaire sent to a particular customer and labeled to be returned to the organization would generally draw responses with a high degree of bias. In other words, respondents represent themselves either more negatively or more positively than they actually are. Similarly, customer exit surveys, or surveys after the sale, may also introduce bias. These surveys generally fail to sample non-customers and dissatisfied or ex-customers, nor do they provide a follow-up to ensure that non-respondents' attitudes are consistent with those of respondents. Customers who have become dissatisfied and no longer use the firm and potential customers who have chosen not to use the firm go unmeasured.

■ *Multiclient surveys.* Several market firms provide multiclient measures of customer satisfaction. The primary problem with these measures is that they fail to evaluate performance accurately. They do not provide enough statistically valid responses to give confidence in the results. Because of the generic, generalized questionnaires necessary in a multiclient approach, it is usually impossible to evaluate specific differences in operating practices as well as product-line variations. Multiclient surveys fail to quantify and relate specific customer requirements by market segment and product line to perceptions of levels of service provided. Customer requirements do vary by segment and product line. While some customers are either satisfied or oversatisfied, others, given the same levels of service, could be extremely dissatisfied. These surveys are less expensive than the proprietary, confidential surveys with which they compete.

■ *Reader or "beauty contest" surveys.* Some service organizations rely extensively on publication-based reader surveys. These are distributed as fold-ins, blow-ins, or bound-ins in various publications. Readers fill out the questionnaires and mail them back to the magazines, where the data are processed and results compiled. The results are not randomly controlled or seeded, and thus have relatively low statistical validity. Also, respondents may not be in a position of authority or involved in the actual decision-making, so their attitudes may mean nothing in the purchase decision. It is easy to stuff the ballot box; a very positive or very negatively inclined reader could fill out more than one form, or the service organization itself, being interested in certain results, could send in a number of forms and produce positive results for its own organization and negative results for rivals. Such surveys at best can provide only simplistic performance measurements; they fail to deal with the underlying factors that can influence service image and performance. To overcome these objections, some organizations (such as DataPro) are using statistically valid mail and telephone surveys carried out on a proprietary basis.

■ *Proprietary customized blind, or confidential, survey.* A fourth way to measure satisfaction is a survey carried out on a confidential basis by an independent third-party professional market research firm. Its primary advantage is that it can be tailored to the strategies of the individual service organization and provide in-depth evaluation by market segment and product line as to service performance.

Such surveys can be used to derive special insight into market needs as a basis for establishing unique strategic directions. These surveys can also be used to evaluate service value in use and to develop effective approaches to service pricing. The surveys have the advantage of being statistically valid and controllable. They allow for both random and specialized seeding to reflect customers, non-customers, and ex-customers. The primary disadvantage is the cost (usually two to three times that of a multiclient or internal survey). See Figure 8.2 for an overall comparison of the four methods.

DESIGN CHARACTERISTICS OF AN EFFECTIVE CUSTOMER SATISFACTION MARKET SURVEY

All four survey methods can provide a sense of direction with respect to measuring customer service, but to be most useful, customer service measures must provide the following capabilities:

1. Measurement of the importance of service in the decision to buy, providing a quantitative basis to determine factors of importance on both a relative and absolute basis
2. Identification and evaluation of the factors used by the marketplace to measure and evaluate service performance, including service response time, repair time, technical diagnostics help, etc.
3. Analysis and evaluation of the service requirements with respect to response, repair, and installation times
4. Evaluation of perceived performance of various competitors against market requirements
5. Evaluation of the importance and value in use of service
6. Evaluation of service representative performance and capabilities
7. Evaluation of the effects of alternative procedures, policies, and strategies for service delivery
8. Analysis and evaluation of individual service and product requirements such as, but not limited to, 24-hour-a-day coverage, 7-day-a-week coverage, remote diagnostics assistance, delivery of parts and consumable items and supply, etc.

The most important issue is to measure and relate the perception of service image and performance to both competition and customer requirements. The surveys should be defined in terms that are meaningful to the customer. They can be used by each specific service organization as a prescription to reallocate resources. It is trivial to ask such basic questions as to whether a customer is very satisfied, satisfied, or dissatisfied with service. Such a question assumes that satisfaction can be determined as an absolute. Also, differences in satisfaction cannot be directly related to service. It is important to determine the customer's perception of what specifically represents excellent, good, or poor service and then to compare performance of various competitors against each other.

It is particularly important to provide a way to measure alternative procedures, policies, and allocation of resources. Addressing the question "What happens when a service engineer arrives on site?" can be extremely useful as an allocation mechanism if you find that in many cases service personnel have to leave and return at a later date because of a lack of parts. Such an analysis would suggest a reallocation of inventory levels.

Regardless of the survey approach used, it is important that the survey is structured to:

1. Deal with customer attitudes and perceptions based on the customer's terminology and issues, not those of the company.
2. Develop a quantitative, action-oriented basis for the survey mechanism.
3. Provide a valid set of techniques to obtain an objective, quantitative, and comprehensive survey for all classes and segments of customers and non-customers.
4. Use existing call reporting and tracking mechanisms to capture actual customer response and performance data and compare the data to market survey satisfaction levels on such issues as ETA times missed, callbacks, excessive downtime due to parts, etc.
5. Develop a framework to evaluate and measure customer satisfaction and performance by market segment and product line.
6. Develop a basis to clearly articulate the service product portfolio in order to measure and evaluate service value in use and pricing alternatives.
7. Provide a strategic framework to measure trends in the levels of customer satisfaction to be used as a tool to minimize potential dissatisfaction and reasons for customers switching to or from specific vendors.

ADVANTAGES AND DISADVANTAGES OF ALTERNATIVE SURVEY METHODS

Considerable debate exists over which method better measures customer satisfaction, telephone or mail. The debate intensifies when considering whether the chosen method should identify the sponsor or be conducted on a blind basis. Many believe self-administered mail surveys that identify the sponsor lead to the best results; others say this method leads to highly biased results and favor telephone surveys conducted on a blind basis (not identifying the sponsor). Each method is described below.

Mail Surveys

Mail surveys are an extremely cost-effective way to collect large amounts of hard quantifiable data, but the return rate can vary from less than 1 to more than 15%. Mail surveys that identify the sponsor lead to a higher response rate than those conducted on a blind basis because customers feel obliged to rate their vendors. The downside of mail surveys is that the turnaround time from beginning to end is much longer and it is impossible to ensure that the respondents are the actual decision makers.

Telephone Surveys

Telephone surveys, while more expensive, provide results in real time, without a lag between receipt of the questionnaire by the respondent and completion, return, and tabulation of the survey. A large-scale phone survey can be conducted and results tabulated in a matter of days, while mail surveys take several weeks to months. The phone survey is interactive in that the interviewer can locate the decision maker, who can ask the interviewer to clarify particular questions. Finally, the sample size can be controlled, with an exact number (quota) of surveys determined and guaranteed in advance.

Open Client-Sponsored vs. Blind Confidential Surveys

BAI has conducted a number of surveys using both blind telephone and mail surveys and sponsor-identified mail and telephone surveys. A comparison of the results can reveal the similarities and differences between each type. The following example is based on experience with a leading independent service organization.

A questionnaire was developed that asked customers to rate their level of satisfaction in each of these areas:

1. Attitude of service technicians
2. Attitude of local management
3. Communications with local management
4. Ability/effectiveness of service technicians
5. Responsiveness (8–5, M–F, after hours)
6. Attitudes/communication ability of dispatchers
7. Attitude/communication ability of headquarters personnel
8. Accuracy of invoicing, billing, etc.

One version was sent by mail, with the sponsor identified, to over 1000 customers selected randomly. Customers were given about one month to return the questionnaire, and about 10% did so. Another version was conducted with 100 customers on a blind, confidential basis over the telephone over a time span of days. The only major difference between the two surveys was the rating scale. The mail questionnaire asked customers to rate their satisfaction with the identified vendor on a 10-point scale, with 1 being low and 10 being high. The telephone survey asked customers to indicate whether they were extremely, somewhat, or neither satisfied or dissatisfied with their primary service providers. Essentially, the mail survey used a subjective scale with the sponsor identified, while the telephone survey used a neutral objective scale on a confidential basis. The results of both surveys were indexed on a 100-point scale.

After analysis of the data, the telephone survey resulted in generally higher customer satisfaction for every category as compared to the mail survey. This difference suggests that survey design and method can and do affect the outcome. Specifically, a negative bias apparently occurred with the sponsor-identified mail survey, and the objective, confidential telephone survey produced more positive ratings. This indicates that customers are apparently more satisfied with their service providers than they care to admit to them. The fact of a bias in any direction shows that it may be costly to rely on the mail survey because it *can* lead to decisions based on biased results. It was concluded that an objective, confidential telephone survey is the most appropriate way to measure customer satisfaction.

SERVICE SATISFACTION AUDIT AND EVALUATION

A major benefit of a structured survey, by telephone or mail, is its ability to measure satisfaction segment by segment. Levels of satisfaction can be measured in the aggregate as well as by individual customer segment (by type of customer, existing past or prospective customers), by geographic region (Northeast, Mid-Atlantic, South Atlantic), by vertical market segment (banks, hospitals, government, manufacturing), or by many other demographic characteristics (e.g., length of time as a customer, number of employees, type of installed base, annual service revenues).

A properly constructed survey can measure levels of satisfaction on a stand-alone basis (by individual vertical market segment, region, type, or size of customer), or it can compare corresponding customer needs evaluated by individual service factors of importance. It is important to know whether region A performs better or worse than regions B, C, or D, but it is equally important to understand whether the satisfaction levels of any of the four regions meet customer needs on key service factors. The satisfaction audit evaluates satisfaction on both the comparative basis (segment by segment, region by region) and by comparing individual service factors.

To measure satisfaction on both a segment-by-segment basis and in relation to individual and aggregate customer needs, the service satisfaction audit uses a basic and direct approach. It analyzes satisfaction on a factor-by-factor basis and is ultimately weighted by what is most important to the customers who rate the satisfaction.

Quantitative measures are becoming increasingly important to service organizations. Service is becoming more professionally managed and controlled as a profitable line of business. Investing resources to measure, manage, and control service image and perception can result in a significant improvement in productivity, performance, and efficiency. In general, any survey method is an improvement over the rule-of-thumb or educated-guess approach.

SUMMARY OF REQUIREMENTS FOR CUSTOMER SATISFACTION AND SERVICE QUALITY CONTROL AND COORDINATION

Based on experience in working with many service providers and the recently approved international standards for service quality measurement and control (ISO 9000), we can describe four key elements required to maintain, control, and deliver service quality, as shown in Figure 8.3:

■ *Delegation of management responsibility for quality.* Any service organization must establish a direct responsibility for managing and controlling service quality. This includes specific delegation of authority between the service and delivery layers. Service quality management should be a primary responsibility of a senior executive.

■ *Documentation of service policy, procedures, plans, and structure.* Management policies, procedures, and practices should be fully

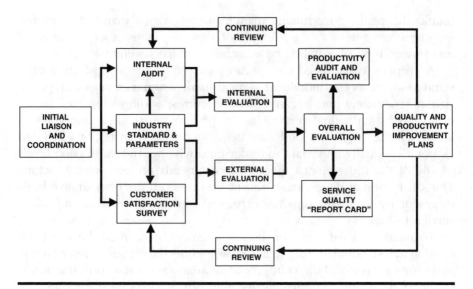

Figure 8.3 Service evaluation and improvement process.

documented. Requirements should include: (1) a service policy and procedures statement, (2) a manual defining targets and standards that should be expressed in both internal and external measurable goals, (3) quality plans to improve service operations to meet established standards, and (4) documentation of actual performance quality against the plan.

■ *Reporting and auditing service performance, internally and externally.* The next step is to provide for regular audits of performance. These should be directly related to the quality targets. Auditing and reporting should be developed by internal and external surveys. The external survey discussed previously focuses on both customer requirements and an organization's ability to meet them and should be done at least annually. It should be done on a blind, confidential, closed-end basis to provide both objective and quantitative mechanisms to measure performance.

■ *Continuous review, evaluation, and follow-up.* The final link in the chain is to review and evaluate performance using the audit and reporting mechanisms. This creates quantitative and qualitative evaluation of performance against plans and goals. It also provides a mechanism to update service targets (as documented in the quality manual) and to follow up on practices. Where gaps exist between the service targets and performance, corrective action should be taken. It is important to recognize when service quality exceeds targets and customer requirements. Numerous market studies show that as much penalty is associated with exceeding service requirements as in underachieving. Exceeding service quality means excessive cost to the customer. Measuring service quality and customer satisfaction are the keys to determining service market direction. A commitment to both will produce significant returns in increased service revenue and profitability.

BENCHMARK AND EVALUATION OF SERVICE PRODUCTIVITY

In addition to measuring customer satisfaction and service quality from the customer's perspective, as described above, it is also possible to measure internal service productivity compared to direct and functional competition. This benchmarking process can prove very valuable, particularly if used in conjunction with the customer satisfaction measurement process described earlier. This next section discusses benchmarking measurement of service productivity.

The high-tech service industry, in general, as well as independent third- and fourth-party service organizations and multivendor equipment service organizations have become much more focused on improving their productivity and efficiency. The issue of strategic and tactical benchmarking has, therefore, received much attention and is critical to an organization's success. The ISO 9000 process for quality management and control emphasizes the importance of benchmarking, which serves as a key to the comparative measurement of service operations and customer-oriented performance against industry and market norms and standards. In running service as a line of business or profit center, it is critical to determine the optimum approach to achieving the best profit levels and at the same time meet customer service needs and requirements. Unfortunately, in the industry, relatively few accepted or published benchmark parameters and targets are available for the typical service organization or manager to establish an effective service strategy and assess and evaluate performance relative to industry standards and norms or customer needs and requirements. This type of data, if properly evaluated to determine key driving parameters and critical targets, could be extremely useful in improving service productivity and efficiency.*

Benchmark information and data parameters, organized by class, technology of products serviced, by type and size of service organization, and by geographic region serviced, can be very useful in measuring these issues. Information provided here is based on extensive in-depth service market audits and studies conducted among more than 450 small, medium,

---

* See Appendix A for more detailed information on benchmark parameters.

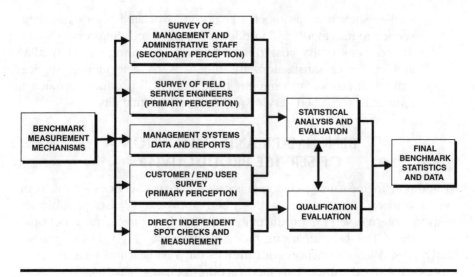

Figure 8.4   Data sources used in developing benchmark data.

and large service organizations supporting original equipment manufacturers (OEMs), dealers, distributors, independent third- and fourth-party service providers, and multivendor equipment services (MVESs) operating in the United States, in Europe, and globally, conducted from 1988 through 2002. These organizations were involved in the service and support of a broad array of technology, including:

■ Information technology
■ Office automation and office products
■ Telecommunications and data network products
■ Medical electronics and technology
■ Building automation
■ Industrial plant systems controls
■ Retail, financial, and point-of-sale (POS) technology
■ Home and consumer goods

In addition, extensive nonproprietary data on service requirements and performance organized by technology and vertical market segment were collected as part of market research studies in individual service markets to determine user requirements for service and to measure customer satisfaction and service performance as perceived by the user. Finally, considerable published reports are available on the organization, operations, and productivity of service-oriented companies and on the service market in which they operate. The nonproprietary elements of all of these sources of data can then be used to develop key benchmark data (see Figure 8.4), using the general process shown in Figure 8.5.

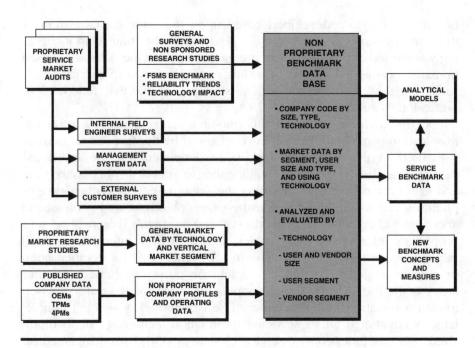

Figure 8.5   General methodology and process in developing benchmark data.

METHOD OF APPROACH TO BENCHMARK ANALYSIS AND EVALUATION

Because of the tremendous variations in financial and accounting practice and a lack of accepted industry-wide standards with respect to parameters and definitions of those parameters, benchmarking in the high-tech service industry is still both difficult and in its infancy. Many competitors are reluctant to share what they consider to be competitive and proprietary data. In many cases, they do not track certain key parameters and operating statistics, a problem that has been compounded by the proliferation of service management systems software packages, each using somewhat different parameters and definitions and providing data in different formats. Finally, for many key parameters, including key standards such as response time, percentage of calls broken due to lack of parts, etc., some significant differences can be observed between the data and reports produced internally and the external perceptions of customers with respect to the same parameters.

Typical research to date has been based on one-time surveys or recurring annual surveys sent to management, executives, or administrators of selected sponsor service organizations using a specific set of survey questions. The data have then been collected via the special survey, and benchmark data are developed based upon the statistical tabulation of these survey responses. Generally, no independent testing or spot checking was carried out by the research organization, and the data were based primarily on internal reports or estimates as compared to external measures, such as customer or market surveys or objective independent professional observations.

Our research suggests that this one-time snapshot survey approach may lead to some inaccuracies, in part caused by the fact that the survey data used in this approach are highly dependent on the individual participating firm respondent's willingness to spend the necessary time and effort to collect and organize the data based upon the survey's premises and assumptions and to be open, objective, and professional about providing what is generally viewed as highly competitive and proprietary information. Inaccuracies also result from internally oriented perceptions and measures, which are sometimes used for compensation or contract negotiations and thus might be purposely biased. Another factor is the fact that the sample population is relatively small or biased toward a specific class or category of service providers — for example, large multinational OEMs servicing information technology or medium-sized regional Independent Service Operators (ISOs) servicing medical electronics. Our own in-depth survey experience suggests that some very significant and real differences exist between benchmarking data reported by organizations who have based their research on a single, one-time, mail survey among a limited, homogenous population as compared to independent, in-depth verification, cross checking, or use of multiple (internal and external) data sources and larger heterogeneous datasets and full understanding of the measurement and reporting mechanisms utilized.

Our methodology to develop more accurate benchmark data is based upon a cross-sectional analysis of in-depth research and experience with 250 small, medium, and large service organizations with operations in the United States, in Europe, or globally, reflecting a broad range of different technologies and service operating environments. In each of these cases, we were involved in proprietary service market audits involving in-depth internal audits and evaluation, as well as external market surveys. In each case, we spent considerable time examining, investigating, analyzing, and evaluating service operating performance, productivity, efficiency, and customer satisfaction, in addition to reviewing financial and accounting records, call management and logistics management system reports and data, and customer satisfaction and market research surveys. The benchmark data from each individual audit study were first sanitized to eliminate any proprietary or confidential information in order to avoid any possible identification of the specific client sponsor or client-specific and sensitive

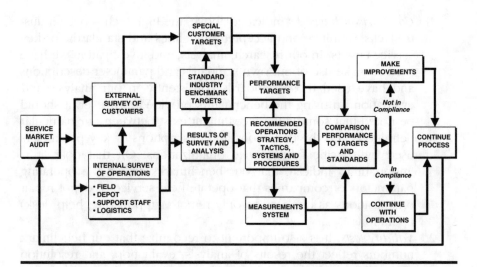

Figure 8.6 Overall benchmark and service quality management process.

information. In addition, all of the data used were subjected to independent analysis and evaluation based upon information from a variety of sources, including financial and accounting data, call management systems reports, logistics management systems data, and customer satisfaction and market surveys that we conducted independently.

In essence, the data reflected results of in-depth objective and professional evaluation of service operations based upon both internal and external studies lasting well over 2 to 3 months. Therefore, we believe we have generated a much more accurate and independently validated view compared to one that is normally obtained from simple one-time snapshot survey based on a standard mail questionnaire, as used in previously reported benchmark previous studies. The admitted downside of this method of approach is that the data were collected over a period of 3 to 4 years, thus the length of time could introduce some bias in the results. (see Figure 8.6).

GENERAL ANALYSIS AND EVALUATION OF THE BENCHMARK DATABASE

Subject to the caveats and methodology identified previously and given that the benchmarking data and statistics were developed based on extensive research involving service firms, it is important to understand some of the technical difficulties involved in developing benchmark estimates and applying and using them. The most important of these issues are outlined below:

1. *Comparison basis.* As indicated above, the high-tech service industry lacks definitive and accepted guidelines and standards for key
   service targets. In our research, analysis, and investigation we have
   tried to make use of our own standards and parameter descriptions
   and have used those standards consistently in our analysis and
   evaluation. In using the benchmarks provided, however, it should
   be noted that some differences might exist between our particular
   definitions and the definitions and descriptions of key parameters
   used by specific field service organizations. On that note, it is
   important to indicate that our benchmarks reflect the operating
   parameters of companies that operate field service or depot repair
   organizations as opposed to only remote support (i.e., help desk)
   operations.

2. *Validity tests.* It is also important to recognize that our benchmark
   numbers reflect the results of analysis, evaluation, and resolution
   of the differences that might exist between the statistics and parameters as reported by internal management systems vs. external
   customer perceptions. Where these differences are substantial and
   significant, we have made a quantitative extrapolation based upon
   the specific situation and our experience to produce a balanced
   measure.

3. *Statistical variations.* As most researchers of benchmark data will
   admit, the statistical variations in the available benchmark data are
   substantial and non-normal. The typical Poisson or normal distribution is not always found. Rather, the data could be skewed to
   the left or right (Figure 8.7) and in some cases may even have bi-
   modal peaks or a totally random distribution (Figure 8.8). Thus,
   differences between mean and median data can be significant,
   based upon our own experience in developing the data and
   applying the benchmarking information. We have generally chosen
   to use the mean or average parameters rather than median parameters, primarily because this tends to be the statistical factor most
   commonly used in the industry. Users of this benchmark data
   should understand that the statistical results reported are not
   smooth and in fact may not be normally distributed. In those cases
   where the data are significantly non-normal, we have identified
   the type of distribution found. In addition, proprietary data were
   not used in the mean calculations in specific cell segments which
   resulted in some parameter measures having minor differences in
   mean numbers due to the data points used in each database cell.

4. *Cross-elasticity of dependent/independent variables.* Our analysis
   and evaluation to develop benchmark data have also identified
   certain key parameters that affect others in terms of cross-elasticity

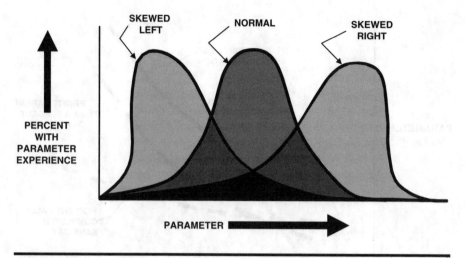

Figure 8.7 Types of benchmark experience distribution.

relationships and logical interaction. Density, for example, tends to have a strong impact on a variety of key parameters, such as inventory investment, average travel time, or number of "broken" calls. Economies of scale also exist, to some extent. These key relationships are discussed later. It should be clearly recognized that certain factors, including specifically the impact of differences in service organization type and technology supported, will affect the benchmark parameters (see Figure 8.9).

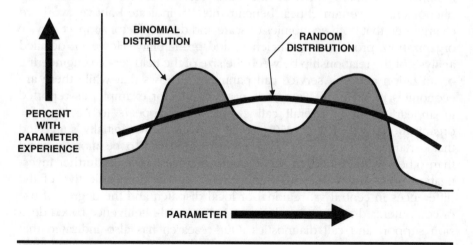

Figure 8.8 Types of experience distribution.

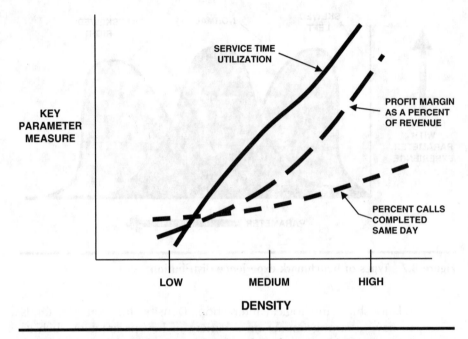

Figure 8.9 Impact of density on key benchmark parameters.

IDENTIFICATION AND ASSESSMENT OF CRITICAL BENCHMARK PARAMETERS

The extended benchmark data and the ability to examine, dynamically, multiple benchmarks provide the basis for identifying key underlying phenomena of certain critical benchmarks. As indicated above, we have clearly seen that both economies of scale and density factors impact service organization, productivity, efficiency, and profitability. However, detailed analysis of the relationship between the size of the field service engineering organization and key service call parameters shows that while there are economies of scale, the impact is not smooth; for example, as reported in an earlier study, overall call closure time appears to be best for organizations with 101 to 250 service personnel. We initially suggested that certain size clusters or work groups appeared to be more optimal than others with respect to service performance; however, further investigation now shows that this finding tends to be more reflective of the differences in central vs. regional or local dispatch and the degree of use of computerized tools and techniques for artificial-intelligence-based decision support and call diagnostics. Our research has also indicated that certain types of technology services require more preventative scheduled and predictive maintenance calls, installations, moves, adds, and changes

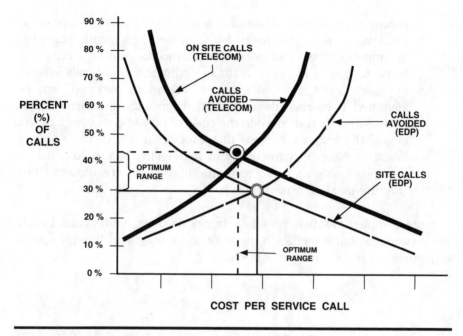

Figure 8.10   Optimum use of TAC and call avoidance.

than others. In addition, electrical and mechanical technology tend to be much more affected by preventative and scheduled maintenance than purely electronics technology. This explains some of the differences found among the various technologies serviced.

Our research also shows that the efficiency of logistics organizations, in general, and the use of full logistics pipeline control down to the level of service engineer trunk stock, in particular, can directly affect field service performance. Where the full logistics pipeline is totally controlled, service productivity in terms of a reduction in the number of "broken" calls due to a lack of parts and an increase in the on-site service call completion rate per day can occur.

Specific areas of investigation, using the new benchmark data, show the following results:

1. *Impact of density on service profitability.* Service profit before tax is significantly affected by increased density of installed base. The degree of impact is apparently due to a combination of density and integrated systems function on profit improvement. The application of sophisticated and integrated call handling and dispatch combined with logistics control systems produces improved profitability, particularly where the density is very high.

2. *Impact of improved call avoidance and technical assistance center (TCA) deployment.* We have also examined benchmarks regarding the impact of TACs and call avoidance mechanisms on service calls costs. As shown in Figure 8.10, an optimum ratio of calls avoided to on-site calls, as a function of technology serviced, can be identified. In essence, the cost of call diagnostics and call avoidance rises sharply as compared to the costs of on-site calls over a certain range. The analysis suggests that a focus on the 33- to 44%-range of call avoidance, particularly in high-technology fields such as data processing and telecommunications and networks, can provide the maximum payoff.

A more complete discussion of benchmarking along with actual benchmark parameters and metrics by type of technology and type of service organization can be found in Appendix A.

9

DEVELOPING SERVICE MARKET STRATEGY AND PORTFOLIOS

CONTENTS

An organization's requirements for service and support are shaped by a variety of demographic and firmgraphic* factors. These factors have a tremendous impact on defining current levels of customer satisfaction, unmet

---

* Firmographics is defined as the profile or template of the typical firm or business in a category (it describes size, financial type, focus, geographic coverage, etc.).

gaps for service, service requirements, and willingness to pay. These requirements are by no means simple or static, as they may have once been perceived by industry observers. Customers have become more sophisticated in terms of their utilization of various services and in their expectations for quality service and support. These expectations are very complex and are evolving as service organizations are finding new ways of responding to global industry trends. We want to examine evolving customer requirements for service and support in order to develop strategies and tactics to respond effectively to these industry trends and directions.

For example, a major change taking place in the high-tech service industry has to do with the way customers make decisions with respect to the purchase of service from outside vendors. Our research, based on telephone surveys of nearly 800 end-users of high-technology equipment from a wide range of industries, has found that a substantial percentage of decisions regarding the purchase of maintenance and support services are made on a decentralized basis. Even among organizations in which decision making is still centralized, a sizable number of organizations report that decisions are not being made in the traditional way (i.e., by information services or purchasing departments). About one sixth of these organizations (15.4%) report that decisions to purchase services are made centrally, but in some way other than by information services or purchasing, or the two departments combined.

Increasingly, these decisions are being made by individual locations, several departments, or committees of representatives from each group of employees affected by the decisions. Organizations with a wide variety of specialized equipment such as hospitals, utilities, or printers and publishers are more likely to make decisions in a decentralized manner.

The size of the establishment also needs to be considered. A small organization is more likely to concentrate service arrangement decision making within one or two departments or even in one individual, such as the owner or a general manager. A small hospital, generally one with fewer than 200 beds, is more likely to have a single executive responsible for making purchasing decisions about service and support for the entire installed base of technology than a large hospital is.

COST CONTAINMENT

The pressure being felt by organizations to control costs is also impacting service demands. Few industries are able to operate without the constraints of having to do more with less. With large dollar amounts being invested in the purchase and support of high-tech equipment, for example, the decision to select a service provider and the required support arrangements is an increasingly complex and critical one.

The need to operate efficiently is driving organizations to deploy increasing amounts of sophisticated technology, thereby creating more opportunities for service providers. At the same time, the need to control costs is affecting decisions about the selection of a service provider. A recent survey showed that most end-user organizations expect service expenditures to remain at current levels or increase by an average of 18.1% over the next 12-month period. Less than one quarter of end-users surveyed expect their service expenditures to decrease. The survey showed an average annual expenditure for externally purchased service of over $1 million. The median expenditure is nearly $250,000.

Organizations expecting an increase in service expenditures most frequently cite an increase in the amount of equipment installed, an aging installed base, and normal inflationary trends as explanations for the increase. The decrease is most often attributed to the addition of equipment with longer warranty periods, an increase in the use of in-house staff for service, and an increase in the use of time and materials service.

With the life cycle of technology getting shorter, and longer warranties becoming available, replacing equipment can be a cost-effective solution for some organizations. A three-year warranty is essentially a lifetime warranty in an environment where hardware is obsolete in two to three years. Organizations that are less able to replace equipment are more likely to experience an increase in their service costs due to the age of the hardware.

USE OF EXTERNAL VENDORS AND SERVICE OUTSOURCING

Some organizations attempt to control costs by choosing to downsize or eliminate internal plant and building service forces by turning to fixed-price service contracts or time-and-materials service arrangements. Organizations are more likely to rely on internal service for functions that are critical to operations and require immediate attention or for which it may be too expensive to have duplicate support channels available.

SERVICE SELECTION FACTORS

The proliferation of technology in the day-to-day operations of organizations has resulted in a greater dependency on that technology and an increasingly important role for hardware and software support services. End-users frequently comment that the quality and responsiveness of service have been deteriorating, while the price of service has been rising. The reality of the situation is that the level of service being provided by many organizations is simply not keeping pace with customers' expectations. In-house service managers frequently comment on the growing impatience of end-users with any lapse in the availability of their systems. For example, the level of service demanded from electric, water, and gas utilities and telephone companies is immediate (i.e., 100% availability, on demand), at any time, regardless of the type of problem the user is experiencing.

Market research has concluded time and time again that the factors that are most important to end-users in selecting a service provider deal with issues of quality of service and responsiveness. In particular, the factors consistently rated as most important are quality of service and the ability of the service technician to fix the equipment correctly on the first visit. The skill and ability of the service person and the speed of service completion are also rated as more important than the price of service, for everything from food service to high-tech repairs. In fact, price is seldom mentioned as an important factor for selecting a specific service vendor. This finding leads us to conclude that price objections by customers should be viewed by service management as a feedback that the customer is not convinced of the value of service received for the money paid. The buyer, in general, makes the general decision to move to a class of service providers that includes a consideration of pricing. In the selection of the specific vendor within that market segment, price is not the overwhelming factor.

The responses tend to be similar in most industry segments, with factors related to quality and time-oriented factors being rated higher than the cost of service. It is important to recognize that time is not necessarily equal to specific service response in some markets. In the banking segment, the length of time the service provider has been in business and continuity of service are clearly important considerations. In health care, the concern is with the response time of service and that the required service is completed correctly on the first visit. The life-and-death situations that hospitals face every day and the expense of sophisticated technology demand that service be provided rapidly (in medical jargon, "stat").

Manufacturers, like financial institutions, are most concerned with the long-term stability of a service provider, in addition to the quality of service and ease of obtaining service around the clock. Retail organizations place the greatest importance on the quality and speed of service. Printers and publishers are also concerned with the quality and responsiveness of service, in addition to having a service provider who understands their needs and who is able to provide solutions to meet those needs. The printing and publishing field is undergoing a major shift to digital technology that is rapidly changing service needs in that field.

SERVICE ARRANGEMENTS AND FEATURES

Overall, it is clear that end-users expect to receive reliable and responsive service from providers who are attentive to and focused on their specific needs. In order to obtain that level of service, end-users are willing to move beyond the idea that only one type of service can provide high-quality, cost-effective service. A growing number of end-users are interested in having a service agreement package or contract with a single service provider covering various types of services, rather than with several different service organizations, each with their own responsiveness, time coverage, and procedures. Even within the healthcare segment, one half of those establishments would choose to have services covered under a package agreement.

End-users want this type of service agreement package to provide a mix of basic and premium features tailored to their needs. The features most end-users would select mirror their concerns with the ability to provide what is needed within the necessary time frame and getting service completed quickly when problems occur. A majority of end-users would select the following service features:

- On-site dispatch
- Unlimited service calls
- Technical assistance hotline
- Replacement/loaner units
- Preventive maintenance
- Guaranteed service response time
- Guaranteed service completion time
- Remote diagnostics
- Uptime guarantee
- Software support

Most end-users express a willingness to pay a premium over and above the basic service agreement fee for such service contract features as the following:

- Disaster recovery
- Guaranteed very rapid response time
- 24-hour coverage
- Asset management
- Network support
- End-user training

The average premium that end-users are willing to pay for these features is in the range of 10 to 15% over the basic service agreement cost. Features for which customers are willing to pay the highest premium, on average, are remote diagnostics, 24-hour coverage, and guaranteed 2-hour response time.

In the high-tech area, recent studies also reveal a growing demand for network services. The demand is being fueled by a rapid increase in the installed base of networking technology, a shortage of qualified network engineers worldwide, and the complexity of diagnosing problems in a network environment. End-users complain that they are the losers in the finger-pointing that can occur between hardware vendors, software vendors, and network vendors when seeking the source of a problem. A lack of network expertise in-house is also creating increase demand for these services from outside providers. The greatest demand will be for services such as network maintenance and repair, network optimization, network back-up and disaster recovery planning, and network design/engineering.

PARTS AND MATERIAL AVAILABILITY

It is also essential for service providers to have the material available to complete the service. End-users expect service providers to have the material available to complete the service. A waiter's pleasant service demeanor will not overcome the lack of food delivery. In fact, an overly friendly waitperson unable to deliver the order on a timely basis can become very irritating to the customer. In the equipment service field, having to wait for parts to be delivered, whether it takes weeks, days or overnight, is a major source of dissatisfaction with service providers. In an attempt to cut costs, some service organizations are stocking fewer parts and having field personnel carry fewer parts to job sites. Customers are experiencing a minimum of two visits to resolve equipment problems: an initial visit to diagnose the problem and determine the correct part to order, and a second visit to install the new part and complete the repair. Customers in less populated locations can be subjected to additional delays, not only because of the travel time required to reach the site, but also because of fewer delivery services available. Field engineers will not return to a site until the parts arrive there, but an order placed mid-day or later may not ship in time to make the overnight delivery service available in the rural area. Service providers and customers appear headed in opposite directions on this issue, with service providers looking for ways to cut costs and customers expecting service personnel to always have the correct material or parts on hand, particularly if the person placing the service call has provided detailed information on the nature of the specific problem or request.

SINGLE SOURCE OF SERVICE

The difficulty of managing service providers and service arrangements for an increasingly complex set of service needs is causing some end-users to seek less cumbersome, and potentially more responsive, reliable, and cost effective solutions to their service needs. Having fewer service providers is one possible solution. BAI studies consistently show that in the high-tech arena, the capability of a service provider to service the entire range of installed equipment and systems is important to most end-users and likely to become increasingly important in the future. Studies of organizations from a variety of industries indicate that the average number of service providers used to support an installed base of technology is six. An example of this strategy being deployed is gated retirement communities, which offer a full range of social, house cleaning, maintenance, grass-cutting, snow-removal, and security services. Some new facilities also offer medical and healthcare services on the premises.

The single-source service arrangement can be provided in one of two ways:

1. *Contractual service agreement.* The buyer retains responsibility for managing service but contracts with a vendor to provide a single point of contact for service via an integrated service agreement covering a broad array of technologies or needs. The establishment assumes the risks of service.
2. *Outsourcing arrangement.* The buyer turns the entire responsibility for managing and coordinating service requirements, as well as delivery mechanisms, over to a vendor. The vendor assumes the risks and responsibility for meeting service expectations.

The level of interest in the single-source concept is currently highest among retail organizations and lowest for healthcare providers, according to BAI studies. Although healthcare facilities are facing the same struggle to control costs and manage a large, complex, and varying customer base, this segment is not moving as rapidly to adopt the single-source concept. Tying healthcare institutions more closely to traditional manufacturer-provided and in-house service are concerns over the qualifications of service personnel to support a variety of specialized equipment, the strict inspections required for hospital certification, and the fact that in some hospitals decisions regarding the future direction of equipment service rest in the hands of the in-house biomedical staff. On the other hand, hospitals are moving to be single-source providers of healthcare services in an approach involving a full mix or combining in-bed traditional hospital facilities, doctor's offices, and outpatient clinics to meet the total service needs of its patients conditions. As the single-source concept becomes more widespread in other industries and proves to be an effective means of receiving high-quality service on a cost-effective basis, decision-makers in healthcare organizations will be more likely to adopt this arrangement.

Organizations of every size perceive benefits to be gained from consolidating and simplifying service arrangements. Interest in a single-source arrangement is clearly present in a majority of establishments in the United States ranging in size from firms with less than 500 employees to those with over 20,000 employees.

ATTITUDES TOWARD SUBCONTRACTORS

The provision of a single-source solution often requires that the primary vendor function in a service management role. Acceptance of a single-source solution then depends on the willingness of end-users to consider alternative arrangements for service, including the use of vendors who use subcontractors. BAI studies indicate that for most service decision-makers, the use of subcontractors would have little or no impact on their decision to use a particular vendor. An additional percentage are willing to consider the use of subcontractors provided they receive specific information about who the subcontractors would be, who would have control, and how the arrangement would work. A few decision-makers prefer the use of subcontractors because they assume that the subcontractor is an expert or has a local presence.

QUALITY OF COMMUNICATIONS WITH CUSTOMERS

Customer demands for greater involvement in the service process include the expectation for a better quality of communication with the provider of service. Customers want to be able to request service without long waits on hold or having to leave a message on an automated system and wait for a return call. They dislike dealing with automated call-routing systems and with live operators who misdirect them or bounce them from department to department. Essentially, customers are saying that they want to know that they have been heard; they want to be acknowledged. They are dissatisfied with not having their calls returned, with not knowing if the automated system recorded their message, and with having to provide detailed information about a problem that never reaches the field technician.

Customers also expect honesty in their communications with service providers. A significant source of frustration is the tendency of service providers to promise more than they can deliver; customers cite guaranteed response and repair items that are not met and service personnel who consistently underestimate their time of service arrival.

Customers want responsive, high-quality service and excellent communications with service providers, and they want the service provider to do it all with a smile. Courtesy is an important factor for many customers. Courtesy can include returning calls to acknowledge service requests; having the field person take the time to explain why a problem occurred and what, if anything, can be done to prevent the problem from occurring again; and, just as important, following up with customers after service calls to make sure that problems have been resolved to their satisfaction. For the most successful service organizations, fixing the problem also means nurturing the customer relationship.

THE NEED FOR TRAINING

Resolving problems to the customer's satisfaction also includes the way in which the problem is resolved. Customers are dissatisfied with service personnel who are not able to diagnose problems and instead try various alternatives until something works. Lesser skilled technicians cannot provide customers with any insight into why a problem occurred or if it could have been prevented. While the need for highly skilled, well-trained technicians is clear, customers do not want to absorb the cost of training new service personnel. They are less willing to accept longer service completion times caused by inexperienced technicians who must spend time reading the service manual on the job, consulting with experienced technicians by phone, or waiting for calls from technical assistance. Customers express concern about being charged for the services of two technicians when one is there to train the other.

Finally, customers expect to receive the level of service they paid for; they expect to receive value for their money. It is clear that, with the rapid pace of technological developments and adoption of those technologies, ongoing technical training for service personnel is critical to customer satisfaction. Service organizations would benefit from providing their personnel with a combination of formal training and on-the-job training. The on-the-job training, however, should not be provided at the expense of sacrificing overall service quality.

A lack of qualified service personnel is a concern not only for service organizations but also for internal service departments. Consolidation and downsizing have affected internal service staffs just as they have affected external service organizations. The lost expertise is often not replaced quickly enough to satisfy the service requirements of customers.

The perception of what is meant by *responsive service* is also changing. The ability to access information and perform tasks in smaller amounts of time creates rising expectations of what is possible. Expectations of how quickly and easily problems can and should be resolved are likely to continue to rise as faster systems are developed and adopted not only in the work place but also in the home.

For manufacturers, this expectation of receiving high-quality service has an added dimension. Failing to deliver on the service promise can have an impact on the sale of products. Customers' perceptions of product quality for computers and electronics is influenced by their perception of the quality of service they can receive for that product. Unfortunately, customers who adopted the latest product may find that the manufacturer rushed the product onto the market before the field personnel were trained to repair it.

Customer expectations for service clearly are exacting and becoming more so. Some service providers are responding to those expectations by positioning themselves as partners with their customers, helping them to reach their organizational goals. They begin with the customers' needs and tailor their offerings to fit those requirements. They are as concerned with nurturing the customer relationship as they are with fixing the technology.

Service organizations that can provide this type of tailored service rather than one-size-fits-all service agreements will be the most successful at attracting and retaining customers. Being able to provide that type of service will require service organizations to become both more efficient and more proficient at delivering service. They will require highly skilled, well-trained customer-service-oriented employees. They will also need to adopt new technologies such as field service management systems, field communications systems, expert systems, and others to help them be efficient. Keeping a human face on interactions with customers will always be important. New technologies such as remote diagnostics, remote repair, and predictive maintenance will help to satisfy customer demands for fast, accurate repairs and will go a long way toward keeping customers happy; however, these high-tech approaches will not lessen the importance of the human touch in the provision of service to customers.

In summary, the service needs and requirements of customers for high-technology equipment and systems, banking services, healthcare services, etc., are complex and demanding. Customers want fast, high-quality service that is responsive to their needs and provided at a reasonable cost. The way in which that service is provided to customers, however, is also important. Customer requirements vary by industry segment, size of establishment and other factors. And, finally, customer requirements are evolving over time. For service organizations concerned with creating and maintaining excellent customer relationships, awareness of these market requirements is essential. Service providers who are committed to delivering the service they promise to customers must recognize the importance of understanding those needs.

Too often, service organizations fail to deal with the customer requirements through the eyes and perceptions of the customer. ATT used to determine service based on their view of the services they should offer. As long as the monopoly existed, the customer had no option. After deregulation, this attitude and approach proved disastrous. Many firms, believing that customers will not pay for service, have offered a limited portfolio of services and created a situation in which customers, in fact, were *not* willing to pay for the reduced services offered.

Many service organizations often despair of making significant profits because they see and perceive the market and customer base as being very price sensitive, with customers being very hard nosed about paying for additional services and support. It is extremely interesting to note that this is not the marketplace view of the situation. True, some customers are very price sensitive and even a minor change in price (either up or down) will result in an immediate shift in vendors. The fact is, however, that the general service market has at least three different types of buyers and decision-makers:

1. *Service-quality-oriented buyer.* This type of individual is primarily concerned about quality and delivery of services, is quite interested in added-value services, and is not very sensitive to price. This buyer is interested in a long-term relationship, would prefer to deal with a single point of contact, and is interested in essentially outsourcing all of his problems. This type of customer can be defined as being price inelastic or quality sensitive.

2. *Average buyer.* The average service buying decision-maker tends to view price as being more important than the quality buyer does but continually maintains a balance between price of service and quality of service delivery. In essence, this type of decision-maker is constantly performing a trade-off between price and quality, with a willingness to pay more for the incremental value-added services required. In general, a minor change in price will not affect the buying patterns in this market segment; price changes must be substantial. These types of buyers can be characterized as being price linear, or price and quality sensitive.

3. *Price-oriented buyer.* The third class of customers are those for whom price is the only issue of concern. These types of buyers presume that all service providers offer essentially the same level of service and use price as a primary differentiator. For these types of buyers even a minor change in price could result in a significant shift toward or away from a particular vendor. These individuals tend to want to micro-manage, are very concerned with the details of the relationship, and are not interested in outsourcing functional

responsibility for service. In fact, they may enjoy the service role as "do-it-yourself" players. This segment of market is price highly elastic or price critical.

The general character of these three types of buyers can be described in terms of their price–demand relationship (the price elasticity of their demand). Market research surveys of over 500 end-users has indicated that the general service market typically can be segmented as follows:

- Price inelastic, 25–40%
- Price linear, 40–60%
- Price highly elastic, 8–15%

In addition to these three major segments, a fourth segment can, and often does, exist in particular markets or unique situations in which service quality questions and issues are absolutely critical. This is the segment in which price becomes an indicator of quality because service (or product) quality is not easily measurable but yet is critically important. In essence, in situations where it is extremely difficult to measure differences in the quality of service being bought, customers sometimes use price as a direct indicator of service quality.

Understanding this important dimension of customer price elasticity and recognizing the existence of these specific market segments are very important in gaining a full understanding of not only how to best approach the field service market but also how to maximize profitability and price, which is discussed further in Chapter 11.

FACTORS INFLUENCING PRICE ELASTICITY OF DEMAND

While it is generally true that personal behavior, attitude, and perception will contribute to alternative views of price elasticity of demand, the fact is that market conditions, characteristics, and industry practices can also have major effects. In addition, market-dominant or market-leader vendors can literally change the perceptions and characteristics of the price elasticity of demand relationships, particularly if they are willing to be creative.

Obviously, if all the vendors in a particular market segment approached customers with a "me-too" attitude and presentation, suggesting that they offer the same quality as the other service providers, but at a lower price, the buyers themselves will become attuned to and focused on price as the primary differentiator. It is, therefore, important to recognize that in many markets the field service vendors themselves fail to understand that customers' focus on price is generated directly by field service vendors' focus on price as a means for differentiating the services of one vendor from another.

In general, most users are primarily concerned about ensuring that the service vendors they choose are capable of meeting certain baseline requirements. They will also obviously be interested in additional or value-added services if, in fact, those value-added services are meaningful to them. It is equally important to recognize that the added-value services of importance to one class of customer may not be the same as for another class. For example, the ability to offer 7-day, 24-hour emergency field service coverage would clearly be much more important to a hospital that is operating 7 days a week, 24 hours a day, than to a business office that is operating 5 days a week, 8 hours a day.

The difference between basic and value-added services by specific segment in the market place should be defined through extensive experience and knowledge of individual customer requirements or through some type of formal market research or survey. Experience alone can sometimes be inadequate or misleading, particularly in new kinds of businesses or changing situations and conditions. This mix of basic and value-added services forming the overall portfolio of services to be offered by the vendor should not be viewed as simply a trivial exercise to develop a broad list of possibilities, such as offered in a Chinese restaurant menu. Pricing and cost relationships, for example, are directly affected by a fixed-price guarantee on materials, bonding of individual service providers, guarantees on response time, or service completion time.

Unfortunately, in the industry this portfolio mix is trivialized by attempting to be all things to all customers and failing to define the specific portfolio elements clearly, crisply, and quantitatively and relate them to price options and alternatives. Another error is to create an all-or-nothing situation in which customers have very few options to pick and choose from among both the basic and value-added service portfolios.

ROLE OF THE SERVICE CONTRACT IN FOCUSING ON SERVICE MARKET SEGMENTS OF INTEREST

Why is it necessary to even consider the possibility of varying price elasticity segments or to tackle such difficult concepts as basic and value-added service portfolios? The answer is that by focusing on the existence and requirements of these segments and by understanding the concept of pricing relative to service portfolio, through the use of a service performance contract, it is quite possible to develop a high level of revenue and profitability for a given set of customers.

The service performance contracting concept is predicated upon certain critical premises:

- A specific mixture or portfolio of basic and value-added services can be defined for a specific group or class of customers.
- The specific portfolio of services (both basic and value-added) can be measured in terms of value in use to those customers based on customers' parameters, operating environments, and paradigms, as opposed to the vendors' costs of service.
- Customers are willing to pay this value if they can be guaranteed performance relating to the specific optimized portfolio required.

PERFORMANCE CONTRACT, DESIGN, AND SPECIFICATION

Once the basic concepts of performance contracting are understood, it is relatively easy to proceed forward to develop and apply the principles in day-to-day operations. It is equivalent to pricing a show as a whole rather than as the cost of individual players. When you go to the theater or movie, you pay for the total performance, not the individual components.

The first step in developing a service performance contract approach is to begin to segment the customer base or market into specific categories, specifically including:

- Those who are extremely interested in service quality and performance but not so much place
- Those who are extremely interested in the trade-off between price and service quality
- Those who are interested in price but not so much quality

Having identified these segments, the next step is to determine the differences in basic and value-added services required from segment to segment and attempt to quantify, as much as possible, these requirements. This could be best accomplished through a double-blind statistically valid survey using either a telephone or mail survey mechanism.

Starting from this basic price elasticity categorization, the next step is to further segment the market by key classes or features of service required for both basic and value-added services opportunities. This segmentation could be along a variety of lines, including, among others:

- Time of day, and day of week coverage
- Response and completion times
- Types of basic services
- Additional services (beyond basic services)
- Materials, procurement, and control

The next step is to develop an underlying set of basic and value-added services which can be used to define and describe the needs and requirements of each of the segments and sub-segments. This can be restructured in terms of a recommended optimized portfolio of basic and value-added services for each individual segment.

Starting from the portfolio of basic and value-added services, it is then essential to build up a scaleable analytical model and framework that can be used to compute and forecast the recommended fixed price for these basic and value-added services, as a function of the size and dimensions of the customer service requirements. This will involve determining the labor hours at a given labor rate and then computing labor costs and adding in material and other costs (e.g., travel) to set prices for the portfolios of basic and value-added services relative to the size and dimensions of the customers' service needs. To that cost, overhead, general and administrative costs, profit, and profit contingency must be added to come up with a final fixed price for the service performance contract (i.e., the optimized service portfolio).

The final step in pricing would be the development of a "sanity check" to make sure that the price for the given portfolio of basic and value-added services focuses on individual market segments and appears to be reasonable. Doing so ensures that the contracting price for the performance quoted does not, on the surface, appear to be significantly higher than a rough-cut direct labor and material cost approach.

With the defined basic and value-added service portfolios and pricing in hand, the final step is to develop a specific brochure and selling aid that clearly defines, to the targeted vertical market segment, the basic and value-added service portfolio and pricing, specifically tied to the costs and benefits of this given portfolio against the price in terms of value-received justification. This brochure and price then become the framework for initiating the service performance contract offer in the market.

The normal selling process, utilizing a performance contract approach, is to take the defined basic and value-added service portfolios and pricing, in the form of a brochure, and to present this to the target customer segment in terms of either a direct-mail piece or a direct sales call. The usual first step is to request a no-obligation audit of a customer's service needs and requirements in order to confirm the price, service quality, and performance commitment associated with the price. This audit assumes the form of a specific performance contract proposal that is fixed price; includes specification of the performance levels, performance bond, and guarantee; and answers the performance questions of concern to the customer. This approach has the potential to lead to a sales close.

REVENUE EXPANSION BASED ON SERVICE PERFORMANCE CONTRACTING

This process of developing a service performance contract approach through a recommended optimized portfolio and pricing can also be extremely useful in extending the basic offer to include other required services for particular customers. Increasingly, buyers of services are now expressing interest in broadening the services obtained to other related services, including preventive services; repair, maintenance, and support for multivendor high-technology equipment; and other such professional services. By adding these additional value-added services to the portfolio, it is possible to significantly increase the revenue base and profitability of the offer. In essence, in a full-service portfolio the customer tends to be willing to pay a premium price for dealing with a single point of contact and integrated-support vendor, rather than with a number of individual vendors. It is important to recognize that individual service vendors usually issue their own bills and statements, and working with a single contractor would reduce the number of bills handled by the customer. In addition, it is quite possible that finger pointing could occur between two separate contractors in the event of a collapse in relationships between two or more separate parties. Here, again, the customer is willing to pay a premium to avoid this type of confrontation.

USE OF PERFORMANCE CONTRACTING TO WIN

In essence, performance contracting does require a good deal more work to put into place. It is necessary to carry out the appropriate market research to clearly define the individual market segments and to develop explicit knowledge of portfolio needs and requirements for both basic and value-added services for individual market segment classes. It is also essential to put together a scaleable pricing approach that can be tied to this specific optimized service portfolio. Finally, work has to be done to quantify service contract performance and to describe it in brochure form so that it can be easily perceived and understood by the customer base. In return for this additional work, however, performance contracts can provide a higher level of profitability plus increased revenue streams and greater success probability, particularly within targeted segments of the market.

Performance contracting can be used to compete directly with larger companies, by more clearly articulating and defining an optimized portfolio of services to meet specific customers' requirements. Performance contracting can also be used to overcome price questions and issues and to erect competitive barriers to entry.

Performance contracting obviously is not for everybody, on either the customer side or the vendor side. The primary customers interested in performance contracting are those who are relatively price insensitive and are more highly focused on service quality and deliverability. Thus, performance contracting works best for vendors that are highly skilled and efficient in their operations and place close control on their costing, scheduling, and assignments. This is very suited to service vendors who have in-depth and detailed cost allocation systems and a very considerable knowledge of the cost of their operations under various situations.

SUMMARY

All field service firms are strongly urged to look more closely at performance contracting as a mechanism for significantly increasing revenues, profitability, and market share. Service performance contracting can be considered the wave of the future. It will be increasingly used by larger organizations to outsource and contract out their service needs and requirements. Organizations that are prepared to deal in this manner will find their marketing opportunities growing and their profit margins increasing.

Field service organizations who continue to deal with the standard time, travel, and materials approach will increasingly find themselves being badgered by customers to obtain the lowest possible price. They will be in constant risk of losing existing customers due to new, less-expensive offerings made by competitors intent on gaining market share. One need only to look at other areas of service such as contract cleaning maintenance, food service, healthcare services, etc. to see the trend emerging to use performance contracting as a general method of doing business.

Service-performance-based contracting, then, is like putting on a show and selling tickets to the full performance rather than for individual acts. Our studies indicate that the "play's the thing" and ultimately, there is no business like show business.

10

MARKETING AND
SELLING SERVICE

CONTENTS

The marketing and selling of professional, technical, and field services have always been extremely difficult functions, primarily because of the esoteric nature of service as a product and because of the complexity, sophistication, and number of options and alternatives for marketing and selling available. Over the last 50 years, a very significant set of workable mechanisms for the marketing and promotion of tangible products has evolved to sell the form, fit, and function, as well as the "label". While form, fit, and function have been developed for services equivalent to those found for products, the perception (or "label") normally found in the product environment does not generally exist in the service environment. The equivalent of a label for service products can be thought of as the *current view perception of future service performance*. This concept is not only difficult to visualize but is even more difficult to communicate, particularly because of the lack of hard and fast dimensions associated with the label or perceptions in the service product. Thus, the normal mechanisms for product public relations and merchandising, packaging, and communication, such as print, radio, and television advertising, may not necessarily be the most cost effective for professional and technical services. However, in the right mix and with the correct focused message they can prove to be very valuable in creating an optimized process.

Significant market research has, in fact, clearly shown that in the service business in general, the highest payoff (in terms of business development and expansion) is achieved when a customer is drawn to the vendor rather than the vendor approaching the customer which occurs at a ratio of approximately 9 to 1 (see Figure 10.1). Thus, for example, a statistically valid evaluation of the experiences of other service firms shows that the probability is nine times greater that a service vendor will close a contract through public relations, marketing, and merchandising by getting the customer to approach that vendor to carry out a specific service task, as opposed to the situation where a service vendor approaches the customer on a cold-call basis to sell that same service. Drawing the customer to the service vendor works twice as well as the same approach for products. This concept, in essence, requires an "invisible sell" in which the service vendor must avoid the appearance of being an aggressive salesperson or soliciting business directly. This concept has been embedded in a number of both written and unwritten laws and certainly falls within the ethics of many professional organizations. For many professionals, such as doctors, lawyers, and consultants, the normal marketing mechanisms, such as advertising, have been frowned upon as being unprofessional. Thus, if managers and executives of service firms wish to conduct the marketing and selling of their business on a cost-effective basis, they must understand, both strategically and tactically, the value of marketing that utilizes public relations, in general, as an alter-

| | | Market Sales Success Experience | | |
| | | Probability of Opening Dialog (%) | Probability of Closing Sale Once Dialog Is Opened (%) | Overall Success Probability (Out of All Prospects) (%) |
Types	Approach			
Product	Direct sales[a]	33	30	3–9
	Indirect sales approach[b]	36	32	10.2
Service	Direct sales call[a]	18	12	2.2
	Indirect sales approach[b]	48	41	19.7

[a] Direct sales call approach.

[b] Using PR mechanisms to draw customers approach.

Figure 10.1   Comparison of direct vs. indirect sales approach and success ratios in selling products vs. services. (From Blumberg Associates, Inc., survey of 753 industrial and commercial customers, Fort Washington, PA. With permission.)

native, or in addition, to the employment of standard direct print, radio, and television advertising.

DEVELOPING THE PUBLIC RELATIONS MARKETING STRATEGY

The starting point for the design and implementation of an optimized public relations marketing program for professional and technical services businesses is the need to construct both a business strategy and a marketing plan. The key to effective public relations is to design an effective message for the target audience. The marketing and public relations strategy plan creates the framework within which this message can be developed. When establishing the strategic public relations marketing plan for a service business, it is necessary to answer the following questions:

- *What is your current image and position?* For existing and maturing organizations, a key issue is tracking the results of previous public relations, marketing, advertising, and promotional campaigns — in essence, determining the image and public relations position your firm currently has. For new organizations, this question is not easily answered.

- *What is the image and public position you would like to have?* It is important to envision the image you are seeking in the overall service business strategy, preferably an image that will optimize the business plan.
- *What is the portfolio of services that you offer?* The business strategy and plan should dictate what package or portfolio of services you offer to the market.
- *What is your pricing strategy?* Professional and technical service firms must develop a pricing orientation dealing with high-priced competitive, average or mid-range price, and low price services. This image can be communicated so it is essential to understand whether pricing is an important part of the image and, if so, which price orientation should be highlighted.
- *What is the targeted market for the services?* The business strategy, service portfolio, and pricing determined to this point can be used to focus on and address targeted markets and market segments. These might be vertically oriented, such as banks, hospitals, or manufacturing organizations; they can be defined in terms of staff functions, such as manufacturing, marketing personnel; or they can even be defined in terms of certain kinds of technologies such as computers, telecommunications, office automation, or networks. The target market could also be defined in terms of specific parameters involving more than one dimension, such as specific types of organizations (such as banks) who are considering out-sourcing. The best mechanisms for market segment focus, definition, and identification are to search for those segments that offer a way to define and focus on a public relations distribution structure in terms of trade and professional associations, magazines, news-papers, etc. Finally, the market target could be specific management levels or corporate functions that best define the buying decision-makers. For example, in the field service market as a segment, the Association for Service Managers International (AFSMI), the National Association of Service Managers (NASM), and specially focused magazines and other media such as *Micro Service Management Magazine (MSM)*, ServiceNews, and *Service Managers Journal* (sponsored by the AFSMI) represent distribution channels for public relations. In another market segment, such as banking, one will find the American Banking Association, a trade association that sponsors both regional and national conferences and trade shows and also publishes a number of magazines that focus on that segment. To the extent that your particular target market, as defined by the business strategy, does not have benefit of specific media attention, professional or trade associations, conferences,

etc., you might seriously consider changing the target market structure because the existence of such focused distribution channels significantly improves the efficiency of a marketing program. Presenting some amount of image-oriented public relations in general-interest media is, of course, helpful, but to pay off that general-image advertising and promotion must be developed in conjunction with more focused messages in targeted media.

■ *What is the public relations and marketing budget?* Important issues that must be resolved with respect to the overall business plan are the size and dimensions of the marketing and public relations budget. A good rule of thumb is to allocate between 2 and 3% of total revenues; however, this is not necessarily an optimum solution for a start-up business (where the percentage should be higher) or for maturing or declining businesses for which it is necessary to make major use of marketing and public relations to revitalize the business base.

■ *What is your willingness to commit personal time and attention?* Another factor in developing an optimized public relations plan is to determine the amount of time that you, as the principal, are willing to devote on a personal basis. In essence, some public relations mechanisms involve more or less commitment and time expenditure. If the principal or senior executives of a professional or technical service organization are willing to devote more personal time, it is possible to develop a much more efficient and effective public relations campaign than if time is not available.

MOST CRITICAL ISSUES

The above issues all serve to define the optimum business strategy and marketing plan and public relations programs, as outlined in Figure 10.2. The three most important issues that critically determine the public relations plan are:

1. *Market segment focus.* Defining the target market as indicated earlier by the service portfolio, pricing, and business strategy approach is one of the most crucial elements of the successful public relations plan. The target market defines the appropriate media, trade shows, business press, etc. that must be dealt with. This, in turn, will determine the success or failure and utility of certain key public relations mechanisms.

2. *Public relations budget.* Certain public relations mechanisms are much more costly than others. On the other hand, the public relations mechanisms requiring a high price tag are usually the

Strategic Issue	Impact	Effect on PR Campaign
What is your current image and public awareness?	Negative or positive image effects, depending on tactics employed	Size and dimensions of appropriate PR mechanism Degree of commitment and attention required
What do you want to sell? What is the portfolio of services to be offered?	Mix of PR approaches and level of focus determined by portfolio	Mix of services offered
What is your pricing strategy and image (high price, average, low price)?	Image consistent with pricing approach	Types of mechanisms to be employed and degree of "gloss" or "richness" utilized
What is your targeted audience and market?	Optimum media and distribution channels determined by market	Choice of media and mechanisms Use of specific distribution channels
What is your budget for PR? How much can you afford?	Use of various mechanisms (e.g., paid vs. unpaid)	Mix of mechanisms Use of controllable vs. uncontrollable mechanisms Elimination of some techniques
How much personal time or involvement can you contribute?	PR strategy and tactics	Influence on success of certain PR mechanisms by direct personal involvement
How long should the campaign last?	Ultimate success of PR program	Budget and schedule
What do you want your image to be?	PR strategy and tactics Message employed	PR portfolio mix PR message and image
What are your PR goals and targets? Who do you want to reach and with what message?	PR strategy and tactics	Reaction time Measurement and feedback process and procedures

Figure 10.2 Key factors in determining a successful public relations program.

ones that are more controllable and manageable, in the sense that paying the bill allows the firm to dictate and control the timing and context of the message. Thus, the size of the public relations budget will have a direct impact on the scheduling and control of the public relations program.

3. *Personal commitment.* The third key factor deals with the level of personal time, commitment, and involvement. Certain public relations mechanisms require a good deal of personal attention in order to be successful. The extent that personal time is available and the individual involved is skilled at the public relations art will determine the overall success of the program.

In summary, the starting process for the development of the successful implementation and roll-out of an effective public relations program is the organization of the business strategy and marketing plan through the development of answers to the questions outlined in Figure 10.2, leading to the design of an optimum strategic public relations program.

SOURCES OF ASSISTANCE

A number of sources of assistance are available to which professional and technical service organizations can turn for help in developing public-relations-based marketing plans, including:

■ *Business strategist consultants and marketing research specialists focusing on the professional and technical services market and industry.* An extremely good way to develop an understanding of the customer market base and segmentation and, more importantly, to determine the existing image and profile is to carry out market research on a blind/confidential basis to survey the customer base. Strategic planning and market research consultants can be of great assistance in organizing and outlining the business plan, measuring customer position, and developing a recommended public relations strategy.

■ *Public relations consultants.* A second major source of help are specialist firms focusing on public relations. Because of their focused nature, public relation firms can be of value in identifying and implementing successful public relations campaigns. It is, however, critically important that the firm selected has credentials and experience in applying public relations in a professional and technical services environment. Many public relations firms tend to focus on product-oriented promotion and may not have the necessary contacts, networks, experience, or insight to effectively assist in publicizing a professional and technical service organization and may tend to be too focused on a more aggressive sell. Be sure to choose carefully and select a public relations firm based upon its actual experience and credentials in the professional and technical services environment and demand to deal with the top executive of the firm. Public relations firms, just as for strategic management consulting and market research organizations, are not inexpensive. Be prepared to spend anywhere from $10,000 to $30,000 or more, per year, for a good public relations organization in terms of assisting and preparing the public relations plan and strategy and actually implementing the key public relations mechanisms recommended.

■ *Books on public relations and marketing professional or technical services.* Several books are available on the subjects of marketing and public relations for professional and technical service organizations.

In summary, a number of sources are available to assist in developing a public relations plan, program, and campaign. The most important of these is the need to carry out the appropriate market survey and analysis on an independent and objective basis in order to understand clearly the target market and its media sources, as well as the current image and position of your firm vs. competing professional and technical service organizations.

DEVELOPING AND IMPLEMENTING THE PUBLIC-RELATIONS-BASED MARKETING STRATEGY

Once the above business strategy and market plan framework is established, it is then possible to proceed with development and implementation of the public relations strategy.

The Need for Public Relations Portfolio

Of the many mechanisms for public relations, some are inexpensive and others are very expensive. Some are more effective than others. In developing an optimized public relations strategy, it is essential to recognize the existence of the options and to develop and select the best portfolio of mechanisms driven by the key planning issues and criteria discussed above. When developing the public relations strategy, it is important to recognize potential limitations, as described previously, due to past tradition, written or unwritten laws, and ethics codes. The historical view was that professional and technical firms, such as lawyers, doctors, and consultants, should not aggressively advertise. Some firms overcame this requirement by going to "tombstone" type ads, which simply highlighted the main focus of the professional organization without creating any sales pitch. However, in the last few years, particularly in the legal and medical fields, the code restrictions concerning advertising have been lifted and it is now possible to find considerable print, radio, and television advertising utilized by professional or technical service organizations, including some that are extremely aggressive in intent and focus.

The most important issue in the development of the public relations plan is the concept of the "invisible sell" discussed earlier. The public relations mix and portfolio should be designed to gain a positive image, including reputation, exposure, and credibility, but should not create an image of total interest in selling actual or specific services or highlighting specific results. The key is to develop a program that produces constant, sustained exposure, coupled with credibility, to plant the idea in the heads of the targeted market that you can be the solution they need.

Mechanisms for Public Relations

A broad array of mechanisms and tactics are available within the public relations tool kit for any professional or technical service organization. These are listed and outlined in Figure 10.3. We can characterize them in terms of their costs and their effectiveness. In general, in these terms of reference, we find the following cluster of public relations tactics:

- *Most cost-effective.* The most cost-effective public relations mechanisms that effectively balance the cost of development and implementation against performance are articles, speeches, and seminars, particularly those that have a current newsworthy content.
- *Good effectiveness but expensive.* The second set of mechanisms can be very effective in producing positive public relations but tend to be extremely expensive. These include special studies, direct mail, and trade show booths.
- *Inexpensive but not particularly effective.* The third set of mechanisms are those that are relatively expensive to produce but do not necessarily create a high-quality result. These include news releases, acting as an intelligence source, and highly visible activity in trade or professional associations.
- *Expensive but potentially effective.* Advertising and newsletters can be very expensive relative to other mechanisms but they can have a high potential pay off if properly designed, constructed, and used or maintained over a long period of time.

Form	Description	Value	Cost	Direct results
Article	5- to 10-page article prepared for publication in a targeted magazine or trade news media	Exposure to magazine's audience Referrals Use as handouts (perhaps with proposal appendix)	Time to write (typically 3 to 4 days)	Possible honorarium ($100–1000) Possible reprint sales ($5–25)
Speech	30- to 60-minute presentations to targeted audience at specific programs or national, regional, or local (chapter) meetings	Exposure to meeting audience Referrals Distribution of literature or materials	Time to prepare plus cost of visual aids ($20 per slide)	Possible honorarium ($100–1000)
News release/press kit	1- to 2-page announcement mailed or delivered to specific sets of media or new employees announcing promotions, new technologies or services, contract awards, joint ventures ... anything newsworthy	Exposure to media audience	Time to prepare release plus production and mailing costs ($300–400)	None
Seminar	1- to 2-day program providing information and education to targeted audience	Exposure to seminar attendees Referrals Closed subject sell for period of seminar	Time and materials to prepare visual aids, handouts, documentation, brochures, mailings, and seminar facility, in addition to logistics costs (typically $20,000–30,000)	Fees from attendees ($300–800 apiece) Potential direct contract award (15% become clients)
Book	200- to 300-page book published on some subject of interest	Exposure Credibility	Time to prepare (3 to 6 months, minimum), plus publication costs.	Contract payment Royalties
Special survey or study	30- to 100-page survey of some issue or question	Exposure Credibility	Cost to prepare survey, plus printing and mailing ($20,000–50,000)	Survey report sales At $500–1,000 per unit

Mechanism	Description	Benefit	Cost	Revenue
Community or association activity	Participate in community or association as officers, committee chairmen, support	Exposure	Time	None
Act as an intelligence source	Provide special or unique information to news media	Exposure	Time to maintain contacts	None
Print advertising	Display advertisement in targeted magazine or newspaper	Exposure (only with repeated interviews or in conjunction with editorial article)	$100–10,000 or more	None
Radio/television advertising	1-minute presentation	Exposure	$100–10,000 or more	None
Talk show	Appear on radio or television talk show	Exposure Credibility	Time to obtain invitation Time on show	None
Contests	Target to win a specific contest, such as best book, best article, best case study	Exposure Credibility	Time to compete	Possible contest prize or award
Direct mail	Letters sent to potential client list, standard or tailored	Exposure Potential referrals	Time to prepare letter Preparation and mailing costs	None
Trade show booth	Booth at trade shows to present capability	Exposure Referrals	Time to work booth Cost of booth space and display ($5000–10,000)	None
Newsletter	4- to 8-page document sent to customers on a paid or unpaid basis	Exposure Referrals Credibility	Preparation time and costs Publication costs Mailing and distribution costs (typically $5000–15,000 per issue)	Potential revenue from newsletter subscribers

Figure 10.3   Public relations mechanisms.

■ *Risky or expensive but potentially offering high payoff.* The final set of mechanisms are generally either risky in the sense that they may not pay off at all or are expensive but, because of their innovativeness, may produce an unusually good result. These include radio and television spot advertising, sponsorship of contests, and appearances on talk shows. Radio and television advertising, in particular, lack the ability to target or focus, particularly for industrial- or commercial-oriented services.

In order to provide an overall view of both the cost and value or effectiveness of these mechanisms, a scale of 1 to 9 can be used, with 9 representing either the highest cost or the best or most effective performer, as shown in Figure 10.4. This evaluation is based upon personal experience in utilizing public relations mechanisms for professional and technical services in a broad range of markets. It should be noted that this does represent a personal view rather than results of any comprehensive study. The analysis, as shown in Figure 10.4, also provides identification of possible joint or combined mechanisms that could produce a higher overall effect.

It should be noted, as well, that both the costs and value or effectiveness of performance will be a function of personal commitment, skills, and capabilities. For example, an executive who is capable of writing well may find that articles are one of the best mechanisms. On the other hand, an individual with little or no writing skills or a lack of interest in writing might not be as effective in using that particular mechanism; in this case, the executive may need someone to "ghost write" such features.

Description and Evaluation of Key Public Relations Mechanisms to Create a Proactive Selling Environment

Analysis and evaluation of key marketing and selling mechanisms used in the professional, technical, and field service markets follow (see Figure 10.5).

Articles

Experience suggests that placement of articles is perhaps the most important and cost-effective public relations mechanisms. To be successful, an article must be focused and customized to a specific audience and media format. Based upon the planning process as outlined above, it is necessary to target a market and define a story or concept to be promoted in that market. By examining the market, you can uncover magazines or newspapers targeted to that market and would be interested in the story. Contact the particular media to find out their policies with respect to the following issues: Do they accept outside manuscripts or are all articles

Type	Cost	Benefit	Overall Cost-Effective Value	Suggested Combination To Increase Value
Article	2	9	9	Speech
Speech	3	8	8	Article
News release	3	5	4	Article (background)
Seminar	8	8	8	Speech or articles
Book	6	9	8	
Special study or survey	9	8	7	
Community or association activity	2	5	4	
Intelligence source	2	4	3	Article
Print advertising	8	2	4	
Radio/television advertising	8	1	3	
Talk show	3	7	6	Book
Contests	6	5	6	
Direct mail	5	5	6	
Tradeshow booth	7	6	6	Speech, article, book, special study, news release
Newsletters	7	5	5	News release, special study

Figure 10.4   Evaluation of public relations mechanisms.

written internally? If all articles are written internally, the process of publication is going to be constrained by the willingness of particular editors to work with you to publish stories under their bylines. If the policy of the media is to accept outside written materials, you will need to determine their explicit guidelines concerning, among others:

- Acceptable length of the article
- Style
- Format (in terms of spacing, type of font, and word processor software utilized)
- Editing style
- Use of figures and/or photographs

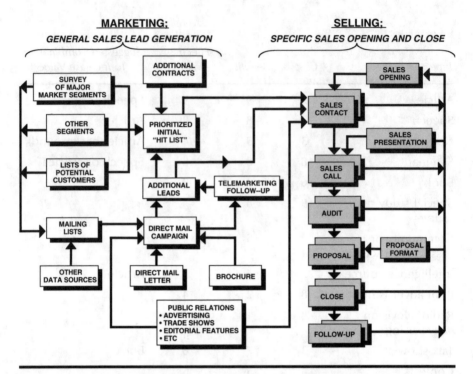

Figure 10.5   Recommended service marketing and selling process.

It is absolutely essential to comply with the requirements to make the job of the editor very easy in terms of review and evaluation of your manuscript. Editors of magazines and newspapers are constantly bombarded by manuscripts submitted by outside authors. They will tend to use even the simplest of guideline constraints as a way of eliminating articles; for example, a manuscript that was acceptable in all ways except for the font and line spacing may possibly be rejected. Finally, be sure to follow up on submissions. It is quite possible that your material has gone to the wrong editor or is sitting on someone's desk. The follow up will at least ensure that your material is appropriately reviewed.

The article itself could be based on one of four major sources:

1. *Cross section of professional or technical experience.* For organizations that have had a lot of experience in various types of situations, it is possible to do a cross-section analysis of those experiences to extract any proprietary data, and produce an article focusing on some insight or experience in terms of what worked or did not work.

2. *New concepts or ideas.* Quite often in your activity, a new concept or idea will arise. These make excellent sources of articles, particularly if it is possible to demonstrate the applicability of the concept or idea in a specific area of the industry or market as related directly to the interest of the magazine or media.

3. *New industry information.* A third possible source of articles would be new information or new insight about the industry or targeted market.

4. *Proprietary case studies.* Journals, in general, look for interesting case studies concerning a particular company in the market or industry. The basic problem with this particular approach is that it requires full approval of the service firm's customer or client, combined with a general reluctance of the client to release such proprietary information. In substance, proprietary case studies represent one of the best types of articles, but it is extremely difficult to put it together for general publication without the full approval and cooperation of the service firm's client.

Many individuals say that the hardest step is to overcome "writers' block". A good way to produce an article is to create an outline and use a tape recorder to dictate material around that outline. In essence, simply talk to the tape recorder as if it was an associate and then transcribe the dictated material. This type of "stream of consciousness" around an outline then becomes the start of the writing process. This approach represents one of the best ways to overcome the dreaded "writers' block".

When editing the initial transcribed material, be sure to eliminate any wordy sections, particularly academic or esoteric words. This is true, in general, unless you are writing for an academic journal. Make the article easy to read and interesting. The test of this is to get a limited sample of people from your targeted audience to review it. It is also a good idea to ask your spouse, your older children, or an individual who has no knowledge of the market or industry to review and critique the article. If they find it interesting and readable, you can assume that it will have general interest.

Enhance the article by adding figures and diagrams to the text to help the reader visualize the idea or concept. Most important is to make sure that you have a beginning or introduction, a middle, and an end. The end of the article should summarize the article and make recommendations for action that the reader can use. It is, in fact, for the article to work effectively as a public relations mechanism it must conclude with specific recommendations for action, focus, or planning. Finally, as a general prescription, do not make the article too long. Comply with editorial guidelines and keep the article to a maximum of 5 to 10 double-spaced pages.

A trick in writing articles that work to generate public relations and interest in a professional service business is making the article fully readable and enthusiastic but to withhold some key concepts or ideas. In essence, do not give away the total story. Grab the readers' attention and generate enthusiasm for taking specific actions; however, do not explicitly supply the entire process or procedure to implement a recommendation. Let the reader come to you for these answers. In short, it is essential to come up with a good, comprehensive article that outlines a new idea, concept, or experience and results in recommendations for action but does not completely articulate (in precise detail) the actual steps involved in implementing the action. This maximizes the potential for readers to come to you.

It is important to note that articles can be used elsewhere if they are not accepted or printed in a particular media. The articles can also be distributed in a direct-mail piece to amplify some idea or concept contained in the main body of the letter, handed out at speeches to further amplify the verbal comments, used at trade show booths as a handout, or used as an appendix to proposals to flesh out specific concepts or ideas. In essence, the very act of putting onto paper an organization's ideas and views can produce a public relations result, even if those views are never published. When an article is published, however, it has even more credibility and improves exposure.

In summary, articles are one of the most affective public relations mechanisms, particularly if they are published. If an organization makes extensive use of articles, make sure to develop a list of articles and handouts to be retained and utilized in response to various requests. Requests for reprints can be extremely useful in both expanding interest in a particular organization and serving as a potential source of revenue. One can usually charge a small fee of $10 to $25 for reprints.

Speeches

Speeches are another good source of public relations in that they provide image and reputation and, in some cases, credibility. A starting point is to identify and develop a list of speaking opportunities at conferences, trade shows, seminars, and other sources that represent the targeted market audience. Contact the sponsors of such events well in advance (typically 9 to 12 months or more), before the agendas of speakers are completed or finalized. Send a letter to the sponsors or organizers with speaking suggestions along with a possible article showing the content or focus. Be sure that the suggestion fits in with the show focus and is relevant. Suggest, in addition to your interest in supporting the conference or show as a speaker, other roles, such as having a booth or participating on the organizing committee. Finally, follow up with a phone call or letter and be persistent, because often the sponsors or organizers are barraged by numerous similar requests.

If you get a positive response from a sponsor or conference organizer in a speech, work out the details, including when and where the conference is to be held, the size and type of audience, your audio–visual requirements, and the ability to provide audio–visual support. Also, agree upon on expenses coverage and documentation, including whether or not the conference will provide its own documentation or if you need to provide your own.

Once the speech is accepted, develop a full speech based upon the approach described previously for articles. Develop an outline and then use a "stream of consciousness" to flesh out the outline. It is also important to recognize the desirability of providing a formal handout. This article can be handed out directly at the conclusion of the speech or provided to the conference organizers to be included in the conference proceedings.

In developing a speech, make effective use of visual aids to support the presentation. Research has clearly shown that verbal and visual clues are much more effective than verbal presentations alone. Be sure to make the visual aids readable and attention getting. Use professional artists or computer graphics with color in order to achieve that goal. In general, it is also important to make sure the visual aids are easy to use. For example, some find it better to use slides and a slide projector with a handheld switch to change slides rather than using overhead foils, unless someone is available to turn the foils. The use of a slide projector allows you to shift to each slide and control the pace of the presentation.

Finally, be sure to pretest the speech. Have a beginning, middle, and end with recommendations for action. Be sure to start the speech with a joke or some type of tension breaker that puts the audience at ease and gives them some sense of where the speech is going. In essence, provide a "road map" for the audience at the beginning of the speech so they understand where you are going and how to follow you. Make the speech enthusiastic and, most importantly, not too long. Normally, a speech should not exceed 50 minutes because the attention of an audience is very difficult to maintain beyond that.

Finally, at the time of the speech, make sure that a copy of your presentation is available to the audience. This can be done by handing out the speech at the presentation or ensuring that it is available in the general proceedings. Experience indicates it is better to have the handout of the speech available after the presentation, rather than before because the audience quite often will tend to look at your materials while you are speaking and lose attention.

Books

A published book is an excellent tool for public relations in that it creates wide exposure and immediate credibility and also generates revenue. The key in making use of a book in public relations is to get a good publisher. Specifically, a good publisher can be extremely helpful in editing and printing the book to meet full market demand and in the distribution of it.

In order to get a publisher's attention and interest, you must develop a business proposal including:

- Concept and focus of the book
- A detailed outline of the proposed book
- The size of the targeted market and estimate of the book sale in units
- A competitive analysis and critique to identify similar books on the market and evaluate what was wrong with them
- One or two draft chapters demonstrating your writing style and the content that you are proposing to use in the book
- Proposed price
- Any special distribution channels or unusual mechanisms that you might have available to distribute the book
- Your own background, experience, and reputation in writing and in terms of market image

It is important to note that the writing is only part of the job of convincing the publisher. The publisher is equally interested in the opportunities such a book presents. Most publishers will only look at an idea if the projected unit sales of the book exceed 5000. This is particularly true if the proposed book is for business purposes.

Experience suggests that writing a book can take a minimum of 3 to 6 months or more, with editing and production taking another 3 to 6 months. In general, a year is a good overall time frame to allow for writing the book and bringing it to a final production draft. Experience also shows that the most critical element in the book is editing. A good business editor can more than double the value in readership of the book. It is essential that you get the best possible editing capability and work closely with the editor to ensure that the book is finely tuned to the proposed audience.

News Releases and Dealing with the Media

Another very important mechanism for public relations is to establish a continuing relationship with media executives, such as editors, writers, and publishers. The easiest way to do that is to look at the masthead of the typical journal or newspaper concerned with your market and contact them directly, indicating your capabilities and intent and your desire to cooperate with them. Provide them with continuing news and facts. In essence, develop a position as a dynamic source of intelligence and information. You will generally find that once you establish this relationship, they will continue to contact you for questions or information. Be sure to respond as accurately and rapidly as possible to any requests from your media and contacts. In affect, create a "payback" obligation from them in response to your support.

When preparing a press release, make it short, readable, newsworthy, and to the point. Press releases should not be more than two double-spaced pages. It is possible to expand the press release by adding a background article or producing a full press kit; however, the press release itself will be the key to whether or not it is accepted for publication.

Remember that the people you are dealing with are generally very overworked and underpaid and can use all the help they can get; they will pay you back with exposure. In working with the media be sure to mind your manners. Do not ask to see the story before publication, as most media will not allow this. It creates a longer turnaround time. Have trust in the media representatives you are dealing with that the editors or reporters will get the story correct.

A final recommendation is not to give up. Experience indicates that you have to bend over backwards to provide as much material as required by the reporter or editor. Patience and long-term commitment will ultimately be rewarded.

Trade Shows and Professional Meetings

A targeted market that is served by a trade show or a professional association that meets regularly presents some excellent public relations opportunities. The best approach is a combination of tactics, including:

- Articles published in professional association publications
- Speeches or workshops at national, regional, or local (chapter) meetings
- A booth at a trade show or professional meeting to meet people and introduce ideas and concepts

We have generally found that a booth is an extremely effective tool for creating awareness, particularly if it is used in combination with a speech given at the meeting and articles published in professional association publications. Finally, the trade shows or professional associations provide a significant array of opportunities for participation as officers, committee chairmen, members, or even helpers. This participation can pay off through both exposure and the ability to gain access to the appropriate individuals for opportunities to publish articles and make speeches.

Advertising

Print advertising is useful as a public relations mechanism for professional and technical services. However, it can be much more difficult to create a successful print advertisement for a service than for a product. Careful attention must be given to the format and positioning, as well as to the size of the ad, frequency of appearance, and, particularly, the message. A picture that illustrates the service is difficult to produce, but can be of very high value in getting across the message. Under any circumstances, make the message easily understandable and avoid "hype" or overselling, or any appearance of exaggeration or puffery. Research indicates that print ads appearing in the same issue as an editorial-based article, or the next issue, creates much better retention value than the print ad alone.

Radio and television advertising is generally not recommended for professional and technical services unless they are professionally developed with a focus on a specific idea, event, or service. The successful use of radio and television advertising requires specialists. Because of the rare use of this technique in the professional and technical service markets, such advertising may sometimes produce a very high payoff in terms of exposure, but its use must be highly targeted.

Other Public Relations Mechanisms to Support the Marketing Process

It is important to recognize that just about everything that is done by your firm influences the public relations image. It is important that your public relations program include consideration of:

- Office appearance and location
- Brochures and handout material
- Appearance and attitude of staff
- Telephone protocol and procedures for interfacing with clients, potential clients, and customers who call in
- Language and communication style
- Quality and commitment to work
- Pricing approach
- Personal appearance, style, and character

In essence, the total image that is produced, using all of the mechanisms discussed above, must be consistent with what you say, what you do, and what you are. John Malloy, in his great book, *Dress For Success*, provides an excellent understanding of how even the appearance of the office and personnel can influence image. The use of a logo as a personal imprint in articles, speeches (on the opening slide), brochures, etc. can be helpful in providing a basic signature or image, tying all of the public relations activities together.

Finalizing the Public-Relations-Based Marketing Plan

We have discussed the major mechanisms that can be utilized to create and implement a public relations plan. In order to implement the plan it is necessary to pull together a complete program, typically at least 6 to 12 months in advance of the desired deployment date. The plan should include:

1. The identification of a portfolio or mix of mechanisms to be employed
2. Assignments and responsibilities as to who is to do what in order to produce, implement, and roll out the mechanisms
3. Overall schedule with targets for specific mechanisms or materials to be employed
4. Budget
5. Overall objectives

In implementing the plan, be sure to use a combination of mechanisms to ensure continued and repeated exposure. For example, one could consider the combination of mechanisms in the same media, such as placing both an advertisement and an article in the same magazine. In general, the optimum public relations portfolio and plan would include mechanisms over which the organization has full control, such as advertising, as well as those where it is at the whim of the media, such as a published article. In general, it is very important to plan far ahead to take advantage of discounts or, on the other hand, to avoid being charged penalties if public relations mechanisms are implemented at the last moment. In general, advertising is less expensive if multiple inserts are utilized. Booth space charges and the cost of booth space support increases as the convention date nears. Also, when an organization is able to plan far ahead for booth space, it is likely to be assigned a much better location on the floor.

Be sure to build the full public relations program and its implementation around the common themes and targets of the public relations plan and the logo. The logo, or image of the firm, should be consistent, recognizable, and used for every mechanism.

Finally, be sure to stick to the plan or schedule and formally revise it as is necessary. The consistency and commitment of your public relations plan and program will pay off. In essence, do not look for immediate response to any specific public relations mechanism. The key concept is to plan the public relations mechanisms as cumulative exposures, continuing to nurture and grow them by repeated restatement and ultimately reaping the business benefits over time. Generally, very little correlation exists between specific public relations actions and creation of specific business opportunities. The real payoff comes from the continuing exposure and awareness, which generate credibility and image. Therefore, in order for it to be successful, the public relations program must be the result of a long-term commitment to make it successful. One-time, or even a few, exposures cannot be expected to have much effect. Try to have something appear every month that is directed toward the target audience to produce an underlying common theme. As indicated previously, doing so often involves a portfolio mix of both paid (advertise) and unpaid (articles, speeches, etc.) exposure.

Recognize that with all the planning it is possible that the public relations program might go awry or, alternatively, that the public relations program is wildly successful. It is, therefore, necessary to continue to track your image and position relative to the public relations program. It is strongly recommended to use blind, confidential market research to measure public relations performance and changes in image and position. Finally, be sure to continue to evaluate and refine a public relations campaign and message based on the evolving strategy, competitive action, market perceptions, and budget. It is critical that a public relations strategy reflects the changing scenario of the business environment and competitive practices and ideas.

MOVING FROM MARKETING TO SELLING SERVICE

Thus far, we have stressed the general marketing and merchandising mechanisms (based on a public relations concept) that work in the service market. Given this portfolio of tools, what is the final step in selling and closing service business? In general, five steps are key:

1. *Identify, establish, and define the service strategy and service portfolio.* The key is to look for perceptions with particular prioritization to service value in use. There is usually some time orientation as well.

2. *Carry out in-depth proprietary market research to isolate, measure, and segment perceptions and service needs.* Proprietary market research can be extremely useful in measuring customer requirements and needs for service, key time parameters, and perceptions. Breaking this information down into key segments can be essential in identifying the most attractive market opportunities.

3. *Develop the optimum marketing and sales approach.* The service business strategy and market research can be used to finalize the optimum portfolio and pricing and to choose the optimum public relations approach.

4. *Carry out the sales approach and close.* The key here is to use the market research (developed in step 2, with the marketing approach in step 3) to focus on specific customers through an orderly process of (a) eliminating competition by creating a unique offer and stressing its value in use, and (b) using knowledge gained in the initial sales and proposal effort in the next sale. This process is described in Figure 10.5. The basic marketing plan identifies the target market, and the public relations campaign creates the initial sales contacts. The actual sales call process is built upon a defined and orchestrated sales opening, sales presentation, and specific proposal format. By building upon success and learning what works and what does not work, an optimum sales approach will be provided.

5. *Deliver against service commitments.*

A sixth and final step would be to ensure delivery of service in accordance with the proposal and commitment. Essentially, the best and most efficient way to sell to the selected market segment will emerge. The key five steps, as outlined in Figure 10.6, work in general for both product and service, but the actual focus and emphasis are quite different for each.

In summary, public relations, if strategically designed and employed, can be extremely powerful in marketing your professional, technical, consulting, and field services. We have tried to identify the key mechanisms and processes to be used in developing and implementing a public-relations-based marketing and sales plan with specific discussion on the most important and powerful of the public relations techniques. The overall process is outlined in Figure 10.7. Because of the need for the "invisible sell" and the tremendous value of having customers come to the organization as a result of its public relations program and campaign of exposure and credibility, public relations is the most effective mechanism available for business development and market penetration.

Steps	Service	Product	Command
1. Identify and establish strategies and products.	Look for product perception, value-in-use, and time.	Look for form, fit, and function.	Step is usually performed at a corporate or product management level for products; often lacking for service.
2. Perform market research	Identify problem in customer terms. Measure time parameters and other requirements. Measure perception.	Look for needs for form, fit, and function. Measure reality.	Step is usually performed at corporate or marketing level, but not normally in service; must be done by sales personnel for service.
3. Develop sales approach.	Customize sales approach to specific customer segments and needs.	Sell form, fit, and function.	Sales approach tends to be defined by product form, fit, and function. Service approach must be developed.
4. Carry out sale approach and close.	Eliminate competition. Focus on value-in-use price.	Sell against competition. Focus on cost plus or competitive price.	Selling approach and close are different.
5. Deliver.	Ensure delivery of "warm and fuzzies". Meet perception.	Delivery reality off-the-shelf.	Delivery is immediate for product; in the future, for service.

Figure 10.6   Summary comparison between product and service sales process.

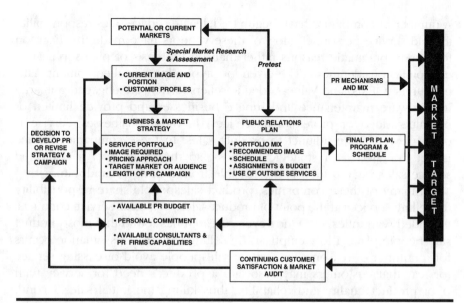

Figure 10.7 **General PR development and implementation process.**

MANAGING SERVICE SALES

In selling high-technology-based services (i.e., hardware maintenance, software support, systems integration, etc.), as with selling other types of service-related products (legal accounting, banking, health care), vendors are always confronted with the issue of determining who within their organization should have responsibility for selling services directly to the end user. A common question that often arises is whether the individuals who actually perform the services should sell the services or whether a dedicated service sales organization should have this responsibility.

This question raises serious debate in today's high-tech service organizations because it involves both philosophical and economic considerations that challenge current wisdom with respect to the basic service-oriented business model. This discussion explores the contrasting attitudes, options, and alternatives from the perspectives of the service company, customers, and sales agents and cites examples (based on case study research) for which these opposing sales strategies have worked or failed. Based on this insight, we have developed a model to help decide which strategy is optimal under various service scenarios.

Current Trends

The first step to understanding the opposing points of view is to examine current trends regarding the delegation of service sales to service personnel.

A number of companies have begun to delegate service sales responsibility to field service personnel. Most of these vendors have made this decision for purely pragmatic reasons rather than on the basis of philosophical or economic considerations. These vendors, typically original equipment manufacturers (OEMs) and Value-Added Resellers (VARs), are engaged primarily in hardware maintenance and service businesses and provide limited or no-value-added or professional services. In these businesses, service is often viewed as an adjunct to product sales. In these companies service is not operated as a strategic business, so the creation of a dedicated service sales organization is not feasible from a budget standpoint.

In many of these companies, product salespeople share responsibility for selling services at the point of product sales (i.e., basic service contracts, extended warranties, etc.); however, research has found that most product salespeople place a low emphasis on selling service. This situation occurs for a number of reasons. First, some salespeople avoid discussing service for fear that customers may associate a product's need for service with poor product quality and reliability, thus killing the initial sale. Second, many salespeople use service as a bargaining chip to encourage the customer to purchase product. In essence, salespeople will give away some services (e.g., extended warranty on new equipment, second-year service contract on older equipment, installation) to the customer at no additional cost to close a sale. This is usually done because product salespeople are not rewarded as highly for selling service as they are for product, if at all, and will sacrifice service commission on revenue in order to meet product sales quotas.

Despite the fact that product salespeople have a difficult time selling services, senior management usually understands the value of service revenue to the company. As a result, senior management may turn to its field service staff to sell services because these individuals are closest to the situation. Field service personnel represent a perceived readily available sales distribution channel for generating additional service revenue.

In theory, a service provider who delegates sales responsibility to frontline field service personnel might expect to lower the total cost of service and increase revenues and profitability, among other possible benefits. However, in reality, very few service providers actually realize these benefits. Numerous examples can be cited where senior management's good intentions to develop and implement these types of sales tactics have simply failed. These examples can be supported by the testimony of management and the field personnel regarding declining customer satisfaction and employee morale, as well as increased customer and employee turnover when these types of strategies have been implemented. Quite often, field service personnel do not feel comfortable with these new sales tasks. Many times field service personnel are not provided with sufficient direction or sales aids or guidance. Unsure just exactly what the sales task involves, some service engineers confuse selling efforts with merely collecting money. In fact, some field service personnel find selling service to be so discomforting, that they actually talk customers out of purchasing services by asking potential customers if they are really sure they want to pay that much additional money. On the other hand, some field personnel are so delighted to sell service that they place more emphasis on selling service than on resolving customer problems, leading to increased customer dissatisfaction. To quote one field service manager, "Customers would just run away every time they saw me coming." This situation is particularly true for organizations that provide attractive financial incentives for selling service.

In response to these new problems, some high-tech companies are beginning to evaluate the economics of creating dedicated sales organizations focusing solely on services. However, it has typically been the larger, progressive-thinking companies with broad service portfolios that have actually implemented such programs. The conventional wisdom tends to be that such a service marketing strategy is not practical or feasible. The main argument is that market demand is not large enough to warrant this approach. Another common argument is that a service sales strategy, particularly if it involves multivendor support, would cannibalize product sales revenues. Unfortunately, the proponents of these views often fail to conduct the necessary market research or fail to perform the appropriate analysis to determine whether these views are valid.

Understanding Customer Attitudes Toward Service Purchase

It makes extremely valid and logical business sense to conduct market research in order to understand customer needs and requirements for services as well as to examine the size and potential of the market for new services. This type of business planning serves to justify the feasibility of creating a dedicated sales organization. However, it is also important to understand and take into account customer perceptions toward salespeople. It is even more critical to understand the role that sales plays within the service and support process. Understanding this relationship is the key to maintaining high customer satisfaction and assuring high services revenue.

Many sales situations have been undermined by attempting to sell service at the wrong time or by using the wrong sales approach. One example is the service technician with sales responsibility who tries to sell a customer a new service before resolving the current problem at hand. Another example is the product sales person who commits to a complex installation project without involving service personnel in the decision.

For Customers	For Vendors
What are the costs of making the wrong decision?	What are the ramifications of providing the wrong solution?
How much information is needed to make decisions?	How much information is needed about a customer's problem to provide a solution?
How often will services be performed and what is the length of engagement?	How much technical information must be communicated to customer?
How easy is it to change suppliers during the engagement?	How costly will it be to modify or change the service offering?
Who holds ultimate responsibility for the purchase decision?	How long is the sales cycle?

Figure 10.8   Assessment of sales situations: key questions.

These situations are commonplace and have a serious impact on customer satisfaction, company morale, services revenue, and profit margins.

As any salesperson knows, customers have very specific perceptions about salespeople and service situations. These perceptions may vary from customer to customer, but service marketers must take these considerations into account in order to develop an optimal sales and marketing approach that fits customer perceptions of reality.

These perceptions are best understood by addressing several basic questions (see Figure 10.8) regarding the nature of the service sales/purchase relationship that exists between customers and vendors, including:

1. How much information is required by the customer in order to make the best service decision?
2. How frequently do new service purchases occur?
3. How easy is it to replace service providers?
4. How much information must the salesperson provide to the customer for the optimum service solution?
5. How much skill and time are required to deliver the service?

These questions fall into two general categories: (1) questions dealing with risk to customers in purchasing services, and (2) questions dealing with risk to provider in selling services. The answers to these questions will determine the type of sales approach and salesperson that would be most effective for handling specific situations (see Figures 10.9 and 10.10). A good rule of thumb is that sales situations involving high risk to both vendor and customer are best handled by a dedicated, experienced, and professional service sales staff capable of fielding and resolving complex

Strategic Issues	Implications to Vendor
Risks of making the wrong decisions are high; company could lose money; decision maker's position is at risk.	Requires good technical background, professional selling skills, business acumen, consultative sales techniques.
Information requirements are low; customer is familiar with service being sold; service is generic.	Does not require a high level of professional selling time or offers.
Service is purchased infrequently; client engagements are short and occur every few years.	Sales people have limited opportunity to appear before customers. First impressions are important.
Engagements can be canceled in mid-stream with little or no risk to client; alternative vendors are readily available and accessible.	Does not justify a concerted sales effort; services can be sold by implementation personnel.
Decisions have strategic implications to customer; decision-maker holds high level of responsibility and authority within customer organization.	Sales people require business acumen; persuasion skills, ability to effect change.

Figure 10.9 Strategic implications of sales situations from the customer's perspective.

technical and business issues. Quite often the highest risk sales are first time sales, as well. Situations of low risk justify the inclusion of service technicians and direct marketing (e.g., telemarketing or direct mail), because these situations tend to be oriented more toward order taking than actual face-to-face selling. Furthermore, low-risk situations also tend to be repeat business, in many cases. Sales situations of moderate risk can be handled by product salespeople, as they tend to arise during the product sales phase, rather then after. However, when they do occur in subsequent years of equipment operation they can be handled by the service sales force if they are covered by a larger service contract or by the service technician if service coverage is merely an add-on to an existing service contract.

Recruiting and Staffing Qualified Service Sales Personnel

Identifying the optimal sales organization to handle specific service sales situations is only the first step toward developing an effective service sales team. The next step is to recruit, train, and staff the appropriate personnel. Just because some services can be most effectively sold by the individual

Strategic Issues	Implications to Vendor
Defects in service delivery resulting from inadequate evaluation of customer needs can be corrected with minimum cost and time investment.	Sales situations can be handled by basic order taking and communication skills.
Sales solutions require an extensive amount of upfront data collection and investigation.	Consultative sales approach is most effective method of evaluating customer situation.
	Both professional sales skills and a strong technical background are required.
Sales presentations are technically oriented; customers focus on technical issues.	Consultative sales approach plus strong technical/business background and communication skills are necessary to assess and resolve situation.
Vendor experiences significant costs by modifying or changing service at customer's request.	
Sales cycles are long; decisions are made over a period of months rather than weeks.	Requires commitment by full-time sales agent.

Figure 10.10   Strategic implications of sales situations from the vendor's perspective.

performing the task does not necessarily mean that these individuals will succeed in, or even enjoy, the sales process. In the same vein, sharp, experienced, professional salespeople do not always understand the technical and business aspects of selling services. A profile of the ideal service sales candidate should be developed for each service category within the portfolio; the profiles should reflect the required educational background, skill level, and professional experience. With this information in hand, service sales and marketing managers can turn to the company labor pool to select the most qualified individuals, recruit from outside the company, or develop and train internally.

Measuring Performance and Compensating for Results

One of the key success factors in selling services is that all members of the vendor organization must understand their roles and the value of their services to customers. This factor is often overlooked, as our traditional views are often oriented toward understanding the value of the product to the customer. New notions regarding exceptional customer service are also product centered and pay little attention to services sold independently

Examples of Service Item	Level of Risk		Recommended Sales Candidates
	To Customer	To Vendor	
On-site maintenance	Low	Low	Telemarketing, service technicians
Depot repair	Low	Low	Telemarketing, service technicians
Design and engineering	Moderate to high	High	Service sales force
System integration	High	High	Service sales force
Software support/help desk	High	Moderate	Product sales force
Remote diagnostics	Moderate	Low	Product sales force, service technicians
Technical assistance	Low	Low to moderate	Telemarketing, product sales force
Disaster recovery	High	High	Service sales force
Training	Moderate	Moderate	Product sales force
Consulting	High	High	Service sales force
Installation	Moderate	Moderate	Product sales force

Figure 10.11 Optimal sales candidates based on service portfolio risk.

of product. In essence, these views are often based on providing quality service to the customers in order to sell more products (see Figure 10.11).

In essence, instead of monitoring customers to ensure that they are happy with their equipment purchase, that it operates properly, and that it is reliable and user friendly, high-tech service vendors must place greater attention on customer care and support as their *raison d'être*. The customer care model places support of the total customer service needs as the key priority. All members of the vendor organization are responsible for ensuring high levels of service satisfaction and that customers' support requirements are met through the delivery of the appropriate service and support products to the customer.

The importance of providing total customer care is becoming increasingly clear because customers continue to demand a single point of contact or one stop shopping for their product and service needs. Furthermore, many service vendors are capitalizing on the significant product pull-through potential of service. Studies by our firm have found that close to

$1 billion of revenue generated by U.S. high-tech service companies have come from the sale of equipment. In fact, many large OEMs and VARs are now discounting equipment prices as a means of selling higher margin services. This is practically a 180-degree turnaround from the days of discounting service to sell product.

At the heart of the customer care model is a human resources and compensation policy that reinforces basic elements. First and foremost is that all employees understand the role and value of service to the customer, particularly from the customer vs. the vendor perspective. Second, all employees, from the chief executive officer on down to the entry-level technician, should be responsible for customer satisfaction. The performance measurement system should evaluate individuals on their ability to influence customer satisfaction in light of their individual contributions to the ability of the total organization to influence customer satisfaction. In essence, the compensation and reward system should be based on organizational or team achievement in addition to individual achievement. For example, logistics support staff, field personnel, and call handling and dispatch personnel, in addition to the sales staff, should receive equally high marks whenever an installation is completed within the estimated time frame because each has contributed the necessary components to a successful installation process (e.g., scheduling, parts, or skills).

A similar rewards and compensation program should be developed for selling services. Pay scales and commission programs should be structured so that employees are compensated equitably for selling services. Sales targets should be high enough to provide ample motivation but should also be targeted enough that they are attainable and achievable. Also, sales targets should be structured to maximize revenues and profits, (for example, compensate for service contract renewals as well as first-time contract sales). In this way, sales personnel spend just as much time servicing current accounts as they do opening new ones.

A team-oriented approach to sales compensation also works effectively to maximize service revenue. Because field service personnel are frequently placed in situations where they can spot service (and product) sales opportunities at customer sites, they should be compensated for business development. While they may be precluded from selling certain types of service by the nature of the risk involved in the sales process, they can certainly assist sales personnel in the prospecting and business development process. By rewarding service personnel for their assistance, they will become more conscientious of developing new opportunities and maintaining close contact with current customers. Another aspect of team-based compensation is to evaluate both sales and service personnel on sales volume and profitability. This serves not only to maximize revenues and profits but also to create an atmosphere of improved communication and coordination of resources between sales and service personnel, elements essential to overall customer satisfaction.

Implementing the Customer Care Model

A final element of the customer care model is the creation of a new functional area within the service organization known as customer care management. This function reports to both service and marketing and is responsible for assuring that customer requirements for service, support, and technology are met. Typically, large customer accounts are assigned a customer care account representative, while medium and small accounts are handled by a customer care specialist who is assigned a number of accounts on a geographic or industry-wide basis. Account representatives and specialists are not engaged in the selling or service processes. Their function is to visit customers periodically to ensure that the vendor is providing the required level of support, service, technology, etc. to the customer. Their mission is to monitor customer activity and coordinate resources on a weekly and monthly basis. This approach is beneficial to preventing situations in which customers turn to other vendors because they did not know that a particular service or product was available from the primary vendor. In this model, the customer care representative acts in a role that is very similar to a social worker, who helps clients receive any available public services.

In essence, customer care personnel proactively offer timely solutions to customer problems or needs at a micro-level. Furthermore, it is not necessary for service vendors to staff a stand-alone customer care department. Customer care management can be organized on a team or matrix basis and staffed by representatives of various functions. Chief executive officers and senior executives who personally visit customer sites on an informal basis to understand customer needs are already engaged in the customer care process. However, the real benefits of the customer care approach are found when visits are performed on a structured, periodic basis and produce immediate short-term results for the customer and the vendor, rather then serving as an exercise in strategic planning for the vendor organization.

SUMMARY AND CONCLUSIONS

In summary, selling services can be a very complex endeavor. In the past, service suppliers have been provided with little guidance and direction as to the optimal strategy and approach to selling services. We have attempted to provide such a customer care model, based on in-depth market research and practical insight. Our analysis suggests that vendors

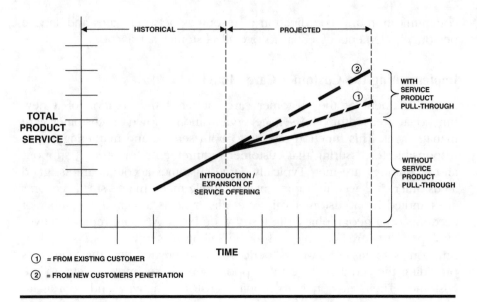

Figure 10.12   Projected product sales with/without service product pull-through.

should take into consideration issues regarding risk and customer perceptions regarding both service and sales situations in order to develop the optimal sales approach. We have also found that the relationship of these issues to the sales situation provides guidance as far as determining the characteristics required of the ideal salesperson.

The biggest obstacle to developing an optimized sales strategy is eliminating the barriers and conflicts that exist between service, sales, and other divisions involved in the sales engagement process. We believe that this can be overcome through a human resources and compensation policy that stresses customer care, service, and team achievement; the customer care model provides such guidance.

Essential to maximizing service revenue and profits is implementation of the customer care model and creation of a customer care management team. This is necessary now more than ever, as customers demand a single point of contact. Many service vendors have begun to understand this concept and have observed significant growth in both service and product pull-through revenue. Current service management trends support the fact that service is no longer viewed as an after thought to product sales, as many vendors begin to discount products in order to sell services rather than the reverse. We predict that, by the end of this decade, we will observe a complete revolution in conventional wisdom with respect to services being merely a means of supporting equipment sales (see Figure 10.12).

11

PRICING SERVICE TO MAXIMIZE REVENUES AND PROFITS

CONTENTS

INTRODUCTION

One of the most important decisions facing the managers of service organizations involves the establishment of prices. In industries dealing with the manufacture, distribution, and delivery of *tangible goods*, the long-term economic strategy would be use of a price based upon the cost of goods plus the ordinary mark-up for overhead and profit. This is primarily dictated by the concept of a production learning curve for goods and the preference of the market or consumer for lowest priced equivalent goods purchased. In essence, cost-plus pricing is the general strategic policy utilized in tangible goods pricing, with some variations employed tactically (e.g., pricing under key competitive performers) to gain market share for a competitive advantage in the short run. In general, in many markets, this approach to pricing has also been utilized in the service industry and particularly in the establishment of prices for service associated with the maintenance and repair of equipment.

This particular approach to pricing, however, often leads companies to *underprice* their services and capabilities. The primary reasons include:

■ *Failure to recognize price-insensitive or price-inelastic market segments.* Considerable research (see Chapter 10) has demonstrated that, with respect to service quality and response, a significant percentage of customers (close to 40%) are relatively price insensitive or price inelastic. In essence, a significant percentage of the market is much more concerned about quality of service than price. In fact, some segments actually view prices as a surrogate for quality and presume that lower priced service means lower quality of delivery. It should be noted that this behavior is not nearly as prevalent in tangible goods markets.

■ *Laziness of marketing and sales personnel.* It is obviously much easier to sell lower priced services (as well as products), and most sales personnel concerned about product sales tend to give away services in order to gain sales of the product.

■ *Fear of market reaction.* A continuing fear on the part of service personnel is that higher prices will not stick or that the market will react negatively. This gut reaction is often dictated by experiences in product markets as opposed to service, but the fear remains.

A number of other problems are associated with the utilization of pricing strategies adapted from product-oriented markets, including:

■ *Creation of competitive disadvantages.* The general cost-plus-mark-up approach to pricing tends to generate competitive disadvantages when an organization lacks recognition of the fact that different economies of scale or cost advantages pertain to various sizes or structures of service organizations. Typically, the large service organizations, who are market leaders, have made significant investments in systems infrastructure for centralized call handling, call avoidance, remote diagnostics technology, and integrated logistics control and have therefore developed a much lower cost of operations. Smaller service organizations, or those organizations who have not made similar technological investments, often fail to recognize the differences in economies of scale or cost advantages; therefore, use of the cost-plus-mark-up approach tends to result in prices that are significantly higher than the major competitors', with no difference in service quality or deliverability.

■ *Incorrect cost information.* A major problem in service pricing is not determining the true costs of a service product or service by market segment. Very few firms have developed cost allocation mechanisms to identify the true costs associated with short-term, mid-range, and long-term response times or service costs by market segment or type of service.

■ *Inattention to market trends and changes.* Many organizations do not track the tactical/strategic or long-term trends in pricing. They fail to recognize underlying changes in market structure and/or competition.

■ *Desire to maintain a full product line.* Many firms recognize the vital importance of providing an integrated portfolio of services. This, however, may require the sale of some services at a loss until significant volume can be built up to achieve economies of scale. Pricing each of the individual service lines within the portfolio on a cost-plus-mark-up basis can therefore lead to significant inconsistencies in the overall pricing strategy.

■ *Inappropriate objectives or goals.* Finally, many service managers fail to recognize that pricing is a vehicle or mechanism that is critical in achieving goals relative to maximizing current profits, maximizing long-term profits, gaining market share, or erecting competitive barriers to entry. In the equipment service market, where the long-term life-cycle costs of service may be considerably higher than the initial acquisition price of the product for which the service is provided, these objectives are particularly important. It is essential that the pricing strategy is based upon an understanding and definition of the particular goals and objectives. In general, the cost-plus pricing approach has failed to differentiate between such alternatives.

In summary, a number of issues must be considered when developing pricing strategy for service organizations and using pricing strategically to achieve overall objectives. Pricing strategies must first consider the options and alternatives available as a framework for strategic choice.

PRICING STRATEGY ALTERNATIVES

In broad terms, three mechanisms are available for establishing prices:

- *Cost plus mark up*. This approach is driven primarily by the cost of operation.
- *Competitive*. This approach is driven primarily by competitive prices, with typical emphasis on the market leader.
- *Value in use*. This approach generally involves focus on the cost or value to the customer of the service to be provided, measured particularly in its absence.

The mechanisms for service price development under these alternatives are described next.

Cost-Plus-Mark-Up Pricing Strategy

The cost-plus pricing strategy could be developed based on the analysis of actual results if the cost accounting system does provide the level of detail required. A cost-plus modeling approach can generally be utilized in the absence of a full cost accounting system. A typical simplistic fully loaded service cost model is driven by the hourly labor rate, incidence of occurrence of service calls, service time, and desired gross profit level. This general model is, in essence, driven by the reliability or failure characteristics of the equipment supported or by triggers of customer demand for service and targeted service response time. A reasonably high correlation exists between service response to be provided and the productivity utilization level of the service force.

Although more elaborate cost-plus models can be developed and utilized, the cost-plus model as presented provides a good rule of thumb for calculating service price. It is important to note that the cost-plus model tends to be somewhat sensitive to mean time between failures or the mean time between service calls. As the equipment becomes more reliable, the cost-plus model tends to dictate that service prices should drop.

Competitive Pricing

Many organizations tend to utilize a pricing approach based on an assessment of major competitors' prices. The standard rule of thumb is to make use of a figure of between 7 and 11% of purchase price as the annual competitive maintenance price, with the additional "ups and adds" for extending the coverage by time of day, day of week, geographic area, etc. A number of difficulties are encountered with applying competitive pricing, including the inability to obtain accurate prices from individual competitors. The basic factors influencing competitive pricing include:

1. Basic annual maintenance charge (BAMC) of the major competitor, which is usually at or lower than the smaller competitor's basic cost
2. Extended cover surcharges
3. Improved response surcharges
4. Extended geography surcharges
5. Other special charges for installation and/or time materials
6. Uptime guarantee surcharges

In-depth analysis of competitive pricing for equipment service clearly shows a lack of direct linear consistency in service pricing due in part to significant differences in the final service price as a function of the "ups and adds". The nonlinear character of this curve is clearly not well understood by many managers in service businesses who tend to view prices on the average without understanding the underlying driving elements. For example, an averaging of IBM's service prices as a percent of purchase price would tend to generate a rule-of-thumb figure of 10 to 11%, which is often used in the industry. However, as can be clearly observed by examining actual prices, this general average figure is not at all the underlying rationale utilized by the major competitors. In fact, a more general analysis of competitive maintenance service prices, including consideration of "ups and adds", showing that the standard price, while an important factor in determining competitive price, is only a part of the overall equation. The determination of the "true" competitive price is not easy. In fact, because of this highly variable characteristic of "service", competitive pricing must be determined by comparing "apples to apples" in the service portfolio offered.

Value-In-Use Pricing

The third pricing approach, and the one that has the greatest applicability to equipment service, is value-in-use pricing. The value-in-use approach is customer centered rather than competitor or vendor centered. Until recently, service pricing has been protected by the product price/performance umbrella. However, with the cost of service and support representing an increasing percentage of the total life-cycle cost of ownership (well above 50% today), customers are more closely examining the full cost of ownership, with a heavier focus on service prices as a function of service quality. In this context, it is particularly important to note that extensive survey research has identified at least three major service user types in every major market segment, including premium, quality, and standard users. In essence, the *premium user* is much more concerned about service quality and capability than service price. In fact, this user is relatively inelastic with respect to service price changes. On the other hand, the *standard user* is very concerned about price and is less concerned about service quality. Research has identified key quantitative relationships between service price elasticity of demand and service quality and performance. The most important result of this research is that, in most market segments, about 40% of the users tend to be premium oriented. The extent of premium, quality, and standard users in any market segment varies from segment to segment.

In summary, recognizing the differences in service response and repair times for different market segments, the value-in-use pricing approach is then driven by a calculation of the full cost of down time by determining the number of types of users, time of day and day of week of operations, incidence of down time, average length of down time, and impact of down time. The service price is then determined by computing the value of service to the individual market segment as a result of offsetting the cost of down time. This obviously will be significantly higher for premium users vs. standard users. These calculations must then be tested against competitive prices and modified if required. The ultimate service value-in-use pricing approach is then driven by the value to the individual user segment of minimizing downtime at a reasonable cost, as a function of service quality parameters.

In essence, a major difference between cost-plus and competitive pricing on the one hand and value-in-use pricing on the other is that value-in-use pricing is based upon a specific and explicit definition of service quality and delivery capability, whereas cost-plus and competitive pricing are generally based upon an average level of service response.

PRICE/FEE STRUCTURES

Competitive, cost-plus, and value-in-use pricing strategies deal with establishing general guidelines for calculating prices or fees for specific service features such as design and engineering, moves, adds and changes, maintenance and repair, or troubleshooting. Most vendors tend to establish a *one-price* strategy for all types of services. However, some of the larger original equipment manufacturers (OEMs) and service organizations tend to develop various strategies for different services, usually due to market conditions, characteristics, and customer preferences. This is particularly true for pricing of professional services vs. maintenance and repair service.

Regardless of pricing strategy, a number of different methods for calculating fees (billing customers for services rendered) are available, including no charge for service, hourly labor rate (time and materials billing), percentage of equipment purchase price, variable rate, or fixed price, among others (combinations of various methods). In essence, at least 12 different major pricing calculations for various services are available, such as cost-plus × hourly rate, cost-plus × variable rate, competitive × hourly rate, competitive × variable rate, value-in-use × hourly rate, value-in-use × variable rate, etc. For example, a vendor may charge an hourly rate for provision of network troubleshooting services, where calculation of the fee is based on the fully loaded cost to the vendor for providing service plus a 15% mark-up for profit. On the other hand, a different vendor may charge an hourly rate for the provision of the same services which is $25 per hour below the rate charged by the first vendor: a form of competitive pricing. Under the third scenario, value-in-use, the vendor charges a particular hourly rate for network troubleshooting because it would cost the customer (or market segment) roughly that much (or more) to provide that service internally. The selection of a particular fee structure tends to be based on a number of factors, including customer preferences and attitudes, market demand, and common business practices within a particular geographic region or market segment (small customers are billed at an hourly rate, while large customers are charged per node); however, some fee structures work better for value-in-use pricing than competitive or cost-plus, and vice versa.

Vendors who do not charge for service usually give away services at no additional charge to customers in order to make equipment or major service sales, the rationale being based entirely on competitive pricing strategies; however, many times the cost of service is actually bundled in the price of the product or other services: a form of cost-plus pricing. In essence, the vendor adds the incremental cost of providing service to the price of equipment or major product purchase so that it appears that the service under consideration is provided *pro bono*. No charge for service is rarely utilized in value-in-use pricing strategies for obvious reasons.

Using an hourly rate (time and materials), the vendor bills the customer for every hour of service provided. The cost to customers increases with the amount of time the vendor spends meeting customer requirements; hourly rates are predominantly utilized in competitive and cost-plus strategies. However, the value-in-use strategy does not preclude utilization of hourly rates, as in the example of a systems developer charging a high hourly rate because of the quality services that can be delivered as the result of experience or education.

Fees based on a percentage of equipment purchase price assume that the cost of service to customers is equal to a percentage of initial purchase price for equipment. This is based on the belief that the services are a function of product price and performance. In a variable-rate pricing scheme, the customer is charged on a price-per-unit basis — for example, in network services, $125 per node. Under these circumstances, total costs to the end-user are a function of the total number of nodes: the more nodes, the higher the price.

All the pricing methods described here require that the customer assume risks of unforeseen costs to the vendor in providing these services. In essence, the vendor rationalizes that customers do not fully understand their needs and requirements or are ignorant to the actual costs or resources involved in providing service. Therefore, in theory, these pricing methods prevent the vendor from losing money in those situations where customers do not fully communicate their needs, resulting in cost overrides against the planned budget.

Fixed-price contracts, however, require that the vendor assume any unforeseen risks. In fixed-price contracts or projects, the vendor quotes a set price or flat rate that the customer must pay regardless of the vendor's actual costs. Fixed-price contracts are most often used in association with value-in-use pricing strategies; however, many vendors do not offer a fixed price because they fail to understand two important points. First, customers do not care how many hours, personnel, materials, etc. will be required to perform services; in other words, most customers are concerned with outcomes or deliverables rather than processes. Second, the use of a fixed price is an effective marketing tool because it sends a message to the market that the vendor is confident enough in the quality and caliber of personnel and services to assume any unforeseen risks.

IMPLEMENTING A PRICING STRATEGY

The alternative pricing strategies described above can be utilized for pricing both new and existing services. In pricing existing services, it is first necessary to look at whether the current pricing strategy is resulting in targeted profit levels and market share objectives. In evaluating current pricing, it is necessary to examine the price at the actual transaction level, not at the invoice or list price. By only considering list price, companies fail to take into consideration the impact of discounts, incentives, payment terms, and other price attributes on market requirements and profit objectives.

Transaction prices represent both the actual per-unit revenue realized by the seller of a service and the price used by the customer to make marginal purchasing decisions. Tracking the transaction price is an extremely useful tool for exploring actual pricing outcomes that affect profitability and market performance. The transaction price is determined by examining and measuring actual pricing practices from the list price to the development of an invoice price and on to the transaction price.

In essence, it examines the actual price paid by customers less incentives, discounts, and price breaks over list and invoice price. Our research suggests that it is not uncommon to find a transaction price 25 to 35% below the original list price, after accounting for discounts and incentives.

After a transaction price database has been developed and put into operation, the transaction price and all its components can be compared regularly over time to monitor price and profitability effects of the discount and incentive programs and suggest adjustments when necessary. Monitoring of the transaction price database will reveal that offering one price to the market does not actually occur. An organization will find different prices for the same services, depending on how incentives and rebates, terms and conditions, etc. are applied by sales and marketing personnel, as well as by customers.

A simple but effective method for strategically managing the transaction prices begins with construction of a frequency distribution for transaction prices and examining the distribution of outer layers, dispersion, and other characteristics. The pricing manager or marketer can examine the price distribution in relationship to the actual accounts or channels served to determine if the pricing strategy and pricing policy is being implemented correctly to generate the types of revenues, profits, and customers the company is attempting to target.

After evaluating the distribution of pricing transactions, many pricing managers are astonished to find that the pricing outcomes are not in line with their desired intent. For example, managers may find that the customers with special or complex orders receive the same price as those customers who require only basic services, or they may find small customers receiving the same incentives, rebates, and terms and conditions as large customers. In essence, analysis of the transaction database may reveal that lower volume customers and customers who are more costly to serve receive better prices than those customers who either purchase at a high volume or are less costly to serve.

Findings like these should help a manager to understand if pricing tactics and policy are being employed correctly, and such an approach satisfies the need for determining whether the pricing strategy should be altered or modified. A more strategic approach to transaction price evaluation can be attained by correlating market transaction prices with unit cost to serve customers or channels and by win–loss probability. The cost to serve a particular customer channel has three components:

1. *Pre-sale costs* include selling expense and design and engineering expense, among others, and can vary widely between customers and distribution channels based on factors ranging from geography to customer attitude.

2. *Production/distribution costs* include materials, labor, shipping, and other direct production or service delivery cost items that may be standard for a wide range of customers and channels but vary for customized or special situations.

3. *Service support costs* include variable costs that are time sensitive and may vary widely between customers and distribution channels based on factors ranging from geography to attitude.

A cost to serve can be calculated for each transaction based on the direct and indirect materials and overhead that generated the transaction to produce the services and support the customer after the sale.

Armed with a transaction price and a cost to serve for each transaction, customers can be analyzed for individual profitability. Plotting transaction price against the cost to serve in terms of low to high yields four possible categories of customers:

1. *Premium customers* demand a great deal of service and support (have a high cost to serve) and are willing to pay the premium of a high transaction price.

2. *Aggressive customers* demand a great deal of service and support, have a high cost to serve, and are skilled at bargaining for price concessions (low transaction price).

3. *Passive customers* demand little service and support (low cost to serve) and do little bargaining over price (high transaction price).

4. *Low-end customers* demand little service and support (low cost to serve) and look primarily for the lowest available price (low transaction price).

Service managers can examine the entire market within the context of these four segmentation alternatives. It is important that service managers consider both customers and non-customers in their evaluations. Managers are also urged to conduct further market research into customer preferences, competitive pricing practices, and price sensitivity to validate and quantify the size and composition of each segment. A service manager can use this information to determine if a pricing strategy is optimized for the customers being served. The manager can then make the decision to serve current customers at the existing price level, modify pricing strategy to target large market segments, or modify market strategy to pursue more profitable market segments.

The pricing strategy for an existing service therefore requires managers to consider seriously the targeted customer base and competitive positioning. Pricing decisions for new services differ somewhat in that managers must rely to a greater extent on market research and comparisons to indirect competitive alternatives, but the general premise for evaluating pricing strategy is the same.

Regardless of whether the firm is servicing an existing market with mature services, a new product with new services, or an existing market with new services, a manager must make pressing decisions based on valid and reliable business intelligence and market data. Pricing decisions can not be made on intuition alone or solely on internal cost data. The consequences may be negative towards financial performance and long term business growth.

Summary of Implementing a Pricing Strategy

In summary, calculation of servicing pricing must become much more sophisticated if service organizations are to survive and prevail in the growing, increasingly competitive service market. It is important to recognize the existence of alternative strategies, as well as methods, for pricing individual services with particular emphasis on the fixed price, value-in-use approach. Pricing in the service market is in a state of transition. The most typical approach is time and materials with higher rates for added value or extended services. Other pricing strategies including fixed-price contracts based on a value-in-use strategy are being increasingly utilized. In the traditional approach of using cost-plus-mark-up or competitive pricing, the tendency is to enter into price reductions. However, it is extremely important to note that one must achieve a significant increase in sales volume as a result of even a minor price reduction in order to maintain the same gross profit margins that were in existence before the price change.

In essence, service vendors should be extremely careful in developing their service prices and particularly in reducing their service prices in the face of competition in order to gain market share. Our market research clearly shows the existence of a significant percentage of the market that is price insensitive. Thus, in general, the development of service prices should be driven by calculation of value in use as well as competitive and cost-plus pricing. These three price alternatives should then be compared in order to determine (1) the desirability of a price increase for the higher quality required by the targeted market segment, in order to increase revenue and profits, or (2) the desirability of maintaining a competitive price at a higher quality (dictated by the value in use) required by the market in order to gain market share.

Service pricing strategies, in general, are extremely complex. The use of fixed pricing based on value in use can result in significantly higher profit margins with essentially the same service quality or a significant increase in market penetration and market share through value-in-use determination of the service quality parameters portfolio required by the key vertical market segment needs for premium and quality service.

In fact, considerable damage can be done if the pricing strategy is not well formulated and based upon market reality rather than gut intuition. A few examples will demonstrate this.

Pricing Services Originally Given Away for Free

A good example of this strategic error occurred in a company called AMP, which was a leading provider of connectors and cable. The key element that established AMP's position in the market was the development of a system called the Amp-o-matic, which was designed to connect connectors to the cable and wiring harnesses. AMP leased these machines and, of course, serviced them, as they represented a very innovative step forward over hand assembly of wiring harnesses and connectors. AMP salesmen quickly noted that when the Amp-o-matic was down, AMP was losing highly profitable connector sales. It was then recommended that the service on the Amp-o-matic be provided for free, although a provision continued to exist in the leased contract that AMP could elect to charge for those services. As AMP began to run into some erosion of their corporate profits due to competition, primarily from overseas, it brought in a consultant to look around to find opportunities for regaining its previous profit margins. The consultant (*not* D. F. Blumberg & Associates) hit upon the idea of charging for maintenance and repair of the Amp-o-matic. The senior AMP executives at the time thought this was such a great idea that they not only put out an announcement to its customers indicating that service on Amp-o-matic would now be provided at a charge but also requested retroactive payments for services previously rendered. This decision to charge for services that were previously given away for free resulted in a major glitch in AMP's revenue and profitability, as several customers elected to drop AMP and no customers paid the retroactive service charges. What AMP had failed to recognize was that the free service was viewed by the market manufacturing executives and purchasing agents as a valid differential between AMP's connector price and competitive pricing. As soon as AMP began to charge for the maintenance and repair services, it was very easy to see that AMP's connector prices were very high relative to competitive alternatives.

Charging for Free Added-Value Services through Restructuring of the Offer

The first example does not, in anyway, suggest that it is dangerous to start charging for services previously offered for free. Firms such as IBM and Unisys had traditionally given away professional design and engineering consultant services in order to sell their computer products, bundling the cost of those services into the hardware purchase price. As the computer market became more competitive, these firms carried out the market research to identify the value in use of these professional services for given classes of clients. They found that not only was the value high, but the customers were willing also to pay for those services. The key was that the free services were provided with little or no attention to the quality and extent of the professional services to be delivered or the time frame in which they would be accomplished. By more clearly defining exactly what the services would produce in terms of deliverables (e.g., value-in-use approach) and further defining a specific time frame of those deliverables, these companies, in effect, were able to repackage and redefine the services as different from the "free" services. The result, in this case, was that the firms were now able to charge for the professional services at a significant profit and the customers were willing to pay for services that they previously got at no cost, because the payment guaranteed the quality of the service deliverables in a given time frame.

Changing Service Pricing Approach

Back in the 1970s when BAI began to do strategic planning work for a variety of high-tech firms, including DEC, Xerox, Honeywell, and others, the conventional wisdom was to charge for services on a time-and-materials basis, utilizing the cost-plus pricing model under the assumption that customers would only pay for actual services provided. Based upon extensive market research, we were able to show that, in fact, customers were interested in, and even willing to pay a premium for, capping their service costs, especially if they could be guaranteed a level of response, time of day, and day of week coverage — in essence, the concept of a fixed-price annual service contract. In today's environment, the generally accepted view is now that fixed-price service contracts represent a much more profitable business. Clearly, it is important not to rely on gut feelings in establishing prices, but rather look at pricing mechanisms from the perspective of the end-user.

DEVELOPING SERVICE PRICES IN THE SERVICE MARKET

With the growing recognition of the opportunities for revenue and profit potential associated with running services as a line of business, increasing focus is being placed on the development of marketing disciplines and structure to serve service organizations. Historically, service has often been sold as an add-on to the sale of products, with installation and initial warranty usually embedded in the product price. Maintenance contract renewals or service time-and-materials contracts were generated almost automatically or through the unofficial and informal efforts of the local sales or service personnel in the field. Pricing for service was normally developed based on typical product pricing concepts of estimated costs plus markup. Some organizations provided some type of incentive or bonus commission to the sales force or service force for generation of additional service revenues. In these cases, services price were marked up to reflect these commissions. However, these mechanisms were often viewed tactically, rather than as an integral part of the general strategic thrust to developing service as a line of business. In fact, in certain cases, service prices have been adjusted downward in attempt to sell products.

Recognition of the revenue and profit potential of treating service as a separate business and growing competition for the service dollar have forced a need for establishing a specific marketing strategy and sales and support tactics for service operations. Development of optimized marketing and sales support plans involves consideration of a number of issues, including:

1. Developing the service pricing strategy
2. Characterization of service products and establishment of the service portfolio
3. Merchandising and packaging of the service product
4. Direct and indirect sales of service

The issue of service pricing strategy has already been discussed. Each of these other issues is discussed further to provide a framework for understanding the issues of strategic focus on service pricing and strategies.

Definition of Service Products and Portfolio

It should be recognized that the sale of a service has been a problem facing a large number of organizations since the dawn of commercial enterprise. A wide range of services, including legal, accounting, advertising, distribution, and even the "world's oldest profession", are merchandised, packaged, and sold every day. The basic key in the development of a marketing plan for service is recognition of the critical fact that it is an intangible; therefore, the *perception* of quality and value in use is as important as the actual service delivery. For example, a lawyer's or doctor's services are often chosen not on the basis of actual performance or price, but rather on the customer's perception of the potential improvement in well-being, position, or circumstances that will result from use of the service. In essence, service-related products primarily are characterized by a *future* element: the potential for change or reduction in risk or an improvement in satisfaction. Thus, the definition of a service product must consider two critical elements:

1. Actual characterization of service delivery (i.e., what is to be provided)
2. Future returns to the customer as a result of utilizing the service

For example, in the case of repair services at a local gas station, customers are paying for both the actual performance of lubrication or changing spark plugs as well as for a reduction in the risk of future breakdown. In the case of accounting services, clients are paying for the actual clerical work associated with establishing the audit and reviewing the books as well as a reduction in the future risk of inaccuracy or inability to pass an Internal Revenue Service audit.

In recognizing these two components, it is essential that the service organization, in developing its products, understand the primary parameters and characteristics of importance to the customer with respect to the future delivery and perceived value as opposed to simply concentrating on the actual delivery of the basic service itself.

Characterization of service products provides for both direct performance and indirect or future guarantees of response and performance in the event of future failure, thereby satisfying both perceived and actual requirements of the service product. In addition to these basic service products, other service support products can also be considered as additive to the primary service product portfolio. Thus, the service product is multidimensional, in that it includes both an element of performance and an element of time and coverage. In summary, the service portfolio provides an overall definition of the product mix and potential maximum set of services that could be offered by the service organization to various market segments and customer bases.

Pricing of Services through Targeted Market Segmentation, Merchandising, and Packaging of the Service Products

Having established the strategic identification of the service product line, mix, and portfolio, as well as the associated strategic service pricing, the next step in developing and implementing an effective service marketing strategy is the merchandising and packaging of the service products in a form that can be discernible and perceived by the individual targeted market segments. In this regard, it is highly important, from a service marketing standpoint, to recognize that, in addition to general service markets, certain vertically designated markets for service exist that possess the unique requirements associated with a high installed base density and extremely high value in use for service responsiveness and quality. Such vertical market segments include hospitals, hotels, major banks, and brokerage organizations, among others. As indicated, unusually high returns can be obtained by specifically focusing on the service needs and requirements of these individual market segments through the creation of a targeted service product portfolio and service pricing.

Packaging and merchandising of services can be achieved through a variety of mechanisms, such as:

1. Brochures
2. Advertising
3. Trade show/trade association participation
4. Direct mail
5. Other merchandising mechanisms

In essence, because of the esoteric and perceived nature of the service product, a positive reference, either directly solicited or received on an unsolicited basis through word of mouth, generates an extremely powerful positive perception. Positive reference selling can be achieved through both satisfied customers and through modifying market segment awareness and perception through articles of an editorial content in trade publications and professional journals, as well as speeches and other presentations. In essence, services can be merchandised and packaged through both formal/direct and informal/indirect mechanisms.

Sales and Distribution

The fourth and final step in developing and implementing an effective service marketing strategy is the final process of sales, distribution, and contract sales close. For field service and logistics support, this can be accomplished by a directly assigned sales force or by indirect selling representatives.

SUMMARY

In summary, the development and implementation of a successful marketing strategy for service operations involves four sequential but related steps or phases:

1. Establishing the service pricing strategy
2. Establishing the service product definition and portfolio
3. Merchandising and packaging the service portfolio based on a pricing model

4. Selling the service portfolio utilizing the merchandising and support mechanisms developed

The process of marketing strategy and selling tactics development and implementation is a continuous one in which feedback from customers by market segment is used for continual adjustment of marketing focus and product definitions, prices, and selling and merchandising support mechanisms to meet present and emerging needs and competition.

When supporting a service line of business, it is critical that a formal and precise marketing and pricing strategy be developed and implemented based upon an appropriate level and commitment of market research, analysis, and evaluation. Because the service product is so critically dependent upon market perceptions, it is critical for the service organizations to understand, measure, and quantify these perceptions by market segment and use this understanding as a basis for developing and implementing a successful marketing strategy.

IV

SERVICE OPPORTUNITIES, POTENTIAL, AND THE FUTURE

This fourth and final part is designed to wrap up the key issues, concepts, and anecdotal and pragmatic evidence presented. We will focus on the key issues of:

- Management vision and strategic direction
- System infrastructure to manage data about customers and allow service organizations to meet the customers needs
- Market density and the mechanisms for marketing and selling to optimize density

In carrying this out, we will look at general market opportunities and potential service business strategies in the future.

12

NEW SERVICE MARKET OPPORTUNITIES AND THE USE OF SERVICE TO CHANGE MARKET POSITION

CONTENTS

INTRODUCTION

As more and more high-tech service organizations are forced to reexamine their business base as a result of declining product sales or increased competition, attention is becoming more focused on emerging opportunities in multivendor equipment service and support (MVES) and third-party maintenance (TPM). For many service organizations that were traditionally focused on the servicing of technology or product "boxes," the transition from running a service in support of high-tech products to running service as a separate and independent strategic line of business has been difficult, at best, and at worst a disaster, creating a major problem due to the lack of even a basic understanding of how best to approach marketing, sales, pricing, and market penetration effectively.

In essence, in servicing products, "someone else" usually has the responsibility for generating the product sale, with the service business base and program being pulled through as a result of product sales. In this business model, product-oriented businesses need not concern themselves with broader strategic issues of marketing, or even portfolio development. Much of this has been determined or dictated either by product management personnel or by the product itself. The new-found orientation to service, however, has created a demand for a strategic readjustment of marketing, selling, pricing, and distribution issues. These matters are all highly influenced by questions of market segmentation; therefore, key questions of segmentation must be seriously examined and evaluated by the modern service business.

To clearly understand the strategic problem of market segmentation facing service executives, it is necessary to go back to basics in terms of the economic theory of the firm. In broad terms, the theory of the firm visualized the need for two sets of resources (labor and material), utilizing a single engine of production to produce units of goods sold to the market for which the market/customer pays an equivalent unit of economic value (e.g., cash) for the products delivered.

This model, shown in Figure 12.1, represents the basic structure of the typical firm and tends to define marketing and selling issues along product lines. In this model, service of the product is a subset of product delivery and is normally defined in terms of the product requirements for supporting services. However, in the newer service-oriented model of the firm,

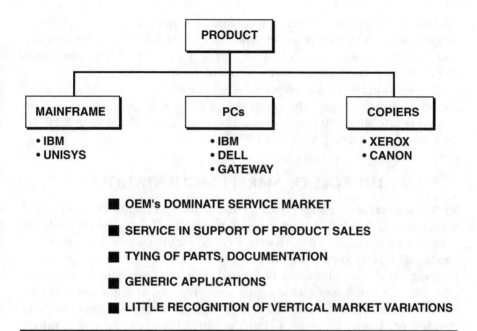

Figure 12.1   Product segmentation.

the structure of the model and processes is quite different. In the service model (Figure 12.1), three resources (labor, channels, and data) are utilized by two engines of production (actual service provided and ability to serve) to deliver two types of services to the end-user, or customer. The customer pays for both services: readiness (or capability) to serve and actual service. As an example, a 1-year service contract consists of a commitment to provide service within a given time frame (say, a 4-hour response) over a given time (say, 5 days a week, 8 hours a day). Actual service is provided within the framework of this ability to serve. It may often happen that a service contract exists with a requirement for monthly, quarterly, or annual payments, yet the only service performance delivered to a customer is the ability to serve and no actual service is provided.

This ability to serve becomes critically important in service because of the impossibility of stockpiling or inventorying excess service capacity and because of the response time dependency of the user of service. For example, service within 4 hours is clearly different from service within 1 hour for certain users; the more rapid service usually dictates a higher price for better responsiveness, if the customer needs that responsiveness. Equally important, to a large extent, is that the ability to serve is often measured in terms of perceptions of realities rather than reality. Depending on the service framework and environment of the customer, the strategic management of service must, therefore, consider both actual service delivery and the ability to serve. Thus, the portfolio of services, pricing, and perception, will be different and more sophisticated than the equivalent service-related issues in the standard product model.

Based upon this newer view of the service business, it is now critically important to reexamine the strategic issue of market segmentation in service and to illustrate how it should be applied, particularly in focusing on new and profitable MVES and TPM services.

THE ROLE OF MARKET SEGMENTATION

Market segmentation issues typically arise in all economies, in general, and in mature and developed economies, in particular. The automobile industry does not manufacture and sell one type of car to everyone; market segmentation has identified different types of cars and different prices by focusing on the requirements of individual market segments. As another example clearly illustrates, clothing products targeted at segments with very high fashion orientation and sold at very high prices are very different from standard or commodity type of clothing sold at lower or discounted prices.

This concept of market segmentation as a service-oriented business strategy, therefore, will identify and produce different levels of service at different prices with even different distribution channels. This segmentation approach can be very useful in identifying, evaluating, managing, and distributing into the service market. The difference between a product segmentation approach, as outlined in Figure 12.1, and a market segmentation approach, as outlined in Figure 12.2, is very critical. Particularly because of the issues of perception, focusing on the ability to serve can be much more precisely measured and much more meaningful in a vertical market segment strategy.

Service market segmentation can generate substantial new and powerful concepts and structures, driven by the perceptions of reality and by such key issues as the ability to pay, density of service demand, etc., which primarily vary by market segment. In essence, in product-oriented segmentation, one can only use secondary characteristics (of the product) to try to estimate service requirements and needs. With the market-oriented segmentation model focused on end-users for service, it is possible to use direct measurement mechanisms to gain a clear understanding of the differences and similarities between segments. These differences can be patterned on the basis of:

■ Criticality of services to the end-users
■ Density of service demand
■ Service value in use

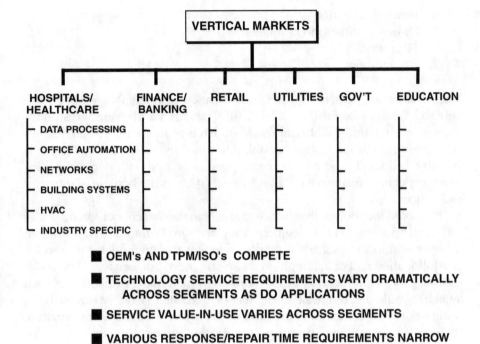

Figure 12.2   Vertical market segmentation approach.

Of these, service value in use, which is measured by examining the cost to the customer in the absence of service within a given time frame, tends to be one of the most critically important variables in defining an optimum service portfolio and pricing for a given market segment.

Vertical Market Segmentation

A starting point for service market segmentation relates to the need to establish a measurable structure for which a significant base of data exists. In the United States, this market segment structure tends to be dictated by the Standard Industrial Codes (SIC), which defines the number and types of organizations by major category and includes organizational units such as:

1. Manufacturing (discrete and continuous)
2. Banking and finance
3. Health care
4. Insurance
5. Wholesale trade

6. Retail distribution
7. Direct distribution of utilities
8. Education
9. Government

These major SIC structures (or vertical market segments) have been the subject of extensive business and market research and extensive studies; a considerable amount of data exists on each of the market segments. In addition, through large-scale, double-blind surveys in each segment, it is possible to identify the critical parameters associated with density, equipment criticality, and service value in use, to measure both similarity and differences.

It should be noted that while these variations are not dramatically different from segment to segment, they are significant enough to enable a buyer within the individual market segment to differentiate the service portfolio offered. For example, a hospital's need for service of a given class of product or technology (say a mini- or mainframe or digital network switch) would be different from that of a retailer, who is driven by a number of factors, including the time of day and day of week of operation, the need for very rapid response, etc. In this regard, the service vendor in general, and particularly the vendor attempting to sell multivendor equipment services and third-party maintenance services, will find a very cool reception from hospital administrators for a service portfolio measured in terms of day of week coverage, response time, technology supported, etc., and otherwise focused on retail needs. Because perception is also a very critical factor in analyzing or evaluating service quality and performance, even the words and images presented in brochures and in the briefing dialog will have different effects in different market segments. For example, the words *platform* or *secretary* have entirely different meanings and orientation in a bank vs. a manufacturing firm.

The Importance of Perception in Marketing and Sales Targeted at a Vertical Market Segment

As pointed out earlier, the character of the customer service base and the service business model place a much higher degree of emphasis on the issue of the ability to serve, which is largely a perception of reality, rather than the service reality itself. This is due, in part, to the fact that service simply cannot be inventoried and stockpiled; therefore, it is not physically possible to measure or evaluate the quality or form, fit, and function of service as one does when buying a product.

In this context, it is very important to understand the significant difference that perception has in service. If we look at the typical marketing course taught at the undergraduate or graduate level, we will find that, as a general rule of thumb, selling products is focused on both the form, fit, and function of the good to be sold and on its label or perception. In the case of products and services, both the form, fit and function and the perception or label exist; however, in the product situation, a competitive product offered with essentially the same form, fit, and function would at best command an increased price or require a discount in the range of 10% to a maximum of 35%, reflecting the value of the perception or label. Thus, for example, for long periods of time, IBM computers could command a price differential of 25 to 30% over directly competitive products from, say, Unisys or DEC because of perception or label. In the case of a product, the label is the image or perception regarding such issues as product quality, level of support, responsiveness, etc. Clearly, for a product then, the most important factor to be sold is the product form, fit, and function. The label represents something of a differentiator, but the price difference is relatively small compared to the form, fit, and function.

In the case of service, however, the label or perception, has a much more dramatic effect. Consider, for example, the perception of services of a doctor or a lawyer; one could easily find price differentials of 100%, 200%, or even more. In the case of brain surgery, for example, one would expect that the differences in perceived service quality could generate extremely large differences in cost or price charged. Even in the legal field, the price per hour for prominent, well-known attorneys usually runs from $500 to $1000 per hour. These are very high compared to a local "storefront" attorney, who might charge $30 to 60 an hour. While the basic services of both types of attorneys are the same (i.e., their form, fit, and function are equivalent), in the sense of their knowledge and practice of the law attorneys with the better representation, image, or perception are typically the ones who can command much higher prices.

It is important to note that pricing of service is not exactly independent. Quite often in service, prices are often used as a surrogate for quality simply because it is so difficult to test, measure, or compute the quality of service before its purchase. Thus, in the case of service, it may happen that higher priced services are quite often perceived by customers as having higher service quality. You do not, for example, look for the lowest priced brain surgeon. Thus, in general, perceptions rather than reality will dominate the service market. A failure to focus or fine-tune these perceptions against the specific requirements of a particular customer base or market segment can often lead to a loss of opportunity in service sales. Conversely, specific focus on the perceptions of a desired market segment can often lead to successful sales.

In this respect, the significant value of market segmentation and, in particular, vertical market segmentation in service lies in the ability (through market research surveys and focus groups) to determine perceptions that a focus on products and technology cannot provide. The only way to really measure perceptions of service is to deal with, and focus on, the buyers of the services rather than on the product that is the subject of the service.

Strategic Market Segmentation and Focus

Because of the differences in perceptions by vertical market segment as well as the importance of perceptions in the actual selling process for service, evidence and experience clearly demonstrate that focusing on the vertical market segment tends to produce greater sales closure than focusing only on the product and technology. Many service executives tend to discount this by arguing that they must understand the product needs and requirements for service regardless of the vertical market segment in which they sit. In addition, it is suggested that the number of specific units, by brand and type, to be found in a vertical market segment may not be significant enough to achieve economies of scale in service. While both these points are true, they still do not minimize the importance of vertical market segmentation.

In point of fact, analysis of vertical market segments will clearly identify the need for additional value-added services such as access to a help desk, installation, training, etc. that are not product dependent or driven. Second, one generally finds that the installed technologies all have a common element of computer-based circuit boards or standard CPU-type technology. The probability of encountering a special, or purpose-built, device that does not have the basic features of a microprocessor or PC/workstation technology is rapidly decreasing as more and more manufacturers move to open system architectures. Finally, in the vertical market segment arena, the customer is more willing to pay for the added value of total service management and coordination because of the desire for a single point of contact and a common level of response and support, particularly for MVES support. Thus, concern about the service vendor not being able to fix and repair every product installed in a customer's base with its own resources is often misplaced. Subcontracting is becoming easier to use, as the real service being offered in the MVES environment is the ability to manage and coordinate the service rather than actual delivery of the service.

Because of interest in having a single point of contact and the appeal of the single service management concept, the market opportunity for MVES and third-party maintenance in specific vertical market segments is increasing and high profit margins are available. Very few of the current MVES competitors offer a full vertical market segment strategy; most tend to build their offerings around specific products or even brand names. Some service organizations, such as Banctec (banks) and the Dataserv division of Wang (retail), have made very effective use of vertical market segmentation approaches. However, most of the MVES/TPM competitors have not yet discovered the strategic market value of vertical market segmentation.

Summary and Recommendations

We have demonstrated that the critical key to increasing revenues and profit margins in multivendor equipment service and third party maintenance involves refocusing the marketing approach and selling process on vertical market segments having a high level of density of technology, criticality of service, high value in use, and lack of competitive activity. By gaining an understanding of vertical market segments through market research, analysis, and evaluation and gathering secondary data on the vertical market itself it is possible to improve the efficiency of market penetration. The development of tailored sales collateral and investments in public relations types of processes oriented to specific market segments can improve the image and perception of a service vendor and penetration of the market. In essence, the segmentation approach that is optimum for MVES/TPM business planning should focus on:

- Types of services offered
- Products to be supported
- Vertical market segments requirements

This overall model is driven by the vertical market segmentation.

It is very clear that the service market and industry is going through a significant revolution as a result of several key general and specific factors and trends (a general picture of the U.S. service market, by horizontal and vertical segment, is presented in Appendix B). This revolution is creating new and potentially highly profitable opportunities for those aggressive TPM- and MVES-oriented service organizations willing to move rapidly to make the needed investments in order to penetrate these new vertical and horizontal market segment opportunities.

VERTICAL MARKET SEGMENT SERVICE OPPORTUNITIES AND TRENDS

The array of key market segments presented in this discussion is not intended to be comprehensive pinpointing of all opportunities but rather key situations that are now just ripening as new and emerging opportunities, created by general or specific trends such as outsourcing, restructuring of the market, new competitive changes, etc. Key vertical market segments and niches that will create important new dimensions and requirements for service include:

- Manufacturing
- Banking/finance
- Hospital/health care
- Government
- Retail/wholesale
- Insurance/real estate
- Education
- Transportation/distribution
- Utilities/communications

Manufacturing Establishments and Plants

Manufacturing is a large, diverse vertical market segment with over 500,000 establishments involved in a wide range of industries, from automotive and parts machinery to chemicals and food processing. Service needs and requirements are expanding and growing as the result of several industry trends: (1) increase in the population of large manufacturing companies at the expense of smaller, less productive, less efficient companies; (2) migration of microprocessor, networking, and other advanced technologies to all levels of the manufacturing operation; (3) growing dependence on automation and networks with greater cost consequences when equipment malfunctions; and (4) increased use of process control to lower costs. High-tech segments and process instrumentation and control equipment clearly represent the greatest opportunities for service.

The use of high-tech equipment such as workstations and microcomputers for computer-aided design, inventory control, and resource allocation at the manufacturing facility, possibly linked via network, makes communication (including voice and data) within the facility possible, leading to a more efficient and cost-effective operation. The wide use of process instrumentation and control equipment in manufacturing can be found in a number of major end-user vertical market segments, including, among others, oil and gas production; petroleum refining; chemicals; paper and pulp; food, beverage and tobacco; pipelines; iron and steel; minerals and other metals; electric utilities; and water and wastewater utilities. Overall, this market is affected by a wide variety of technological and competitive factors, including shorter life cycles of electronic systems as compared to older pneumatic and analog system technology, new market entrants, and rapid deployment of network linking and building within a manufacturing campus.

As a result of these market trends, the role of service is becoming strategically more important and critical to end-users. Current trends having implications for the high-tech service industry include:

- *Increasing service costs.* As service costs rise, end-users desire more focused service portfolios for new plants and maintenance of existing bases, specifically including maintenance and repair, software support, installation, upgrades/end-of-life extension, design and engineering, and network management. In addition, the broad scope of process instrumentation and control systems applications and the often highly critical nature of these applications to end-users reflect the high value in use of such services.
- *Deterioration of service quality and performance.* Because the service of process instrumentation and control systems market has a high degree of product pull-through, the sales of service will ultimately generate product sales in the future for those providers offering high quality for both product and service.
- *Inability to coordinate and manage mixed vendor systems.* The availability of multivendor support is becoming more important due to the use of multivendor equipment at manufacturing sites, including workstations and personal computers, and throughout process control networks, where a variety of programmable controllers, computers, field instruments, and sensors may be found. This wide use of a variety equipment has also led to the entry of standard off-the-shelf microprocessor manufacturers.
- *Unacceptable and costly equipment down time.* The overall manufacturing service environment, whether process control or discrete manufacturing-based, or both, allows for a fully integrated network operation that links all three levels of the firm (i.e., corporate/headquarters, plant office, and plant floor) with one another, as well as with related service environments such as building automation/building perimeters, plant/facilities perimeters, and other plants and buildings. Because these networks are pervasive in the operation of a plant, any down time affects the bottom line of the business.
- *Increasing costs of labor and support associated with internal plant and administrative maintenance force.* These increases have led to an increase in the use of outside contract services by this market in recent years, although the general approach is to manage services in house, particularly among larger end-user facilities.

■ *Product life extension.* Product technology market demand is stabilizing as the focus shifts from new construction to extending life cycles of existing equipment. A substantial and increasing portion of the total market is replacement, often funded by plant maintenance budgets, where approximately 15% of the hardware market is for equipment replacement. However, for some products, as much as 50% of expenditures are for maintenance and repair and a growing portion of the market involves upgrading. Approximately 26% of total expenditures are for upgrades and changes to existing plant operations.

Banking/Finance

Federal regulations have now blurred the distinction between different types of financial institutions, meaning that banks and thrifts will face increased competition from insurance companies, mortgage companies, and mutual funds. Banks have typically responded with increased consolidation within the industry, searches for greater efficiency through technology and increased dependence on automation and networks, and a movement towards "super-regionals" and global competition.

The banking/finance services industry continues to undergo continued consolidation in response to competitive pressures to reduce costs and boost profitability through greater efficiency. Mergers are seen as a way to strengthen profitability by making possible the cost efficiencies promised by investments in new technology. The most successful institutions to emerge from the industry shakeout will be those that respond to the need for technological improvements.

Banking/finance is one of the fastest growing vertical market segments in terms of installed base and value in use (dependency on service) of high-tech equipment. Although data-processing systems are utilized by virtually all financial institutions, different types and sizes of institutions depend on this type of equipment to varying degrees. For example, large banks (typically $500 million in assets or more) generally operate their own mainframe, which supports a variety of peripherals and related systems and equipment. Smaller banks may or may not have their own mainframes in place and, in fact, may utilize shared data-processing systems tied into a bankwide network. Regardless of type, data-processing systems and equipment used by banks require a high level of service response due to their integral relationship to ongoing day-to-day operations. In most cases, large minicomputers, mainframes, and clustered mini- or mainframe groups are used for host functions in banks; however, in very small banks, PCs and PC-based networks can successfully emulate many of these host functions.

Service opportunities abound as financial institutions increase their already high use of data processing, office automation equipment, telecommunications, networks, and related systems and equipment including automated teller machines (ATMs), branch and platform automation equipment, and cash vault management systems and equipment. Network systems are increasingly serving as the primary "backbone" for these systems within the bank.

Most banks are turning to private bypass, local area network (LAN), and wide area network (WAN) technologies to improve the efficiency and control of their decisions support, database, and management information systems. Together, these factors have changed not only the overall structure of the banking services market but also the service portfolio required by banks. The total U.S. bank/finance equipment service market in 1995 was $21.5 billion and was projected to grow to over $43 billion by 2002.

As technology and market developments redefine the relationships between different segments of the banking industry, giving rise to "virtual banking", reliance on the aforementioned technologies to coordinate information exchange among banks, mortgage companies, collection agencies, and credit bureaus will grow greater. As the public's acceptance of banking technologies grows, demand for technology-based services will also increase. ATMs, for example, are taking on more tasks, such as cashing checks, taking utility payments, printing instant statements, dispensing travelers checks, and taking loan applications.

Banks are now using extensive data and voice communication networks for managing internal bank and branch administration and control, as well as communications and coordination with and between other banks and financial institutions, bank headquarters and remote sites (e.g., branches, loan origination centers, and operations centers), bank customers (e.g., bank by phone and customer service), and bank and regulatory agencies (e.g., state banking commission, Federal Deposit Insurance Corporation (FDIC), Federal Reserve). In addition, banks rely upon internal bank voice communications, the management of which involves data communications and telecommunications equipment, in general, and telecommunications-oriented network systems for which both voice and data traffic is handled utilizing essential digital technologies.

The rapid increase in the deregulation of the banking industry in the United States and Europe has led to a significant increase in service opportunities. As banks expand their services, new types of institutions are moving into the banking market, including use of network technology for delivery of banking and financial services. These trends create the need for new service and support:

■ *Fewer institutions and emergence of "super-regionals".* Economic and financial problems continue to plague the industry. Strong banks are responding by merging with and acquiring other banks. Even without federal legislation, interstate banking is a reality in most states. The gap between high-performance banks and the rest of the industry in regard to their ability to invest in technological infrastructures is growing.

■ *Need for efficiency is creating a need for more technology.* Competitive pressures are forcing banks to cut costs, downsize, and open nontraditional branches where automation is used to free-up a limited staff for selling. In addition, with the increasing cost of federal regulation compliance, the need to cut costs and increase efficiency is greater, especially for small banks who cannot afford to have a full-time compliance officer as many large banks do. Automated systems can help banks track federal compliance. In addition, federal legislation such as the Americans with Disabilities Act and Community Reinvestment Act has caused banks to seek technology-based efficiencies, which might include requirements to redesign the services of ATMs, for example, for compliance, as well as offering greater opportunities to provide hardware and software support services to help cut compliance costs.

■ *Growing public acceptance of electronic funds transfers and ATMs.* This acceptance has allowed banks to create more uses for ATMs. Banks are installing ATMs twice as fast as they are opening branches and are moving branches away from their traditional role as transaction processors toward the role of sales/service centers tailored toward customer needs.

■ *Movement toward distributed processing.* In order to provide better and faster service (e.g., one-hour loan approval) and to use computing resources efficiently, banks are moving away from centralized processing and toward distributed processing, where PC-based systems are used and are more affordable.

■ *Increased use of outsourcing.* To cut costs, banks are often outsourcing some or all of their data processing. Fewer computer systems are needed by the banks, so less maintenance is required.

■ *Increased use of teller and platform automation terminals.* It is estimated that U.S. banking facilities have installed more than 350,000 ATMs and 200,000 platform/customer service terminals. Increasingly, these teller and platform automation terminals and systems are completely automating the main "core" or branch banking functions, which historically had been accomplished by hand or through the use of electromechanical calculators, adding machines, and the like. Banks are now moving more quickly toward real-time, online branch automation systems that instantaneously process customer transactions at the branch level.

Hospital/Healthcare

The maintenance and repair service market potential for hospital systems and equipment is significant, not only on the basis of magnitude but also as a result of the well-defined structure and easily accessible nature of the industry. Still, on the basis of size alone, the total hospital technology service support expenditures in 1995 amounted to $20.7 billion, and by 1999 total service expenditures were almost $41 billion.

Major hospitals and hospital chains are faced with growing costs for service and support of the array of technology found in the typical hospital. Equally important is a major new trend to acquire outlying medical practices which significantly changes both the technological base and the service requirements of the hospitals. These changes manifest themselves in the following areas:

■ *Changes in initiatives and regulations in healthcare technology.* Hospitals and healthcare facilities in both the United States and Europe are undergoing significant changes as a result of both planned and actual initiatives. In the United States, the failed Clinton initiatives are already creating a new concept for expansion of hospital outreach to achieve market control. Many hospitals are buying up general medical practices in their region in order to effect control over an increasingly larger consumer base to put themselves in a position to negotiate with the health payment agencies. New payment initiatives to reduce hospital operating costs are also causing a change in hospital administration, with the result of a significant reduction in new capital expenditures and an increased focus on the concept of outsourcing of nonessential services. Major new technologies for healthcare service delivery are also being developed. Finally, in Europe, the trend is toward privatization of hospitals and a reduction in national and government controls, leading to increased opportunities for the provision of service directly.

■ *Need for increased networking support.* The acquisition of outlying medical practices physically removed from the central hospital buildings and campus increases the need for dynamic real-time network communication and control between the doctors' offices and hospital central files, diagnostics, and medical and surgical facilities scheduling. In order to achieve the economies of scale implicit in the acquisition of these new outlying medical practices, the application and use of enhanced network technology will become critical.

- *Change in technology service parameters.* Another major change created by the acquisition of outlying medical practices impacts directly on the method of approach and delivery mechanisms for technology service. Typically, the hospital was one building, or a high-density complex of buildings in one campus, and was relatively easily served by an on-site technology service organization such as the biomedical engineering department. Service technicians merely traveled from floor to floor and from building to building (on foot) in order to install, maintain, repair, or replace technology. With the growing responsibility for service and support of technology found in physically outlying doctors' offices, the basic paradigms of hospital technology service are changing. Service personnel must drive to the various sites, creating a need to expand the logistics support infrastructure to include the repositioning or delivery of the appropriate parts to the correct remote physical location, as well as a need for dynamic optimized call handling, dispatch and assignment, tracking and call close-out, and logistics support. In this new scenario, the biomedical engineering or other internal service organization begins to look more and more like the typical manufacturer or distributor service organization with a significant increase in travel time and increased logistics cost and inherently less efficiency.

- *Change in hours and days of coverage.* Traditionally, the technology service needs of hospitals tended to be served during normal business hours (8:00 a.m. to 5:00 p.m.), 5 days a week, with only certain areas of the hospital operating 24 hours a day, 7 days a week. The acquisition of outlying medical practices that tend to have a higher utilization on weekends or on the second shift again changes the basic paradigms of service.

- *New technology distribution.* The acquisition of outlying medical and healthcare practices by major hospitals and hospital chains is now leading to consideration and use of new networked technologies such as PACS (picture archiving and communications systems), distributed client server workstations, and other applications that can provide a greater level of systems and technology delivered to remote doctors' offices through network distribution mechanisms.

Government

Typically, governments consist of three primary segments: federal, state, and local. Government tends to be a large user of all forms of technology and is formally structured and bureaucratic, with multiple levels of decision making. The total government/other equipment service market in 1995 was $15.4 billion and grew to over $31 billion by 2001. Service market needs and requirements relate to several major trends including:

- *Increased reliance on automation.* Due to the overwhelming amount of paperwork that flows through most government offices, automation to manage the information and improve communications among all the agencies has become a major priority for the government. Installation of new equipment to update old equipment, setting up LANs/WANs, and managing massive amounts of data require different types of services, such as design and engineering, technical assistance, and configuration control, in addition to the more traditional services.
- *Frequent lack of funds to purchase services.* Generally, the price of services is a critical issue among government customers, so those vendors who can provide the best mix of quality services for the least amount of money will tend to get the business.

Retail/Wholesale

Pressures from increased competition for limited disposable income are forcing retailers to continue to streamline their operations and lower costs by implementing efficient, high-tech equipment and systems. Increased competition in this era of consolidation, as evidenced by consumers shopping more at discount and outlet stores, has placed heavy emphasis on automation in inventory, warehousing, logistics and invoicing, and on other technologies such as point-of-sale systems.

While many retailers are disappearing due to mergers and failures, a segment of retailers that have incorporated cutting-edge retail techniques and technology to enhance customer service is prospering; they have been dubbed by industry analysts as "power retailers" and include discounters such as Wal-Mart and Target; warehouse clubs such as Price Club, Sam's Club, Costco Wholesale Clubs, and Pace Membership; and category specialists such as Toys "R" Us, Home Depot, and Circuit City; and specialty clothing retailers such as The Limited and GAP. These retailers have taken the lead in incorporating high-tech into retailing, a method of savings that is likely to spread throughout the industry as other retailers seek to emulate the successes of the power retailers.

Because of the traditional nature of retailing and because of the emphasis on measuring and tracking a number of variables and marketing statistics at the point of sale (POS), retailers are significant users of computer systems, networks, and application-specific equipment, such as POS terminals, scanners, or bar coding. To stay competitive, retailers are using the latest information systems technologies to maintain service quality while cutting costs.

Competitive pressures in the retail/wholesale segment translates into increased opportunities in the high-tech services market. The overall estimated service revenue for this market segment was almost $17 billion in 1995 and is expected to grow to slightly more than $34 billion by the year 2003.

The three major areas of technology innovation in retail include retail automation (computing), electronic article surveillance, and electronic data interchange (electronic networks). Retail automation includes business functions, POS technology, marketing merchandising and communications, specifically in inventory control, electronic marketing, electronic merchandising, and electronic information collection, retrieval, and storage. Electronic article surveillance is an important first step toward tighter inventory control, which has become imperative in the retail industry.

Electronic data interchange (EDI) encompasses industry networks, including integrated network systems and especially value-added third-party networks. EDI moves structured information about transactions between customers and vendors throughout the retail system, linking inventory, invoicing, and other functions. Bar coding is an integral step for information collection within the EDI process and involves scanning equipment. The bar codes produce the data that retailers, wholesalers, and manufactures use in the information channel. The network equipment used to transfer the huge amounts of data is also a serviceable element in the EDI link. Use of EDI systems and the equipment that constitute these systems will continue to grow among retail operations. The forces driving implementation of EDI include the ever-growing requirements to (1) maintain accurate inventory records, particularly via scanning; (2) measure product; (3) utilize direct order entry; (4) apply the concept of "partnering"; and (5) enhance strategic applications of customer/vendor information.

The retail industry is a significant user of computer systems, networks, and industry-specific equipment such as POS systems and electronic cash registers, and current trends are likely to have the following implications for the high-tech service industry:

- *Entry-level employee labor shortage.* With a shortage of 18- to 34-year-old entry-level employees, automated equipment and systems for food preparation, ordering, POS processing and payment systems, sales, inventory control, and other management functions are becoming more essential.

- *Less skilled workers.* With the move to hire less skilled workers, disabled workers, older workers, and even non-English-speaking workers to ease the labor shortage, the need for automated equipment, "smarter" systems, and visual rather than written job aids will grow.
- *Demographic changes.* Aging of the baby boom generation and slow economic growth indicated an end to the carefree spending of the 1980s, leading to customers seeking more value and service. Competition for customers is heating up and persuading retailers to invest in more technology to enhance service, minimize labor costs, and process information faster.
- *Nutritional concerns.* More salads and fewer fried foods are being consumed today, so restaurant operations require different types of equipment such as rotisseries, boilers, more refrigerated cases, sous-vide, and cook–chill cooking.
- *Environmental pressures.* Consumers with environmental concerns have forced retailers to learn how to reduce, reuse, and recycle through greater use of trash handling equipment and automated building systems to monitor and control energy usage.
- *Cocooning.* Cocooning is the trend of consumers to prefer to stay at home. The trend has fueled an increase in food take-out and delivery, purchases of prepared foods, and shopping through home shopping networks, infomercials, and mail order. Equipment such as fax machines is needed in restaurants to process take-out orders, as is food preparation equipment in convenience stores, supermarkets, and general merchandise stores. Automated equipment makes nontraditional food-service locations possible by reducing necessary kitchen space.
- *Casual living.* The move toward more casual dining by even high-end restaurants means they are also in competition with prepared gourmet foods available in supermarkets and through delivery services. Full-service restaurants are following the lead of fastfood restaurants by automating ordering, food preparation, inventory, and other tasks in order to give faster service and to cut costs. "Display cooking" (bringing the restaurant kitchen into the dining room) is becoming more popular.
- *Use of hands-on devices at retail establishments.* When consumers do venture out, they want to be entertained. Retail stores are becoming entertainment centers as well as merchandising centers. More automated systems are being used to encourage purchases. Music and video sales and rentals can be sampled by customers before making a decision.

- *Need to get information to customers as quickly as possible.* Information has to be processed faster to stay competitive. The need for real-time information dissemination through networked systems is expanding; therefore, systems integration is becoming more important.
- *Move from proprietary systems to open systems.* As more manufacturers conform to open system standards, buyers can assemble a system with various manufacturers' equipment at lower cost. Manufacturers have to compete on price, which offers more opportunities for third-party maintenance companies. Customers want lower costs and the convenience of one phone call.
- *Move from centralized processing to distributed processing.* With the move from centralized processing to distributed processing and client-server systems, more powerful PCs are able to run POS systems. Smaller companies that were unable to afford mainframe or mini-computer-based POS systems can invest in PC-based systems.
- *Use of data transmission via radio, television, and satellite.* With the move from data transmission via leased land lines to data transmission via radio, television, and satellite, video conferencing is being utilized more, and POS payment systems can work fast enough to be used in quick-service operations. Faster data transfer makes efficient systems possible for more retail establishments.
- *More database marketing. POS systems collect valuable information about customers of a particular business or a specific product.* Retailers can use the lists to expand into mail-order or to follow-up purchases with offers tailored to the customer, leading to a greater need for information-processing equipment and systems.
- *Legislation government-ordered recalls.* Legislation banning refrigerants containing CFC took effect in 1995, requiring retrofit of older equipment by installing new compressors using non-CFC refrigerants. New recalls and government actions will continue this need for manufacturers and retailers to track owners of products in Europe. "Green Laws" require manufacturers to be responsible for final product disposition.

Insurance/Real Estate

The insurance industry consists of two major segments: property and casualty insurance and life and health insurance; overall, there are some 5800 insurance companies. The most attractive service segments are national insurance companies with diverse product offerings such as life and health insurance companies.

Activity in the real estate market hinges on the rise and fall of interest rates. The most recent recovery of the real estate market can be attributed in part to the return of capital; most notably, banks are lending to investors both from the United States and abroad, such as from Europe, Hong Kong, and Latin America.

The insurance and real estate industries are major users of data-processing, telecommunications, and industry-specific equipment such as POS terminals/systems. Service market revenues for insurance/real estate was estimated at $14.8 billion in 1995, growing to over $30 billion by 2002.

Service market requirements are affected by these trends:

- *Increasing automation of companies and agents through the growing introduction of microcomputers and networks.* Due to the fast-paced life of insurance and real estate agents, the use of microcomputers and networks has grown rapidly. With the use of high-tech equipment at offices throughout the country, service is not only required at headquarters but has also become critical for the success of field offices.
- *Greater use of networks and large, sophisticated databases.* Even with today's heavy paper use by both insurance and real estate organizations, storage of massive amounts of information is also required on the main computer via a network. To improve communications within the organization, information is fed into the database of the main computer, making it easily accessible for review and analysis when needed.
- *Expansion of business scope, such as moving into financial services and creating new service products.* Expansion is accompanied by the need for more equipment and services, leading to greater opportunities to provide hardware and software support services.

Education

Education is represented by the three major segments of public school districts, private schools, and colleges or universities — overall, more than 100,000 establishments. Education is a moderate user of data-processing, office automation, and telecommunications equipment, as well as building automation systems for energy management. The most attractive service segments are the largest users of automated systems and equipment, namely colleges, universities, and large public school systems. Service revenues were $9.4 billion in 1995 and grew to over $18 billion by 2001.

Service market needs and requirements are affected by several major trends including:

- *Operating fund limitations.* As for the government sector, pricing of services is a crucial factor. Those vendors who can provide the optimum mix of quality services for the best price will have the chance to provide services to education facilities.
- *Increasing use of data processing for operations, student education, administration, and research.* Expansion is tied to a need for more equipment and services, leading to greater opportunities to provide hardware and software support services.

Transportation and Distribution

Like the retail stores that they serve, distribution operations were stung by the recession in the late 1980s and early 1990s and some slow to moderate growth through the rest of the decade. Reactions among distributors paralleled those of retail stores. These actions made them more efficient, and in today's markets transportation and distribution have experienced both growth and increased profitability. These firms have also begun consolidating, downsizing, and searching for greater technology-based efficiencies provided by high-tech equipment and systems. Some of the trends shaping the size and structure of the industry include: (1) customer sophistication and demand for value in terms of reduced travel time and more rapid shipments, (2) technological improvements allowing leveraging of information to gain power in the distribution channel, and (3) globalization and an accompanying narrowing of distribution channels with a broadening base of opportunity.

Today's state-of-the-art distribution impacts both retailers and their suppliers, because merchandise is produced on an as-needed basis, reducing warehousing costs. Within distribution operations, information technologies are moving from simply processing and recording daily transactions toward strategic applications and productivity gains that make operations more competitive and responsive. New technologies such as quick response, warehousing information networks, point-of-shipment systems in fixed facilities, and voice/data communications systems within the distribution flow are changing the face of distribution. Food service distributors, for example, have begun using information systems to help determine acquisition and carrying costs, item movement, and volume discounts and to automatically produce demand-forecast formulas. Power retailers such as Wal-Mart have incorporated high-tech equipment to lower distribution costs an estimated 33 to 50% below competitors' costs.

The distributor's role in turn is being transformed by the new technology. Whereas the distributor had been a conduit for moving products from manufacturers to end-users, the distributor is becoming an important information link in the overall scheme of the market, increasingly providing data services to end-users from point-of-shipment information terminals. To better prepare for and perform in its new role, the industry is increasingly investing in data-processing systems, computerized logistics/inventory systems, and automation integrated with retail information systems.

Many of these technologies can be networked to create quick response systems linking distributors to manufacturers, brokers, buying and marketing groups, and customers, requiring heavy investments in serviceable telecommunications/network equipment. The emphasis is shifting from managing data within a distribution operation to one of linking up with these manufacturers, brokers, buying groups, and customers. Though most information exchange within the distribution industry takes place via phone and fax. In the year 2002, most data were exchanged using electronic data interchange (EDI), the use of which is growing within the industry at a rate of 25 to 35% each year. Also, although the industry is currently semi-automated, it is moving quickly toward full automation, meaning high expenditures on equipment services and support.

Overall, the distribution industry is marked by the following trends: (1) evolving role as vital information link; (2) expanding role as data collector, processor, and analyst; (3) competitive pressures to find technology-based cost efficiencies; (4) increased integration into end-user information systems; and (5) increased point-of-shipment automation.

This industry is primarily concerned with the physical distribution of goods to market and includes segments of the economy where this type of operation occurs, including wholesale distribution, sales branches of manufacturers that distribute stock, and trucking and warehousing operations. The distribution industry is a significant user of the following technologies: (1) telecommunications equipment (faxes, networks, and radiofrequency communications); (2) logistics systems and networks; (3) wireless communications; (4) data-processing equipment (mainframes, mini/microcomputers, and especially portable PCs); (5) building or process automation equipment; (6) systems integration; and (7) application-specific technology (e.g., bar coding, scanning).

The total high-tech services market for transportation/distribution was $8.2 billion in 1995 and grew to over $16 billion by 2001. The largest opportunities exist in servicing and support of data-processing equipment, data-communications equipment, voice/data and LAN services, and software support. The high-tech service market for transportation and distribution is large and growing rapidly.

Overall, the emerging role of the distributor as a point of shipment information links, the pressure for quick response systems, and increased competition are providing attractive opportunities for high-tech equipment service providers. Some of the trends that translate into service opportunities include:

- *Order placement made directly by end-users.* New technologies are allowing as much as 80% of order placement to be done directly by end-users. This means that not only will it be necessary for end-users to have the equipment but it will also be more crucial for the equipment to be maintained and operable at all times.
- *Maintaining the flow of information with their own information systems.* Distributors have already begun to add capabilities such as electronic transmission of statements and accounts receivable information, as well as electronic funds transfer. In fact, industry analysts predict the most successful distribution operations will be those that incorporate state-of-the-art technology to deliver goods to market through quick response systems.
- *Use of high-tech equipment.* In general, distributors are investing in serviceable information technologies and high-tech services. A survey of CEOs at the top 50 distribution companies showed that 74.4% are introducing new technology to boost productivity and efficiency.

Utilities/Communications

The utility industry consists of the electric, gas/petroleum, telephone, water, and cable television segments. This industry has been at the forefront of adopting wireless technology, which is not surprising in light of the fact that many of the telecommunications equipment and service providers are major players in the wireless and mobile communications markets. Utilities are generally regionally concentrated, making them prime prospects for private networks, an approach that most utilities have taken in the form of conventional base repeater systems or trunked networks.

Maintenance of utility equipment is a major area of need in the utility industry both on a routine and emergency basis, particularly in remote and rural areas; utilities are active, of course, in emergency and disaster relief efforts along with emergency response workers. The recent innovation of remote meter reading via drive-by-terminals that activate transmitters on the meter offers major cost advantages in manpower savings; one worker with a mobile data communications link can do the work of 15 to 20 workers on foot. In addition, other applications being adopted by the utility industry include computer-aided dispatch, as well as telemetry and online, real-time process control.

Although most utilities gather data on a quarterly basis, wireless applications allow more frequent and, in some instances, continuous real-time data collection. For example, the petroleum industry must have the capability to transmit data and voice communications from remote drilling and exploration sites and also to collect data via telemetry and SCADA. In addition, for active well heads a continuous stream of data is collected via wireless devices that measure and monitor well activity. One of the greatest cost efficiencies in terms of task automation is within the area of dispatch and on-site repair. Generally, the automated dispatch system provides a means for the service personnel to be routed from repair locations to another remote site without returning to a centralized dispatch.

The total high-tech services market for utilities and communications was estimated at $7.6 billion in 1995. The market has the fastest compound annual growth rate (CAGR) of all the vertical markets and is projected to grow to over $22 billion by 2002–2003. The largest areas that offer service opportunities include:

- *Maintaining large amounts of real-time data.* Not only are massive amounts of data maintained but the data are updated constantly, meaning that any down time results in dissatisfied customers and loss in revenues. Service vendors who can provide 'round-the-clock quality service will do well here.
- *Use of remote meter reading via drive-by-terminals.* With the use of this technology, utilities require well-maintained systems that are always up and running.

HORIZONTAL MARKET SERVICE OPPORTUNITIES AND TRENDS

Two horizontal service areas offer fruitful, profitable service opportunities. Service organizations should give serious consideration to both the *network* and *prepress printing/publishing* technology service markets, which have CAGRs exceeding 13%.

Network Services

One of the most rapidly growing market opportunities for service organizations is the expanding installed base of network systems and technology. Local area networks (LANs) are utilized in all vertical market segments and are moving toward fully integrated business networks. Furthermore, LANs have become critical components of specialized applications such as process control or plant automation.

In essence, LANs incorporate a combination of software and hardware and provide the framework for improving the use of information-processing technology on a distributed basis to the end-users. In general, there are four major reasons why LANs are installed and utilized: (1) provide a low-cost framework and mechanism for systems integration and network management through efficient interconnection and control of central processing units, storage devices, terminals, and personal computers, as well as applications; (2) enhance the ability to share common resources, including PC and data terminal access to high-speed/high-capacity storage and retrieval devices and high-quality printers; (3) provide for implementation of new types of online, real-time applications involving integrated access to common databases not possible in earlier "star"-based networks; and (4) provide low-cost communications through private network operations offering the ability to communicate directly over a privately owned line of technology rather than through the public switch and leased facilities.

Local area networks represent only a portion of the installed base of network technology going on in the U.S. market. Wide area networks (WANs) are also being installed at a rapid rate and are used to control integrated voice/data PBXs and multiplexers, as well as advanced integrated voice/data packet switch equipment and concentrators to support WAN operations. In addition, a relatively new communications technology, based on the ability to communicate data, voice, and graphics instrumentation over a LAN or WAN via wireless (FM radio band or cellular) mechanisms, is being deployed rapidly. This new technology will have a dramatic impact on the future of the network market. As individual networks evolve further and begin to interface with other related network systems environments, they will continue to increase in importance in the end-user's operating environment.

At the moment, much of this market is still held captive by the attempt of original equipment manufacturers (OEMs) to withhold parts, documentation, diagnostics, etc. from "unauthorized" third-party maintainers; however, this is still a very attractive market due to the currently high margins for service created by the barriers to entry by the OEMs.

The total service market for network equipment services was $27.7 billion in 1995 and is projected to grow to more than $85 billion in 2002. The network service market includes the following breakouts: basic services (including installation and operations support), value-added services (including planning services and design/performance), and hardware maintenance.

Prepress and Printing Technology

The service of front-end electronic prepress and printing technology used by printing and publishing establishments represented an approximately $7.4 billion service market in 1995 which will grow to more than $28 billion by 2002. These figures represent basic hardware repair activities and value-added services, including software support, remote diagnostics, and other value-added services. Printing presses and platemaking services comprise over 54.6% of the total hardware service market, and electronic prepress equipment comprises another 20.9%. The service market opportunity for electronic prepress equipment will grow at a much more rapid pace than the printing presses and platemaking segment, as more printing establishments are adopting newer advanced prepress technologies.

Analysis of the overall service problem–diagnosis–resolution process in printing technology shows some very interesting opportunities, such as an increased need for diagnostics consultation and hotline technical assistance for the entire printing process, an increased focus on stock-keeping and physical delivery of consumables and supplies, and the need for value-added professional services 24 hours a day. These value-added services are required in addition to a variety of basic support services such as equipment installation, preventive and predictive repair, equipment maintenance, training, environmental disposal of toxic chemicals, and equipment troubleshooting.

The need for equipment support is further intensified by the fact that the industry is faced with competition from other functional approaches to delivery of information to ultimate end-users such as high-speed multicolor copiers and video, cable television, and satellite communications using direct video images. In essence, the effect of these key factors and trends is an emphasis among printing/publishing establishments on service and support of printing technologies in order to develop and sustain a competitive advantage among the various delivery mechanisms and direct functional competitors. This service focus can be described in terms of a need for consultative design, engineering, and integration services to bring new technologies and updated printing applications to bear, as well as a need for other value-added services to support the general process, such as: (1) 24-hour technical and hotline assistance services, parallel to printing plant operations; (2) toxic waste disposal services to haul and process toxic materials; (3) just-in-time delivery and logistics control of consumables; and (4) rapid responsive maintenance and repair services to support existing and new technologies that reflect more sophisticated capabilities, increased interaction between steps in the production process, and a trend toward reduction or elimination of internal plant maintenance.

An important new market trend is bringing changes in the printing industry. New electronic and automation technologies have been brought in to provide extremely rapid turnaround and just-in-time printing capabilities. These new electronic technologies integrate data, graphics, and communications and are being deployed widely in the general printing and publishing industry, as well as in printing and publishing functions in the manufacturing, distribution, and professional areas. This is a market in which little or no independent third-party maintenance capability exists and therefore provides an attractive new service opportunity.

In summary, these new market segment opportunities and the trends creating them offer service organizations who are willing to make the necessary investments numerous avenues for profitable growth. With the possibilities presented in both vertical and horizontal market areas, service organizations can target their choice along industry or equipment lines; however, the most important lesson here is that these opportunities are dynamic and in a very brief time they could evolve into other profitable possibilities not yet realized.

NEW AND EMERGING SERVICE MARKETS

The traditional business model of the sales and service organization assumes direct control over both field sales and service forces through local or regional field offices, in order to provide market control. However, in markets such as automobiles, office equipment, construction equipment, material handling equipment, etc. more typical business models employ indirect channels through dealers or distributors with only general supervision and control in the field by the major manufacturer. This alternative service and sales structure is less expensive and involves less investment than the direct model. In this indirect model, the sales and services responsibility is assigned to independent dealers and distributors, who take the full responsibility for sales and service of the manufacturer's product within their specified area of responsibility, usually defined geographically (by region) or by product mix or some combination of the two. Dealers and distributors can represent one manufacturer or several, particularly if the individual manufacturer's products are not directly competitive.

In this indirect channel sales and service field strategy, the manufacturer's responsibilities in the end-user market are primarily marketing and sales support directed toward influencing customers to purchase from particular dealers and distributors. Some manufacturers retain responsibility for direct sales to major national or international accounts.

In general, in this type of arrangement, the individual dealer or distributor operates its own sales and service organization and typically utilizes service as both a mechanism for market penetration and market control and as a source of incremental revenues and profits. In fact, in some markets the profitability of a dealer's service business is significantly greater than the profitability of the dealer's product business. Some manufacturers prefer this indirect model because it significantly reduces front-end investment in distribution; it also reduces control and management of customer service and satisfaction in the field.

In this typical situation, the major manufacturer provides certain types of support to its dealer service network, including:

- *Warranty/credits.* The dealer usually supplies the warranty service and is credited by the manufacturer for the work done.
- *Parts and logistics support.* The manufacturer supplies parts to the dealer to support dealer service or for direct sale to end-users.
- *Training.* The manufacturer provides dealer training.
- *Technical assistance and support.* Technical support is usually provided by the manufacturer particularly during new product introduction and roll-out.

Although some manufacturers attempt to create a standard service management systems infrastructure, or at least reporting mechanisms to coordinate dealer sales and service, others let their dealers make their own decisions about systems and infrastructure, particularly if vendors are available that offer software and application service provider (ASP) types of infrastructures designed for a dealer's specific requirements.

In this service business environment, it is of interest to look closely at the future of this indirect channel business model from the standpoint of service and support, taking into account:

- What should the manufacturer do to improve support to its dealer/distributor base without impacting the independent entrepreneurial spirit of the dealer organizations?
- How can individual dealers achieve economies of scale or make use of advanced technology within the framework of their local financial structure and economic base?
- What action should be taken by TPM/MVE suppliers, OEMs, and other dealers to optimize their service operations and customer satisfaction?

Areas of Potential Improvement in Indirect Services and Distribution

In this regard, it is worthwhile to examine new technology and infrastructure developments that could improve the efficiency of service operations at both the manufacturer and dealer level in the indirect channel business model. These include:

- *Improving warranty, claims, processing, systems and technology.* For the last few years vendors have started to develop warranty processing systems software designed for use by both the manufacturer and its dealer base. Some organizations, such as Key Prestige, Satisfusion, and ServiceBench, offer warranty and claims processing capabilities on an ASP or service bureau basis, in effect offering the capability to outsource the entire warranty/claims process to achieve more timely and accurate performance.

■ *Parts/logistics improvements.* Extensive studies of many different indirect channel operations clearly show that logistics/parts support by the manufacturer to the dealers and to the dealer service forces in the field can be significantly improved. Very often a long delay occurs between the time that the dealer service person in the field needs a part and when that part is finally delivered, simply because of the need to go through at least two bureaucratic levels at both the dealer and manufacturer level. In addition, little attempt has been made to optimize the full logistics pipeline control in a complex manufacturer/dealer operating structure. Here again, two new developments have taken place that can improve service operations. First of all, several vendors, including Xelus, Servigistics, MCA, and Baxter Planning Systems, have developed specialized logistics/parts software for management and control of the full logistics pipeline that includes both manufacturer and dealer operations. In addition, members of organizations traditionally operating as physical distribution groups, such as UPS, FedEx, etc., now provide a full logistics service and support capability to the field level. By taking over the actual physical parts inventory, establishing repair depots, and utilizing extensive land and air transportation facilities, these organizations are able to minimize the cost of spare parts inventory in the full logistics pipeline and significantly decrease the time involved in delivery of parts required from the field.

■ *Field communications.* Significant new breakthroughs are also taking place in the area of field service communications, including, specifically, the development of new personal digital assistants (PDAs) and laptops with full global positioning service (GPS) and voice recognition, as well as the ability to download images, pictures, and technical design and schematic layouts directly to the field. Vendors of these technologies are now offering integrated deals with nationwide discounts to enable even smaller dealers and distributors to make use of this new technology especially if they are able to purchase within the framework of one overall cost-effective deal struck with the general manufacturer.

While these represent only a small portion of the areas of improvement that can be achieved, it is very clear that significant new developments in technology and infrastructure will be arriving over the next several years that can significantly improve the efficiency and effectiveness of both OEMs and dealer/distributor field service organizations.

THE IMPACT OF NEW SERVICE OUTSOURCING TRENDS

It is of interest to note that the indirect distribution channel, utilizing dealers and distributors, has often been a business model of choice, especially where customers require a high degree of local sales support and general customer service. This distribution delivery model has been used especially where purchasers operate their own internal plant or building maintenance organizations and do not require a high level of field service oriented toward break-and-fix situations. However, a number of trends are beginning to change the character and level of field service and support that dealers and distributors have to provide. Key trends such as aging of the internal plant and building maintenance service organizations and the increased integration and networking of systems are leading to more outsourcing of the internal plant and building maintenance forces.

What happens when these new trends require a much higher level of field service and support on the part of the dealers and distributors? What action should be taken by both the parent OEM and by the dealers and distributors themselves in the face of these changes?

An examination of these changes and requirements in a number of vertical markets, including lighting systems and technology, electrical distribution, medical and healthcare technology, process control and plant automation, printing and prepress technology, and office equipment, has led to answers to these key questions.

Original equipment manufacturers supporting indirect dealer and distribution channels should provide the following centralized capabilities to their dealers and distributors in order to improve overall field service efficiency:

- Improved parts, logistics forecasting, planning, control, and distribution
- Establishment of a regional or national technical assistance center (TAC) offering diagnostic support to dealers either during normal business hours or on a 24-hour basis
- Online, real-time access to technical documentation, reliability, and configuration control data
- Rapid and efficient warranty processing

From the perspective of the individual dealers and distributors, improvements should be made in the following areas:

- Capabilities for call handling, diagnostics, and work force scheduling for greater efficiency in the allocation and scheduling of dealer labor personnel in the field

- Effectiveness of real-time communications to and from dealer/distributor field service personnel through the use of laptops, truck-mounted receivers, and handheld PDAs offering voice/data communications on a wireless basis, plus GPS.
- Central and dealer-level repair depot processing, moving from job shop to just-in-time sequencing

In summary, outsourcing of the traditional internal plant and building maintenance organizations is leading to greater dependence on the dealer and distributors field service capabilities which, in turn, requires focus and cooperation by both OEMs and dealers/distributors to address the new field service requirements. This is especially true during the early stages of product launch and warranty coverage. OEMs must plan optimal new field product launches that include consideration of providing training and diagnostics on the new products to the field dealers and distributors, the correct parts, and timely processing of warranty claims for reimbursement. The lack of efficient OEM warranty processing of dealer claims can lead to serious problems between dealers and the parent OEMs, in addition to failure to collect accurate mean time between failure (MTBF) and mean time to repair (MTTR) and other reliability data.

MARKET SEGMENTS WITH MAJOR IMPACT

We have discussed above the key market segments most affected by important outsourcing trends. In these particular segments and niches, the impact on dealers and distributors is growing, and manufacturers in these segments using the indirect distribution model must take immediate action, in conjunction with their dealers and distributors, to address these new demands.

It should be noted that if the OEMs and dealers do not take action, the end-user is not without options; in fact, end-users could look to other parties, including:

- Manufacturers moving into multivendor equipment services (MVES)
- Third-party maintenance and independent service operators (TPM/ISOs)

In this regard, OEMs moving into MVES support and TPM/ISOs might want to look closely at some of the market segments to develop new service portfolios focused on those segments. Consideration should also be given to the possible acquisition and roll-up of dealer service forces in these segments to create a new regional or nationwide service force.

Under any circumstances, the key trends of outsourcing and downsizing of the internal plant and building maintenance forces are creating new opportunities and threats for both OEMs and dealers involved in indirect channel support and significant new market potentials for OEMs and TPM/ISOs moving into multivendor support.

13

OVERALL ISSUES IN MANAGING SERVICE

Our analysis and evaluation started with a focus on the need to create a new service-oriented business model to reflect more closely the real issues involved in a business-oriented service organization. We suggested that the service organization makes use of three sets of resources:

- Labor
- Materials
- Information and Data

We pointed out that in the service business, information and data are as much a resource as labor and materials and should be managed in real time. We also suggested that while a product business makes use of information and data, they are primarily in support of the managerial functions of control and reporting, whereas in a service business information is a critical resource.

Our evaluation also indicated that a service business has two engines of production:

- Production of the actual service required by the customer in real time
- Creation of perception or the capability to serve at some future time

Our evaluation suggested that the need for a second engine of production (creating a perception of the capability to serve) is generated directly by the fact that it is not possible to stockpile or inventory services. This second engine of production is just as important as the actual production

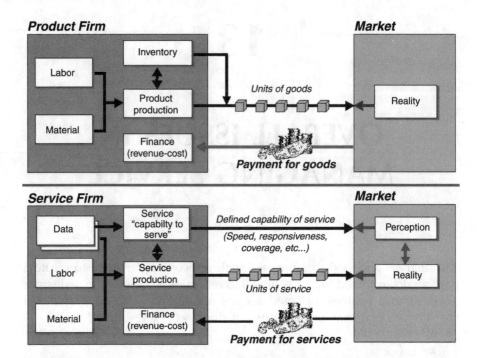

Figure 13.1 Comparison of product and service business models.

of the services, and the customer is willing to pay for both the actual services and the perception. Payment for the perception is, in essence, an insurance policy and a guarantee that the service will be provided within the time frame of the customer's requirements. We have also shown that the service business model shown in Figure 13.1, which was originally developed in the high-tech service market, has applicability for all types of services, including banking, health care, retail, transportation, and distribution.

Our analysis also revealed that the applicability and use of this new service business model required three areas of focus:

■ *Development of the senior executive vision and direction for the service business in terms of objectives, market focus, and general operating plan.* Obviously, a service organization designed to support only product sales will require a different format and focus than a service organization supporting products and also generating revenues and profits on its own as an independent line of business.

■ *Design, development, and implementation of the infrastructure and systems to support the new strategy.* The basic customer relationship management (CRM) technology and infrastructure, implemented on a real-time basis, provides the infrastructure support for the required strategic direction.

■ *The need to increase market share and served based density.* The third component is to take the appropriate actions in terms of market surveys and customer satisfaction audits, to develop a new service portfolio and pricing, and the design, development, and implementation of marketing and sales program, to increase the density of the service customer base supported. Service density is a critical element of achieving efficiency in the service environment.

The process of proceeding with this new strategy will generally involve three stages or phases:

■ *Stage 1. Development of the service strategy and direction* — This step requires analysis and evaluation of internal productivity and performance benchmarks against industry standards; an external assessment (through market research) of customer satisfaction, current and emerging requirements, and willingness to pay; identification of strategic options, alternatives, and scenarios; and final selection of an optimized strategy that achieves the highest return on investment at minimum risk.

■ *Stage 2. CRM systems design and development* — The second stage involves design of the full CRM plan and includes an assessment of requirements for a system based upon the stage 1 evaluation, as well as an assessment of the state of the art. This process, in turn, leads to a plan of system specification, development, and implementation for the system.

■ *Stage 3. Plan implementation and roll-out* — The third stage involves the development, implementation, and roll-out of an overall service strategy, implementation of the full service delivery organization (including call management, logistics management, field communications, and field service deployment), and creation of market and sales procedures to increase service density.

As shown in Figure 13.2, the overall approach to design, development, and implementation of an effective strategy for managing service using the service business model requires an orderly, logical, and quantitative investigation of the various internal and external factors and market conditions that could affect the strategy and an approach to implementation that takes into account the structural components required.

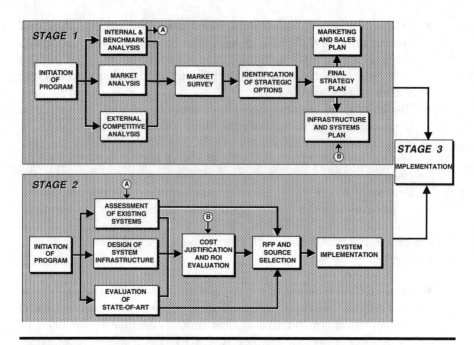

Figure 13.2 Process to develop an optimized service business.

SERVICE OPTIMIZATION

We have tried to emphasize the importance of the new optimization paradigms facing service executives running services as a strategic line of business research. Research and experience demonstrate that service optimization is achievable and that many mechanisms in technology exist to support it. It is very clear that the state of the art, including benchmarking, diagnostics, workforce scheduling and optimization, and use of advanced wireless laptops and PDA technology, in service is moving forward rapidly, particularly as more and more of the basic infrastructures for call management, logistics support, and field communication have become automated. We strongly advise all service executives to look very closely at the issues and concepts of optimization, full benchmarking, and new integrated service management systems. The new technologies representing the state of the art can be used to ensure that service executives are maximizing the profit contribution and service quality and performance of their operations.

SUMMARY

As indicated above, significant opportunities are available to improve productivity, efficiency, and quality of service operations. In addition, experience suggests that focusing on improving the overall equipment base density served through a proactive movement to third-party maintenance and multivendor equipment support through expansion of the service portfolio can improve the productivity of a service organization by 10 to 25% or more. Thus, major areas of productivity improvement involve internal improvement in call management and logistics support and external top-line increases in revenues and density attributable to higher levels of customer satisfaction and sales.

In addition to the basic improvements in productivity and efficiency of existing operations, a general mechanism also exists for achieving productivity and efficiency improvement on a strategic basis. This involves utilization of advanced strategic manpower and logistics service planning models to examine the optimum trade-off between service response to a customer (service quality) and service cost. Such trade-off analysis can be performed through the use of simulation or a "closed form" model designed to explore the trade-offs between the required manpower and logistics support levels and a customer's willingness to pay for given levels of service. A computational strategic planning model can be extremely useful in establishing the optimum strategic allocation of service staff and logistics support to meet a given hardware-based customer service response and price requirement. In general, the key to service productivity and quality improvement is the establishment of a formal optimized business plan and model defining the role and importance of service and the desire to enter into general service to increase density (e.g., third- or fourth-party maintenance) vs. service on one's own product or technology. The combination of the strategic level analytical models and the productivity improvement steps outlined previously with respect to improving call handling, service personnel utilization, and logistics support efficiency are the keys to optimizing the productivity, efficiency, quality of delivery, and bottom-line profitability of service operations.

Service executives now have a variety of vendors and sources to assist them in achieving their service business optimization goals. It is important to recognize that, given the array of standard and best-in-class software and the communications options and alternatives, systems integration becomes a vitally important issue in achieving overall successful implementation, application, and use. It is also important to recognize that about 40% of both investment and operating costs are for central and field communications. Thus, full systems integration must consider hardware, software, and communication.

APPENDICES

Appendix A

APPLICATION OF BENCHMARKING OF SERVICE OPERATIONS FOR IMPROVING SERVICE ORGANIZATION PRODUCTIVITY AND EFFICIENCY

CONTENTS

INTRODUCTION

The high-tech service industry, in general, as well as independent third-party, multivendor equipment service, and fourth-party service organizations have become much more focused on improving their productivity and efficiency. The issue of strategic and tactical benchmarking has, therefore, gained increased attention and importance. The ISO 9000 process for quality management and control emphasizes the importance of benchmarking as a key to the comparative measurement of service operations and customer-oriented performance against industry and market norms and standards. In running service as a line of business or profit center, it is critical to determine the optimum approach to achieving the best profit levels and at the same time meet customer service needs and requirements. Unfortunately, relatively few accepted or published benchmark parameters and targets for this industry are available to be used by the typical service organization or manager in establishing an effective service strategy and in assessing and evaluating performance relative to industry standards and norms or customer requirements.

If it were available and properly evaluated to determine key driving parameters and critical targets, this type of data could be extremely useful in improving service productivity and efficiency. BAI, as part of its process of providing management consulting to the service industry, has tried to fill this gap by developing an extensive base of benchmark information and data parameters, by class, technology of products serviced, type and size of service organization, and geographic region serviced. This information is based, in part, upon extensive service market audits and studies conducted by BAI among more than 450 small, medium, and large service organizations; supporting OEM manufacturers; dealers; distributors; and independent third- and fourth-party service and multivendor equipment service (MVES) providers operating in the United States and Europe, as well as globally, conducted from 1988 to 2002. These organizations were involved in the service and support of a broad array of technology, including:

- Information technology
- Office automation and office products
- Telecommunications and data network products
- Medical electronics and technology
- Building automation
- Industrial plant systems controls
- Retail, financial, and point of sale (POS) technology
- Home and consumer goods

In addition, BAI has developed extensive nonproprietary data on service requirements and performance by technology and vertical market segment as part of carrying out more than 500 market research studies in the service market to determine user requirements for service and to measure customer satisfaction and service performance as perceived by users. Finally, BAI has collected considerable published data on the organization, operations, and productivity of service-oriented companies and on the service market in which they operate. The nonproprietary elements of all of these sources of data were then used to develop key benchmark data (see Figure A.1) using the general process shown in Figure A.2.

BAI originally published an executive summary of their benchmark findings in 1993, covering data developed for the period 1988 to 1992, based on surveys of 90 companies. A second analysis based on a 100-company sample, for the period 1993 to 1995, was completed and updated in 1996. This information was updated again in 1999 using a 120-company sample for the period 1995 to 1998. The most recent analysis is based on 130 firms who participated in BAI's benchmarking program during the period 1999 through 2001. The benchmark parameters and standards developed from that process and data sources are discussed below.

METHOD OF APPROACH TO BENCHMARK ANALYSIS AND EVALUATION

Because of the tremendous variations in financial and accounting practice and a lack of accepted industry-wide standards with respect to parameters

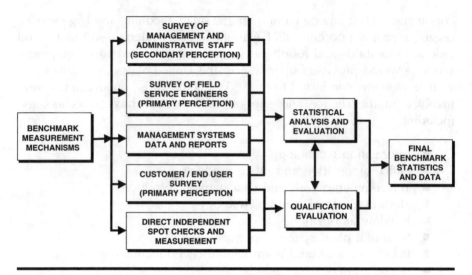

Figure A.1 BAI data sources used in developing benchmarks.

and definitions of those parameters, benchmarking in the high-tech service industry is difficult and still in its infancy. Many competitors are reluctant to share what they consider to be competitive and proprietary data. In

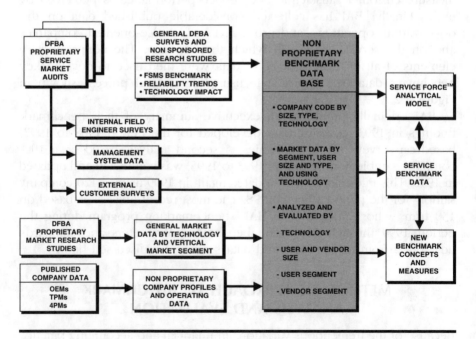

Figure A.2 General methodology and process in developing benchmark data.

many cases, they do not track certain key parameters and operating statistics. This problem has been compounded by the proliferation of service management systems software packages, each using somewhat different parameters and definitions and providing data in different formats. Finally, for many key parameters, including key standards such as response time and percentage of "broken" calls, some significant differences apparently exist between the data and reports produced internally, and external perceptions of customers with respect to the same parameters.

Typical benchmarking research to date has been sponsored by professional associations in the service market, such as AFSM International and SIA, and has been based on one-time surveys or recurring annual surveys sent to management, executives, or administrators of selected sponsor service organizations. Benchmark data were developed based upon the statistical tabulation of these survey responses; no independent testing or spot-checking was carried out by the research organization, and the data were based primarily on internal reports or estimates, as compared to external measures such as customer or market surveys or objective independent professional observations.

Our research suggests that this one-time snapshot survey approach may lead to some inaccuracies. This is, in part, caused by the fact that the survey data used in this approach are highly dependent on the willingness of individual participating respondents to spend the necessary time and effort to collect and organize the data required by the survey and to provide openly, objectively, and professionally what is generally viewed as highly competitive and proprietary information. The data have also been based on internally oriented perceptions and measures, which are sometimes used for compensation or contract negotiations and thus might be purposely biased. Also, the sample population has been relatively small or biased toward a specific class or category of service providers — for example, large multinational original equipment manufacturers (OEMs) servicing information technology or medium-sized regional ISOs servicing medical electronics. Our own broader survey experience suggests that some very significant and real differences exist among benchmarking data reported by organizations basing their research on a single, one-time mail survey from a limited, homogenous population compared to independent, in-depth verification and cross-checking or the use of multiple (internal and external) data sources and larger heterogeneous datasets.

The methodology used to develop more accurate benchmark data for the high-tech service industry for 2002 utilized a cross-sectional analysis of in-depth research and experience with 130 small, medium, and large field service organizations with operations in the United States and Europe,

| | Type of Service Organization | | |
Technology Serviced	OEM Service	ISO, TPM, and MVES Services	Total
Information technology	12	14	26
Office products and office automation	10	15	25
Retail and financial automation and point of sale	6	4	10
Telecommunications and networks	13	10	23
Medical electronics	14	6	20
Home and consumer goods	4	3	7
Building automation	6	3	9
Industrial plant controls	7	3	10
Total	72[b]	58	130[a]

[a] Includes 42 with operations in Europe and rest of world.
[b] Includes eight OEMs with TPM/MVES services operated as separate profit centers; data for such centers were used in the ISO/TPM analysis.

Figure A.3   Service organizations represented in BAI updated benchmark database (1999–2001).

as well as globally, reflecting a broad range of different technologies and service operating environments (Figure A.3). Figure A.4 specifies the technologies serviced. In each of these cases, BAI was involved in proprietary service market audits involving internal audits and evaluation, as well as external market surveys. In each case, we also spent considerable time examining, investigating, analyzing, and evaluating service operating performance, productivity, and efficiency, as well as customer satisfaction; we also reviewed financial and accounting records, call management and logistics management system reports and data, and customer satisfaction and market research surveys. The benchmark data from each individual audit study were first sanitized to eliminate any proprietary or confidential information to avoid any possible identification of specific client sponsors or client-specific and sensitive information. In addition, all of the data

Technology	Type of Products Serviced	Types of Firms	Typical Size of Firms (Number of Field Personnel)
Information technology	Main frames, minicomputers, micro/PC/ workstations, EDP peripherals	OEMs, ISO/TPMs	Medium to very large (500–20,000)
Office automation and products	Office automation, PCs, and workstations; copying machines; document management/imaging; word processors; micrographics; office equipment	OEMs, dealers/ distributors, TPM/ISOs	Small to medium (200–2000)
Retail, financial, point of sale	POS terminals, cash registers (ECR), bank automation such as ATMs, special equipment	OEMs, dealers/ distributors, TPM/ISOs	Small to large (50–5000)
Building automation	HVAC, instrumentation, lighting, alarms	OEMs, dealers/distributors, ISOs (limited)	Small to medium (100–2000)
Industrial plant controls	Process control, switch gear, plant robotics, other automated systems	OEMs, dealers/distributors, ISOs (limited)	Small to medium (100–2000)
Telecommunications	Data networks, voice networks, PBX/key sets, network switchers, bridges and routers, modems	OEMs, utilities, private bypass operations, TPMs	Small to large (25–15,000)
Medical electronics and technology	Medical instrumentation and analyzers, diagnostic imaging and analyzers, diagnostic imaging systems, surgical suites, anesthesiology, sterilizers	OEMs, hospital/ biomedical groups, ISOs/TPMs	Small to medium (15–500)
Home and consumer goods	Washers/dryers, dishwashers, ovens, televisions/VCRs, stereos	OEMs, dealers/distributors, ISOs (limited)	Small to medium (25–2000)

Figure A.4 Major benchmark segments: products and technology.

used were subject to independent analysis and evaluation based upon a combination of information from a variety of sources, including financial and accounting data, call management system reports, logistics management systems and data, and customer satisfaction and market surveys that we conducted independently.

In essence, the data reflect objective and professional evaluations of service operations based upon both internal and external studies lasting well over 2 to 3 months; therefore, we believe we have generated a much more accurate and independently validated view than is normally obtained from one-time snapshot surveys based on mail questionnaires, which have been used in previously reported benchmark studies. The admitted downside of this method of approach is that the data were collected over a period of 3 to 4 years (1998–2001), thus possibly introducing some bias into the results. We believe, based on testing of 12 specific parameters and comparisons with our earlier 1988–1993, 1992–1995, and 1995–1998 databases, that the field service industry remains relatively stable over any 3- to 4-year period so the effects of the time factor paradigm shift, if it does exist, appear to be minor.

As indicated in Figure A.2, we have also tested the benchmark data in our own analytical model (ServiceFORCE) for logical consistency and to identify possible independent and dependent relationships. We report on some of this research below. This process is continuing to include new data and permit identification of new interrelationships. The overall strengths and weaknesses of our methodology as an approach to benchmark development, as compared to other sources, are shown in Figure A.5.

GENERAL ANALYSIS AND EVALUATION OF THE BENCHMARK DATABASE

Subject to the caveats and methodology identified above and given that the benchmarking data and statistics were developed based on extensive research involving over 130 firms (as outlined in Figure A.3), it is important to understand some of the technical difficulties involved in developing benchmark estimates and applying and using them. The most important of these issues are discussed here.

Comparison Basis

As indicated above, the high-tech service industry lacks definitive and accepted guidelines and standards for key service targets. In our research, analysis, and investigation we have tried to make use of our own standards and parameter descriptions and have used those standards consistently

Type	Factor	Comment
Strengths	Based on primary surveys of field engineers and customers	Not dependent on limited or potentially inaccurate company data reports alone
	Uses combination of sources: surveys, databases, spot checks	Data independently validated
	Fully correlates internal and external evaluation on key measurements	Based on resolution of both internal and external perceptions and data
	Accuracy ensured by full statistical and correlation analysis combined with independent validation and spot checks	Attempts to be logically and internally consistent
		Avoids internal bias
		Not based on a simplistic snapshot
	Uses analytical model framework	
Weaknesses	Data developed over several years	Does not fully deal with parameter changes over short time frames
	Proprietary raw data eliminated	No direct client input in final data evaluation where unique or specialized programs are adapted

Figure A.5 Strengths and weaknesses of BAI benchmark as database presented compared to alternative "snapshot" survey approach.

in our analyses and evaluations. It is important, however, to note that differences may exist between our particular definitions and definitions and descriptions of key parameters used by specific field service organizations. It should be mentioned that our benchmarks reflect the operating parameters of companies that operate field service and/or depot repair organizations as opposed to only remote support (e.g., help desk) operations.

Validity Tests

It is also important to recognize that our benchmark numbers reflect the results of analysis, evaluation, and resolution of the differences, if any, that might exist between the statistics and parameters as reported by internal management systems vs. external customer perceptions. Where these differences were substantial and significant, the quantitative extrapolations were based upon specific situations and our experience to produce a balanced measure.

Cross-Elasticity of Dependent/Independent Variables

Our analysis and evaluation to develop benchmark data have also identified certain key parameters that affect others in terms of cross-elasticity relationships and logical interaction. Density, for example, tends to have a strong impact in a variety of key parameters, including inventory investment, average travel time, number of "broken" calls, etc. Economies of scale also exist, to some extent. These key relationships are discussed below. It should be clearly recognized that certain factors, including specifically the impact of differences in service organization type and technology supported, will affect the benchmark parameters. We have tried to highlight some of these key differences, based on our analysis.

Continuing Research Update

Finally, it is important to recognize that our own research into field service benchmarks is continuing based upon new information received, etc. We encourage others to share their experience and data in order to advance general industry knowledge of the key factors influencing the industry.

PRIMARY SERVICE BENCHMARK DATA

Using the process and methodology outlined above, benchmark data and information have been developed based upon technology serviced and type of operation (OEM vs. independent), as well as for general industry parameters. Eight types of technology serviced by field service or depot repair organizations have been examined as outlined in Figure A.4:

1. Information technology
2. Office automation and office products
3. Telecommunications and networks
4. Medical electronics and technology
5. Building automation and technology
6. Industrial plant controls and systems
7. Retail, financial, and point of sale (POS)
8. Home and consumer goods

Two types of operations have also been analyzed and segmented:

1. Independent service maintainers such as independent service operators (ISOs), third-party maintenance (TPM) providers, multivendor equipment service (MVES) providers, fourth-party maintainers, and dealers and distributors
2. Original equipment manufacturers (OEMs), including systems integrators and assemblers

Where an OEM was engaged in some limited third-party maintenance, the benchmark information was fully analyzed under the OEM category. Where the OEM had established a separate and distinct Strategic Business Unit (SBU) for independent service, that SBU was evaluated under the independent service category. It should also be noted that some independent service maintainers in the database are also distributors.

The new updated BAI benchmarking database is based on over 130 major field service organization data points. This is statistically valid at the 90% confidence level to within plus or minus 10%. Confidence with respect to the individual cells is obviously less. In some specific cases, because of the lack of statistical stability, estimates were made of the probable mean based upon a combination of internal data, external surveys, and industry experience.

The benchmark data are broken down into four major categories:

1. *General service organization and operating parameters.* Key benchmark parameters related to the overall structure of the typical field service organization are shown in Figure A.6. These benchmarks look primarily at revenue, profit margins, and key ratios as a general framework for assessing performance. It is important to understand that these data as reported are averages or means. Some OEMs run service as a cost center or contribution center and thus have low revenues per field engineer. Others run service as a full profit center. Through attempts to control the market by withholding parts and diagnostics, some OEMs exhibit much higher revenues per service engineer because of a lack of direct competition, but others do not. The average combines this skewed or binomial distribution into one figure, thus masking some of those more sophisticated issues and differences.
2. *Service call parameters.* A very important area in benchmarking relates to the efficiency of handling the service call. Using our defined call factors and parameters, we developed data on the individual time increments involved in call handling and manage-

ment, as shown in Figure A.7. The information reported in this table is also, in every case, mean data. We did, however, have the ability to confirm independently many of these data points through external market surveys, particularly those parameters that were not extensively reported on internally (such as call handling and call waiting time on-site). It is important for potential users of this class of information to note differences between the descriptions used for a particular call factor or in particular clock tracking mechanisms as compared to the "wall clock" times that we used. These might reflect differences between the companies' own experience and the benchmark data presented in Figure A.7. Some firms use a time clock for their reporting (i.e., 8:00 a.m. to 5:00 p.m.).

3. *Service call operational data.* A key area of productivity and efficiency analysis relates to the key benchmark parameters involving service call operations. The data, presented in Figure A.8, focus on the number of calls handled per week, the number of call completions, and, in particular, the number of calls broken or avoided due to lack of parts. We have generally found that this information is extremely useful in identifying opportunities for productivity and efficiency improvement. Unfortunately, we have found that many organizations do not adequately track this particular class of data and we strongly urge service organizations to establish tracking mechanisms for these key call operational parameters shown.

4. *Logistics data and parameters.* The fourth major area of benchmarking relates to logistics performance. The data presented in Figure A.9 provide information on logistics benchmark experience from a broad range of service organizations. We have found, generally, that the statistical stability of these numbers is less certain; therefore, while the mean information has generally been presented, it should be noted that for some specific parameters the distribution variations are quite extensive. We also believe that some of the data reported, particularly with respect to the percentage of parts found to be dead on arrival in the field may not be completely accurate, due to a general failure to report this key parameter.

In summary, the overall benchmarking database represents four major clusters of data involving over 32 key benchmark parameters and provides a good cross-section of representative experience for all types of field service organizations.

EVALUATION OF KEY DRIVING VARIABLES OF ECONOMIES OF SCALE AND DENSITY

The analysis and evaluation of the key benchmarking data allowed us to identify the key independent variables or "drivers" that affect other parameters over time. This research is continuing, in general, and in conjunction with expansion and updating of our ServiceFORCE model and estimating parameters. Two key parameters are discussed below.

General Economies of Scale

It would appear to be obvious that economies of scale in terms of employee or revenue size should affect a variety of other parameters. We investigated the full benchmark database in depth to determine whether or not economies of scale exist. By examining service revenues per employee as a function of overall service employment size and service revenue per employee vs. total service revenues in our earlier studies, we were able to discern general impacts or trends of economies of scale. Our evaluation suggested that total service revenues or total service employees may not necessarily be the best key parameters in regard to economies of scale, however. Overall corporate revenues and overall employee size seem to provide a better correlation with respect to particular market segments and product technologies. Our general assessment suggests that economies of scale definitely exist within the field service market, at least up to the size of 5000 service engineers.

Density

While economies of scale may exist, it is very clear that density is a critical driving factor with respect to impact on benchmark parameters. As part of the work previously reported, we developed parameters of density, defined as the customer/equipment base, or *parc*, in a geographic area, in order to examine the impact of installed base density on key service variables and factors. Overall, profitability is definitely affected by density. Service time utilization, efficiency, profit margins, and percent calls completed are affected by density (Figure A.10). Our data suggest that density is probably the single most critical factor with respect to improving or impacting profitability and productivity in service.

BENCHMARK COMPARISONS BY SPECIFIC SEGMENTS

Our expanded database and data parameters for 1988 to 2001 provide additional mechanisms for benchmarking. Data have been developed to examine the impact on key benchmarks of specific segmentation:

Parameters	Technology								
	Information Technology	Office Automation and Office Products	Telecommunications	Retail, Financial, and Point of Sale	Medical Electronics	Building Automation	Industrial Plant Control	Home and Consumer Goods	General Industry
Revenue[a] per service person ($1000)	196	179	206	164	291	180	217	143	199
Revenues[a] per field person ($1000)	307	222	303	233	429	233	244	218	282
Profit margin as a percent of revenue[b] (%)	40	42	58	39	54	50	52	45	54
Percent of total calls fixed remotely (by each field person) (%)	18	17	20	14	22	15	17	14	17
Percent of total calls fixed remotely (by support) (%)	37	19	41	21	25	9	8	6	22
Ratio of field personnel to support staff	1.8	1.9[c]	1.6[c]	1.7	1.8	1.6	1.5	1.5	1.7

Efficiency of field force (ratio of direct service time to total service time available) (%)	70	69	76	75	67	70	72	77	71
Total call closure time (hours)	4.4	8.8	8.1	8.9	6.1	5.4	11.1	18.7	10.2
Percent with computerized field service management systems (%)	96	88	100	89	100	82	84	80	90
Percent using advanced diagnostics and AI technology (%)	20	11	25	12	30	24	24	19	20
Percent using advanced field communications technology (%)	35	19	48	16	25	19	18	11	25

[a]Including parts sales.
[b]Before G&A and allocations.
[c]Skewed left.

Figure A.6 Benchmark data; total field service staff to field engineers (mean data, except where noted). (From Blumberg Associates, Inc., 1999–2001 data, Fort Washington, PA. With permission.)

Call Factor	Description	Technology Serviced								
		Information Technology (hr)	Office Automation and Office Products (hr)	Telecommunications (hr)	Retail, Financial, and Point of Sale (hr)	Medical Electronics (hr)	Building Automation (hr)	Industrial Plant Control (hr)	Home and Consumer Goods (hr)	General Industry (hr)
Call handling time	Time between call placed by customer and receipt by service person	0.4	2.1	1.4	2.6	1.1	0.5	1.5	12.4	3.0
Call initial response time	Time between receipt of call by service person and initiation of call action	0.6	1.9	0.6	1.8	0.5	0.4	0.7	4.0	1.6
Call travel time to site	Travel time to site	1.8	2.0	2.4	3.0	2.0	2.2	4.6	1.0	2.6

Call holding/ wait time onsite and parts travel time	Time not working onsite due to lack of parts, skills, etc., and travel to pick up parts and return	1.0	1.8	1.6	0.7	2.2	1.8	2.4	0.4	1.8
Call repair time	Time between arrival onsite and repair completion, less holding and parts pickup/ delivery travel time	0.8	2.2	2.3	1.3	2.1	0.9	2.1	1.6	2.0
Total call closure time[a]	Call placed by customer and call closeout	4.4	8.8	8.1	8.9	6.1	5.4	11.1	18.7	10.2

[a] Call totals may not add due to averaging and partial responses.

Figure A.7 Benchmark data: service call parameters (means). (From Blumberg Associates, Inc., 1999–2001 database, Fort Washington, PA. With permission.)

Parameters	Technology								
	Information Technology	Office Automation and Office Products	Telecom-munica-tions	Retail, Financial, and Point of Sale	Medical Electronics	Building Automation	Industrial Plant Control	Homeand Consumer Goods	General Industry
Demand repair/fix calls received per week per service person	14.6	17.0	16.8	18.9	13.8	6.2	5.8	7.4	13.9
Average completed calls per day per field person	2.5	2.4	1.9	5.0	1.8	1.0	0.8	1.0	2.5
Average repair/service completions per week	10.8	11.8	8.9	23.5[a]	8.7	4.9	3.7	4.9	12.9

Total calls per repair completion	1.3	1.4	1.8	1.1	1.4	1.2	1.4	1.5	1.3
Other calls (MAC) per day	3.9	3.6	3.3	9.0	16.8	14.7	13.8	1.8	7.6
Total calls per week	18.8	21.2	20.9	28.5	31.2	21.5	18.7	9.4	32.5
Site service calls avoided (%)	32	15	7	13	16	34	38	5	20
"Broken" calls due to lack of parts (%)	30	24	12	13	26	20	24	15	21
Calls fixed in same day (%)	46	58	97	87	25	12	7	65	58

a Random distribution.

Figure A.8 2002 Benchmark data; service call operational data (based on analysis of weekly calls per service person). (From Blumberg Associates, Inc., 1999–2001 data, Fort Washington, PA. With permission.)

Parameters	Technology								
	Information Technology	Office Automation and Office Products	Telecommunications	Retail, Financial, and Point of Sale	Medical Electronics	Building Automation	Industrial Plant Control	Home and Consumer Goods	General Industry
Acquisition costs (for parts) as a percent of total hardware service revenue (%)	46	33	25	22	28	30	32	38	31
Logistics operating costs as a percent of total costs (%)	10	11	9	13	12	10	12	15	11
Priority orders shipped same day (%)	96	85	89	86	94	79	80	90	88
DOA in field from logistics (%)	1	2	1	2	1	2	2	2	2
Percent of service calls requiring parts (%)	55	39	30	65	59	34	30	71c	49

Percent of call orders causing "broken" (incomplete or extended) calls due to lack of parts (%)	16	21	11	10	32	15[a]	12	10	17
Field personnel trunk stock fill rate (%)	42	36	72[c]	66	27[b]	31[a]	32[a]	72	50
Parts delivery source (%):									
Outside (UPS, FedEx, SonicAir)	85	70	83	79	94	78	80	5	81
Internal (company van, other field personnel)	12	25	13	18	2	8	6	21	14
Other (%)	3	5	4	3	4	14	14	4	5

[a] Skewed left.
[b] Binomial distribution.
[c] Extrapolated, based on internal and external data.

Figure A.9 Benchmark data; logistics parameters (mean). (From Blumberg Associates, Inc., 1999–2001 database, Fort Washington, Pa. With permission.)

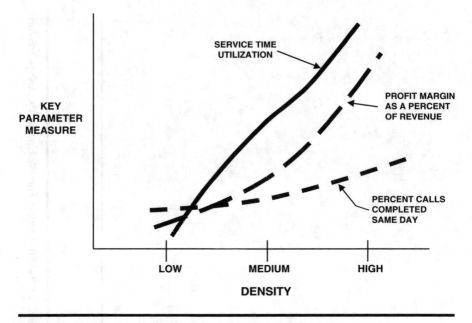

Figure A.10 Impact of density on key benchmark parameters.

1. OEM vs. independent service organizations, including third-party maintainer/multivendor equipment service and support
2. Geographic impact of operations in the United States vs. Europe
3. General financial parameters
4. Depot repair and fourth-party maintenance operations

This analysis is discussed further below.

Difference in Benchmark Parameters Between OEMs and ISOs

Our analysis clearly shows that there are some very real differences between the key benchmark parameters of service organizations operated as part of the original equipment manufacturers (OEMs) vs. parameters for independent service operators (ISOs) including third-party maintenance providers (TPMs) and separately operated multivendor equipment service (MVES) organizations. It is important to recognize that over the last 6 to 8 years, some OEMs have moved into the TPM/MVES business and have established separate profit or contribution centers for that purpose. Where such OEM type of operations exist and data were available, the data for those particular operations were included in our ISO analysis. The data clearly show that, while the revenues and profitability are higher for OEMs, the productivity and efficiency are lower as compared to the ISOs. This

Benchmark Parameters	Average	Best in Class
Revenue (including parts sales) per field person	$199,000	$319,000
Pretax profit per field engineer (%)	20	42
Completed calls per field engineers per day	2.5	6.6
Field fill rate (%)	59	97
Trunk stock fill (%)	50	59
Local re-supply (%)	9	38
Costs per field call	$206	$142
Skills costs	$76	$55
Parts costs	$68	$56
Travel and other costs	$62	$41
Percent calls avoided by field personnel (%)	24	38
Percent of calls resolved remotely by support center (%)	30	43
Utilization rate (without travel) (%)	57	88
Utilization rate (with travel) (%)	73	89
Percent contract of total revenue (%)	82	96
Basic services (%)	100	100
Added-value services (%)	51	91

Figure A.11 Key operational benchmark parameters for ISO/TPM organizations and firms. (From Blumberg Associates, Inc., 1999–2001 database, Fort Washington, PA. With permission.)

reflects, in part, the fact that service and support of OEM product sales have been traditionally viewed as a form of "annuity", with an associated attempt on the part of the manufacturers to prevent direct competition by extending warranty periods, withholding parts and diagnostics, etc. ISOs, on the other hand, have had to work harder and more efficiently due to a greater level of competition. The analysis of an historical trend seems to suggest that this difference will disappear over time as more OEMs enter into third-party and multivendor equipment service markets. Benchmark comparison data for OEMs and ISOs are shown in Figure A.11.

Geographic Differences

Figure A.12 shows the significant differences found in benchmarks for service operations operating only in the United States or Europe (i.e., through subsidiaries or independently), as compared to a global or industry-wide picture. Competitive data for the rest of the world, including the Far

Benchmark Parameters	Global	United States	Europe
Revenue (including parts sales) per field person	$199,000	$207,000	$191,000
Calls per field engineers per day	2.5	2.6	2.1
Field fill rate (%)	59	74	58
Trunk stock fill	54	62	48
Local resupply	9	12	10
Costs per field call	$206	$200	$225
Skill costs	$76	$74	$82
Parts costs	$68	$70	$78
Travel and other costs	$62	$56	$65
Percent calls avoided by field personnel (%)	24	28	18
Percent of calls resolved remotely by support center (%)	30	34	28
Utilization rate (without travel) (%)	57	59	52
Utilization rate (with travel) (%)	73	70	79
Percent contract of total revenue (%)	82	81	77
Basic services	100	100	100
Added-value services	51	47	42

Figure A.12   Key benchmarks reflecting geographic region differences. (From Blumberg Associates, Inc., 1999–2001 database, Fort Washington, PA. With permission.)

East/Pacific and Middle East, are simply not extensive enough to allow us to draw statistically valid comparisons. In addition, many of the service organizations outside the United States and Europe do not accurately report all the key parameters. The differences in the European service operations reflect, in part, the greater level of complexity in servicing across country barriers, lower density levels, and (in certain countries) a higher dependence on OEMs for service. Changes have taken place that are diminishing the degree of differentiation between the United States and Europe performance.

Financial Benchmark Ratios

A full analysis has also been carried out to examine and develop benchmark financial ratios and cost data, examining both revenue and expense components as a percentage of total revenue received. This information, as shown in Figure A.13, is segmented for the general industry as well as for OEMs and ISOs/third-party maintainers.

Financial Measurement	Type		General Industry Average (%)
	ISO/TPM/ MVES (%)	OEM (%)	
Revenue contract	77	61	70
Installation	6	14[a]	10[a]
Moves, adds, and changes (MAC)	3	7	5
Warranty	8	12[a]	9[a]
Time and materials	6	6	6
Labor	34	30	32
Freight	3	3	3
Auto/travel and per diem	7	8	7
Parts and logistics support	14	15	14
Handling/overhead	8	8	8
Administration and systems support	7	5	7
Advertising/marketing	8	8	8
Profit before taxes and S&GA	19	23	21

[a] Includes transfer payments from product divisions.

Figure A.13 Selected financial ratios and performance measurements. (From Blumberg Associates, Inc., 1999–2001 database, Fort Washington, PA. With permission.)

Benchmarking of Depot Repair Operations

Data obtained in the past have been updated and provide an improved ability to assess and evaluate key parameters associated with depot repair operations. The two types of repair depots are:

1. *Internally oriented.* These depots are utilized only in support of the internal logistics pipeline for a given service organization. Repair volumes are constrained and focused only in support of the logistics infrastructure required to sustain a given field service force, supporting an installed equipment base/parc or product line.
2. *External repair depots.* A new class of depots that have been emerging over the last 10 to 12 years includes those that are run independently as a profit or contribution center or independent line of business. These organizations may be supporting a specific logis-

tics infrastructure, but their repair volumes are not constrained by just internal support; they are capable, and in fact, extend proactively into the development, of increased volumes from the overall marketplace. This type of process, called fourth-party maintenance, allows the depot to achieve significantly greater economies of scale.

The general benchmark parameters for both internal and external (fourth-party maintenance) depots, on an average basis and at the most productive level, are reported in Figure A.14.

Parameters	Internal Depot		External Depot[c]	
	Average Experience	"Best Practices" Efficiently Run	Average Experience	"Best Practices" Efficiently Run
Profit margin or contribution of depot repair (%)	0 (breakeven)	6	16	29
Average unit repair cost ($)	78	59	53	40
Repair time turnaround (days)	10	5	4	3
Field dead on arrival (DOA)[a] (%)	3	2	2	1
Receipt no trouble found (NTF) at recovery[b] (%)	7	20	11	23
Bench tech labor and supplier costs as a percentage of total costs (%)	46	41	35	24
Transportation costs as a percentage of total cost (%)	12	7	11	7

[a] Measure of repair quality.
[b] Measure of receiving processing quality.
[c] Run as a line of business.

Figure A.14 Benchmark parameters for operations of internal repair depot and external (fourth-party) depot repair operations (based on 32 repair depots). (From Blumberg Associates, Inc., 1999–2001 database, Fort Washington, PA. With permission.)

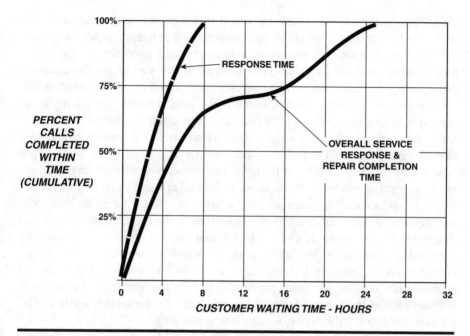

Figure A.15 Typical cumulative response and overall repair time distribution performance (based on 1994 data from 45 companies).

Key Service Response and Repair Time Distribution Evaluation

Data on cumulative distribution of service response and repair time have also been updated, as shown in Figure A.15. These service performance curves are extremely useful when compared to equivalent required service response and repair time demands from customers or market segments. In essence, a similar cumulative requirement pattern can be developed (through customer- and market-oriented large-scale surveys). Adjusting service performance to just meet this cumulative service requirement provides an efficient performance profile to use for optimizing service performance against customer service requirements. The information portrayed in Figure A.15 shows general performance based on experience, primarily for the data-processing, office automation, telecommunications, and financial/point-of-sale service technologies.

IDENTIFICATION AND ASSESSMENT OF CRITICAL PARAMETERS

The extended benchmark data provides the ability to examine, dynamically, multiple benchmarks as well as providing the basis for identifying key underlying phenomena of certain critical benchmarks. As indicated earlier, we have found that both economies of scale and density factors impact a service organization's productivity, efficiency, and profitability. However, a detailed analysis of the relationship between the size of the field service engineering organization and key service call parameters shows that, while economies of scale do exist, the impact is not smooth; for example, as reported in our earlier study, overall call closure time appeared to be best for organizations with 101 to 250 field personnel. We initially suggested that a certain size of clusters or work groups appeared to be better than others with respect to service performance. However, further investigation now shows that this tends to be more reflective of the differences in central vs. regional or local dispatch and the degree of use of computerized tools and techniques for artificial-intelligence-based decision support and call diagnostics. Our research also indicates that certain types of technologies serviced require more preventive and predictive maintenance calls, installations, moves, adds, and changes. In addition, electrical and mechanical technologies tend to be much more affected by preventive and scheduled maintenance than purely electronic technology. This explains some of the differences among the technologies being serviced.

Our research also shows that the efficiency of logistics organizations, in general, and particularly the use of full logistics pipeline control (down to the service engineer trunk stock) can directly affect field service performance. Where the full logistics pipeline is totally controlled, improved service productivity in terms of a reduction in the number of "broken" calls and an increase in on-site service call completion rates can occur. Results of using the new benchmark data for specific areas of investigation are discussed below.

Impact of Density on Service Profitability

In our previous reports, we have already shown that service profit before tax is significantly affected by increased density of installed base (see Figure A.16). Our new analysis, as shown in Figure A.17, also indicates the degree of impact on profit improvement due to density and integrated systems function. The application of sophisticated and integrated call handling and dispatch, as well as logistics control systems, produces improved profitability, particularly where the density is very high.

Impact of Improved Call Avoidance and TAC Deployment on Utilization

We have also examined benchmarks dealing with the effect of technical assistance centers (TACs) and call avoidance mechanisms on service calls

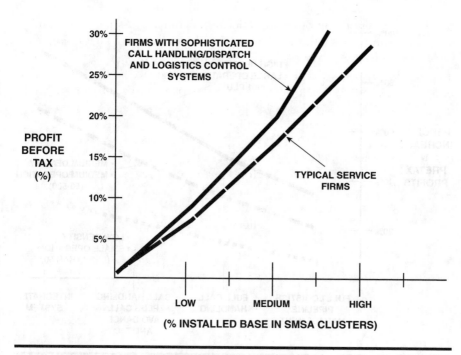

Figure A.16   Impact of density on service profitability.

costs. As shown in Figure A.18, we can identify an optimum range with respect to a trade-off between calls avoided and on-site site calls, as a function of technology serviced. In essence, the expense of call diagnostics and call avoidance rises sharply, as compared to the costs of on-site calls over a certain range. Our analysis suggests that the maximum payoff can be achieved in the range of 33 to 44% call avoidance, particularly in high technology such as data processing and telecommunications and networks. In this regard, the actual number of calls completed per service engineer per day is also a critically important benchmark parameter. As shown in Figure A.19, we can clearly see that the number of service calls completed by a service engineer per day will influence both revenues and pretax profits.

Because a high percentage of on-site calls require parts, logistics support and particularly full logistics pipeline control will also have a direct effect on calls per completed call. As shown in Figure A.20, parts can be delivered to service personnel on a timely basis to avoid "broken" calls through assigned field personnel trunk stock combined with rapid courier resupply on a timely basis or by nearby field personnel. As the total observed site fill rate increases towards 100%, "broken" calls due to lack of parts drop significantly. Our data suggest that the optimum solution for achieving a given full stock fill rate at the site would be to use a

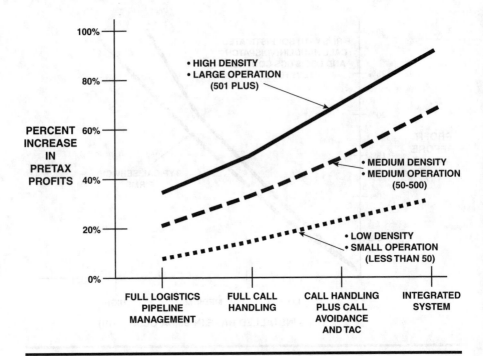

Figure A.17 System and infrastructure impact on pretax profits.

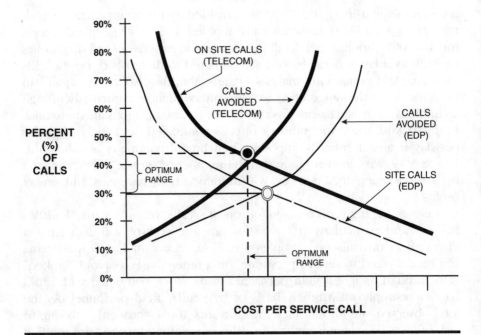

Figure A.18 Optimum use of TAC and call avoidance.

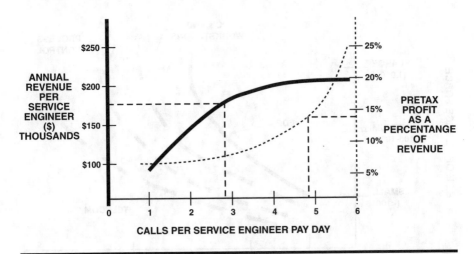

Figure A.19 Revenue and profit percentage as a result of service engineer calls per day.

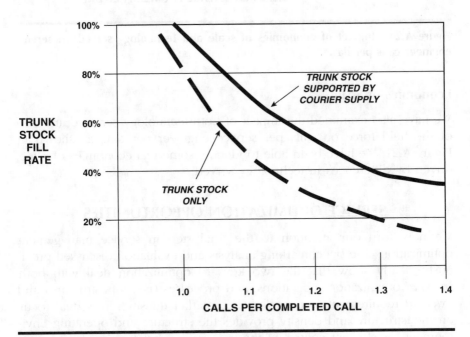

Figure A.20 Impact of logistics support on call efficiency.

combination of optimized trunk stock based upon detailed forecasting of parts failure and demand, plus a superimposed rapid resupply by same-day courier service in the event of a trunk stock out.

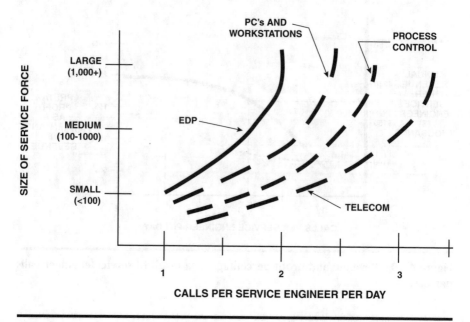

Figure A.21 Impact of economies of scale and technology served on service engineer calls per day.

Economies of Scale

We have also examined the impact of both technology serviced and size of the field force on calls per service engineer per day, as shown in Figure A.21. We have been able to identify some real economies of scale, driven by differences in technology served.

SERVICE OPTIMIZATION OPPORTUNITIES

We now turn our attention to the final step in service management optimization. The benchmarking analysis and evaluation discussed previously clearly show that the two keys to optimization deal with both *internal* organization, operations, and processes (i.e., infrastructure) and *external* requirements for service (i.e., market density). This dual focus on infrastructure and density provides the structure and operating environment for efficient control of the two major resources involved:

■ Service personnel
■ Material and logistics

Our studies show that labor typically represents 50 to 65% of total costs, and parts/logistics account for an additional 12 to 18% of costs; however,

(MEAN)

PARAMETER MEASUREMENT	BEST PRACTICE COMPANY*	TYPICAL FIRM	PERCENT IMPROVEMENT
REVENUE PER FIELD ENGINEER	$254K	$178K	43%
PRETAX PROFIT PER FIELD ENGINEER (FE)	41%	18%	128%
CALLS PER FE PER DAY	6.6	2.4	175%
PERCENT OF CALLS AVOIDED BY FE	36%	21%	71%
PERCENT OF CALLS RESOLVED BY REMOTELY BY SUPPORT CENTER	40%	28%	43%
FE UTILIZATION**	86%	55%	56%
COST PER CALL	$143	$208	45%

* Based on Cross Representative Sample Evaluation of Firms in IT / Telecomm / Medical with 250 or more   Fes
** Without travel

Figure A.22   Key operating benchmarks associated with field service optimization.

approximately 60 to 75% of all required service calls require at least one part or item of supply. Thus, logistics represents the largest investment and the second largest operating expense. It also affects the productivity of the labor component, which is the highest cost. Lack of parts at the right place at the right time reduces the efficiency of labor utilization.

Based on this evaluation we have isolated two key operating benchmarks offering the greatest impact on service performance in the field and bottom-line profitability:

- *Benchmarks associated with service personnel.* The key benchmarks that can be related to service force improvement are shown in Figure A.22. As indicated, by comparing best practices to averages, we can determine the level of improvement that could be expected.
- *Benchmarks associated with service logistics.* A similar analysis of key logistics benchmarks is shown in Figure A.23. Here, again, the opportunities for improvement to achieve optimization are calculated by comparing best-practice firms to averages.

It is clear that through this analysis that a great deal of opportunity exists for improvement in the typical service firm through optimization evaluation. A separate study of mechanisms for service optimization is available (*Field Service Optimization: Oxymoron or Major Opportunity?*, Blumberg Associates, Inc., 2002).

PARAMETER MEASUREMENT	(MEAN) BEST PRACTICE COMPANY*	TYPICAL FIRM	PERCENT IMPROVEMENT
TOTAL CALLS PER REPAIR COMPLETION	1.1	1.4	21%
% OR CALLS "BROKEN" DUE TO LACK OF PARTS	14%	26%	46%
FIELD FILL RATE	92%	52%	77%
RESUPPLY RATE IN DAYS	180	300	40%
REPAIR TURNAROUND (IN DAYS)	3.2	5.8	45
FIELD DEAD ON ARRIVAL (DOA)	1%	2%	50%
TRANSPORTATION COSTS AS A PERCENT OF TOTAL COSTS	8%	11%	27%
LOGISTICS OPERATING COSTS AT A % OF TOTAL COSTS	10%	13%	23%

* Based on Cross Representative Sample Evaluation of Firms in IT / Telecomm / Medical with 250 or more Fes

Figure A.23 Key operating parameters associated with service logistics, parts planning, and forecasting.

RECOMMENDED BENCHMARK TARGETS

Based upon an assessment and evaluation of BAI's total database, the results of extensive dynamic parameter assessment and evaluation of service optimization, and the use of the BAI's ServiceFORCE model in approximately 75 specific strategic planning assignments, we have identified 14 key parameters or targets that seem to be most useful in managing service as a strategic line of business. These key parameters represent critical measures of performance, customer satisfaction, productivity, and profitability and are in certain cases drivers of general efficiency levels. This benchmark best-practice list, shown in Figure A.24, is not, of course, the only solution, but it does represent a fairly definitive view of a competitive or "best-in-class" operation for the technologies and regions considered in this evaluation. This information is provided in terms of both a target and critical threshold below or above which action should be taken. We intend, of course, to update this set of "Blumberg's Best Benchmark Basics" over time as additional data and research are developed.

SUMMARY

We have presented a complete array of benchmark data for six major technologies serviced based upon extensive research carried out over a 3-year period, involving over 130 service organizations. We believe that this benchmark data can be extremely useful in analyzing and evaluating service operations and identifying the opportunities for productivity improvement.

Focus	Measures	Recommended Benchmark Targets[b]	Critical Threshold Test	Comment
General	Revenue per service engineer	$199,000	$138,000	Measures value-added contribution.
	Gross profit margin[a] as a percentage of revenue per service person	54%	35%	Net of corporate contribution; may not be applicable if service is a cost center.
	Direct service personnel budget divided by total service budget	0.7	Above 0.8; below 0.5	Good measure of efficiency: Too high a ratio indicates not enough support; too low a ratio indicates support inefficiency.
Customer service	Customer call waiting time (wait time on phone)	15 sec	30 sec	Customers reporting service problems should not be kept waiting (affects customers satisfaction).
	Customer call hang-ups (abort)	1%	3%	Measures customer dissatisfaction.
	Percent compliance with ETA as given	90%	75%	ETA commitment and compliance are critical factors.
	Customer response time (call received to initiation of call action onsite)	3.5 hr	6 hr	Good direct measure of responsiveness.

Category	Measure			Description
	Percent calls completed same day	80%	50%	Indirect measure of service productivity affected by, for example, density, equipment, mean time between failure, and mean time to repair.
Operational	Service time utilization (actual service time divided by total service time available)	75%	50%	Good measure of field personnel productivity; related to responsiveness.
	Actual call closure time divided by targeted closure times[b]	0.9	0.6	Excellent measure of service performance; requires establishing customer targets.
	Calls per completed call	1.1	1.3	Measures service engineer efficiency.
Logistics	Percent calls broken due to lack of parts	15%	25%	Excellent measure of logistics efficiency.
	Percent PI shipped same day	90%	70%	Measure of warehouse efficiency.
	Repair turnaround time	5 days	8 days	Measures depot repair efficiency.

[a] Before taxes and corporate allocations.
[b] Targets based on formal customer determined time frames.

Figure A.24 Blumberg's best benchmarks: key service benchmark targets for ISOs. (From Blumberg Associates, Inc., 1999–2001 database, Fort Washington, PA. With permission.)

Appendix B

A NEW STRATEGIC VIEW OF THE U.S. SERVICE MARKET SIZE, STRUCTURE, SEGMENTATION, AND TRENDS

CONTENTS

INTRODUCTION

In the early days of high-tech companies, service was viewed as a necessity useful primarily for maintaining customer satisfaction; however, service was secondary to product and production-related issues and was often given away as a product pull-through device. Today, successful high-tech companies understand that service is a strategic, integral part of their business, an excellent source of profit, and a key mechanism for market and account control. Furthermore, service strategy and quality are ways in which competing companies and their leaders can differentiate themselves in a crowded marketplace. This aspect of strategic service has also caught the attention of executives outside the realm of high-tech companies, as original equipment manufacturers (OEMs) in more traditional industrial and manufacturing sectors seek ways to offset shrinking profit margins and increased competition in commodity markets.

Keeping abreast of emerging trends and market requirements for service is a major factor contributing to success in the complex service marketplace. It is crucial for service organizations to benchmark themselves against competitors and against the needs of the market. The assessment of service market size, structure, and segment dimensions offered here will provide service managers with tools to evaluate the changing service market and judge their company's "fit" within this dynamic environment. This analysis includes:

- *Overview of the service market.* The overview focuses on definitions of service and types of service organizations. It will also discuss the dynamic relationships among players in the service market.
- *Discussion of the U.S. service market.* The analysis of the service market in the U.S. includes estimates of the total value of service market demand, expected growth rates, and factors driving growth. It also segments the U.S. market by industry and by service type (i.e., professional services, field service, and logistics support services). Finally, the discussion focuses on trends influencing employment of personnel in the service industry.
- *Analysis of service organizations.* An analysis of service organizations based on BAI's expertise and research examines the size distribution and ownership distribution of service organizations by equipment category at both the company and establishment levels. It also includes estimates of the size of the service forces supporting various equipment categories.

OVERVIEW OF THE SERVICE MARKET

Service can generally be described as a result of useful labor that does not produce a tangible commodity or as the provision of business functions auxiliary to production or distribution. In many contexts, service is taken to mean simply maintenance and repair; however, BAI describes it in more general terms: as assistance provided to another individual or group.

As such, services can be categorized in a variety of ways, one of which is to look at customer service vs. after-sales service. Customer service is used here to mean service provided before the sale. Conversely, after-sales service, including field service and depot service, is provided after the product sale is made or represents an independent sale without a direct product link. When "service" is mentioned in casual conversation, it is usually used to refer to customer service; however, this analysis will concentrate on after-sales service, including many types of basic, value-added, and professional after-sales services and support.

Several different kinds of players can be found within the framework of the field service market, each of which generally operates two types of service organizations, external and internal:

- *Product-based service vendors* — OEMs and value-added resellers dealing with technologies such as computers, telecommunications equipment, office products, medical electronics
- *Functional or traditional service vendors* — hospitals, banks, distributors, utilities
- *Independent service vendors* — third-party maintainers, fourth-party depot service providers

In addition to these key players, the total service market also encompasses vendors of products and services that sell to the field service market. These include field service management system vendors, test equipment manufacturers and distributors, training firms, consulting firms, and communications service providers. The total set of organizations and players in the field service market is depicted in Figure B.1.

Regardless of the type of service organization under consideration, three general types of services can be included in a provider's service portfolio:

- *Basic services*, including primarily traditional maintenance and repair functions
- *Value-added and professional services*, including design and engineering, system integration, consulting, training
- *Other support services*, including logistics support, facilities management, depot repair and parts, software support

While not all of the individual services in each group apply to every market segment, virtually all market segments have some elements of all three groups that are relevant to end-users and service providers.

BAI anticipates high growth for vendors supporting the service market between the 2002–2010 time frame. The highest growth rate will be for communications systems service. This segment is predicted to grow by 21.6%

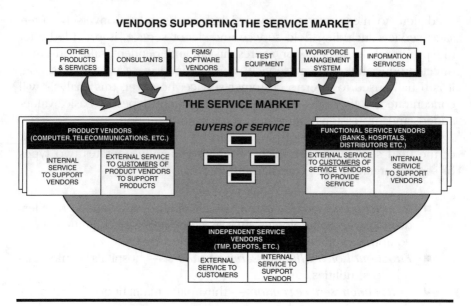

Figure B.1   Overall service market.

annually to almost $6.8 billion by 2004 (see Figure B.2). Several service industry segments are predicted to increase their demand for use of field communications and field service management systems by over 18% annually, including medical electronics, information technology, and communications (see Figure B.3). In addition, the way in which field service management and facilities management systems are being developed is expected to change dramatically over the next 5 years. As newer, more cost-effective, and more sophisticated off-the-shelf software systems have become available, the market for internally developed service and facilities management software has and is expected to continue to decline at a rate of over 17% annually (see Figure B.4).

In the past, the total service market was fragmented and characterized by many highly specialized companies with numerous and complex buyer–seller relationships. BAI has recently presented numerous studies showing a strong preference among service users for dealing with a single point of contact for service. Consistent with these findings, a great deal of consolidation has taken place in the service industry in recent years. Large national and international independent and OEM-operated service organizations have emerged in such industries as information technology, communications and networks, printing and publishing, and process control and automation, among others. At the same time, the number of small service organizations has experienced remarkable growth, particularly

Type of Systems	Year							CAGR (%)
	1998	1999	2000	2001	2002	2003	2004	
Facilities maintenance management[a]	3669	4197	4802	5493	6284	7189	8224	14.4
Field service management[b]	2530	2882	3283	3739	4259	4851	5525	13.9
Field communications[c]	2100	2554	3106	3777	4594	5586	6794	21.6
Total	8299	9633	11,190	13,009	15,136	17,626	20,543	16.3

[a] Facilities maintenance management systems (include sales of software applications).
[b] Field service management systems (include sales of field service management software applications and hardware).
[c] Field communications applications and hardware (include connectivity, hardware, software).

Figure B.2 Total market for facilities maintenance management systems, field service management systems, and field communications technology. (From Blumberg Associates, Inc., studies of FSMS and related markets, Fort Washington, PA. With permission.)

Technology Segments	Year							CAGR (%)
	1998	1999	2000	2001	2002	2003	2004	
Information systems	1041.8	1250.3	1475.8	1714.3	1998.7	2323.6	2894.9	18.6
Office automation/data-processing equipment	486.2	543.6	606.9	667.9	729.1	791.0	985.5	12.5
Telecommunications/network equipment	801.0	951.3	1130.8	1328.4	1544.1	1789.7	2229.7	18.6
Medical electronics	268.5	326.2	389.7	460.1	540.4	632.8	788.4	19.7
Process control/plant automation	726.9	869.8	1041.4	1231.9	1449.7	1680.9	2094.2	19.3
Building systems/HVAC	310.2	326.2	370.6	423.0	480.4	543.8	677.5	13.9
Retail, point of sale, customer service equipment	680.6	804.5	951.9	1113.2	1286.7	1502.9	1872.5	18.4
Other	314.8	364.2	421.7	482.4	549.0	622.9	776.1	16.2
Total	4630.0	5436.0	6388.8	7421.1	8578.2	9887.7	12,318.8	17.7

Note: Total equals the total market for field service management systems and field communications, including hardware, software, and support services (connectivity, etc.).

Figure B.3 Total market for FSMS and field communications by type of technology serviced ($ million). (From Blumberg Associates, Inc., studies of FSMS and related markets, Fort Washington, PA. With permission.)

| System Origin | Year | | | | | | CAGR (%) |
	1998	1999	2000	2001	2002	2003	2004	
Internally developed	2386.6	2258.2	2053.4	1781.7	1296.7	878.9	728.7	−17.9
Standard, off the shelf	3812.4	4820.8	6030.9	7450.1	9245.9	11,160.7	13,020.3	22.7
Total	6199.0	7079.0	8084.3	9231.9	10,542.6	12,039.6	13,749.0	14.2

Source: BAI studies of FSMS and related markets.

Figure B.4 Total market for FSMS and FMMS systems by system origin. (From Blumberg Associates, Inc., studies of FSMS and related markets, Fort Washington, PA. With permission.)

TYPE			INTERNAL	EXTERNAL	INDEPENDENT
I N D U S T R Y S E C T O R S	MANUFACTURING	DISCRETE PRODUCTS			
		CONTINOUS PRODUCTS			
	FINANCIAL/BANKING/INSURANCE				
	HEALTH CARE				
	WHOLESALE/RETAIL/TRADE				
	UTILITIES				
	COMMUNICATIONS				
	TRANSPORTATION/DISTRIBUTION				
	EDUCATION/RESEARCH				
	OTHER SERVICES				
	GOVERNMENT	FEDERAL			
		STATE/LOCAL			

Figure B.5   General structure of the service market.

supporting technologies such as computers and networks serving local and regional markets. The general structure of the service market is shown in Figure B.5.

Service organizations generally focus on providing support for a particular type of product or deliverable service function. For example, the service company may specialize in providing support for one type of technology such as computers, ATMs, or televisions. Alternatively, the service organization may support a deliverable service function such as health care, banking, food service, or legal services. In this situation, the service organization supports the many types of equipment necessary, for example, to provide healthcare or banking services. Regardless of technology or functional service focus, the service organization of the 1990s is much more likely to provide multivendor service offerings than its predecessors. Furthermore, this trend holds for independent and OEM-owned organizations. Building on this and other market trends, a significant number of hybrid service organizations have emerged in the 1990s that "cross over" by covering multiple technologies and multiple service functions. Over time, then, the sellers of service are becoming much more sophisticated and complex in order to facilitate the simpler relationships buyers desire.

DISCUSSION OF THE U.S. SERVICE MARKET

The service market in the United States is growing rapidly in terms of size and complexity. BAI estimates that the total high-technology services market for 1998 (including field maintenance and repair, professional and technical services, and logistics and other support services) is worth $298 billion and will grow to $604.4 billion by the year 2004, representing a compound annual growth rate (CAGR) of 12.5%. Detailed demand estimates and growth by service industry segment are given in Figure B.6.

Factors driving the growth of the service industry include:

■ Service organizations owned by dealers or independent service organizations (ISOs) are being created because many types of OEMs are willing to outsource service of their equipment to third parties.

■ OEMs that choose to maintain service organizations rather than outsource services are realizing the benefits of strategic multivendor, multiple-technology service organizations organized as profit centers.

■ The growing complexity and interconnectedness of technology create a greater need for highly skilled repair and support technicians.

■ Integration of technologies into local area networks (LANs) and wide area networks (WANs) complicates maintenance and repair and necessitates more value-added and professional services.

■ Growth in markets that have the largest installed base of high-tech equipment creates a greater need for sophisticated maintenance and repair services.

■ End-users of service, ever more cost- and quality-conscious in their own operations, have discovered that increased service levels often help them to maintain or improve their bottom line and are willing to pay for these services.

The market for field maintenance and repair reached $176 billion in 1998. BAI estimates that this will increase to $293.8 billion by 2004, representing a CAGR of 8.9% (see Figure B.6). Field maintenance and repair for process and environmental controls, ATMs, and point of sale and building automation technologies will be the fastest growing segments of basic field service. The largest maintenance and repair segments, however, will continue to be computers and data-processing equipment, voice/data integrated LANs, and office technologies.

Among the three categories of service researched in this study, professional and technical services will experience the most rapid growth. BAI estimates this segment is worth $86.2 billion currently and anticipates that it will grow to $244.6 billion by 2004, representing a CAGR of 19% (see Figure B.6). Included in this aggregated view of the professional and

Service Category	Equipment/Service Type	Year							CAGR (%)
		1998	1999	2000	2001	2002	2003	2004	
Field maintenance and repair									
	Computer/data processing	33.6	36.6	40.5	44.6	49.0	54.0	59.4	9.9
	Standalone communications	17.8	18.8	20.0	21.1	22.3	23.6	25.0	5.8
	Office automation and technology	37.5	41.6	44.9	49.0	53.6	58.3	63.6	9.2
	Voice data/integrated LAN	28.0	31.6	33.5	37.8	41.8	45.9	51.0	10.5
	Process/environmental controls/networks	13.0	14.8	16.9	19.2	21.9	25.0	28.4	13.9
	Other facility and plant technology	10.3	10.7	11.1	11.6	12.0	12.5	13.1	4.1
	Building automation	4.0	4.6	5.4	6.2	7.2	8.4	9.7	16.0
	Other building technology (HVAC, etc.)	22.4	22.9	23.4	23.9	24.3	24.8	25.4	2.1
	Medical electronics	5.7	6.3	6.9	7.6	8.3	9.2	10.1	10.0
	ATM/point-of-sale	2.9	3.3	3.8	4.3	4.9	5.6	6.3	14.0
	Other maintenance and repair	1.0	1.1	1.2	1.4	1.5	1.6	1.8	10.4
Subtotal maintenance and repair services		176.2	192.3	207.4	226.6	246.9	268.9	293.8	8.9
Professional and technical services market									
	General management consulting	16.0	19.5	23.7	29.0	35.3	43.1	52.6	22.0
	General design and engineering	8.4	9.5	10.8	12.3	13.9	15.7	17.9	13.4

Commercial information systems	8.9	10.3	11.8	13.6	15.6	17.9	20.6	14.9
Government and military systems	3.9	4.0	4.1	4.2	4.3	4.4	4.5	2.5
Process control/plant automation	20.9	24.3	30.5	37.8	46.1	57.1	70.3	22.4
Network systems (LAN/WAN, wireless)	28.1	33.7	39.1	47.0	55.8	66.1	78.7	18.8
Subtotal: professional services	86.2	101.2	120.0	143.8	171.0	204.3	244.6	19.0
Logistics and other support services								
Depot repair and parts	6.8	7.8	8.7	9.9	11.2	12.6	14.2	13.0
Software support and service	8.3	8.7	9.1	9.7	10.2	10.7	11.3	5.4
Facilities management	7.3	7.9	8.6	9.4	10.1	11.0	12.0	8.5
Logistics support	4.8	5.7	6.7	8.0	9.4	11.2	13.3	18.5
Other support	8.3	9.2	10.2	11.3	12.4	13.7	15.2	10.5
Subtotal: logistics	35.6	39.3	43.4	48.1	53.4	59.3	66.0	10.8
Total: service market	298.0	332.8	370.8	418.5	471.3	532.5	604.4	12.5

Figure B.6 Total U.S. high-tech service market forecast by service/equipment category ($ billions). (From Blumberg Associates, Inc., worldwide high-tech service industry database, Fort Washington, PA. With permission.)

technical services category are general management consulting, general design and engineering, systems integration for commercial or military systems, process control/plant automation systems integration, and network systems integration. General management consulting, network systems integration, and process control or plant automation network systems show the best opportunities for growth in the professional and technical services category. In the case of professional and technical services, the fastest growing are also the largest segments of the market.

Combined demand for logistics and other support services was estimated at nearly $36 billion in 1998 and is anticipated to grow to $66 billion by 2004, representing a CAGR of 10.8% (see Figure B.6). Logistics support and depot repair will have the highest growth rates in this segment. BAI expects the independent or fourth-party depot repair market to reach $14.2 billion by the year 2004.

Growth in the service market is changing the environment for employment of high-tech service professionals. Two important trends affecting employment in the service market are the increasing complexity of technology and the proliferation of ISO-owned and dealer-owned service organizations. These trends are discussed below:

- *Increasing complexity of technology.* Increasingly sophisticated technology has created a need for higher skill levels and better training. The number of technical workers with college degrees will continue to increase, as will the emphasis on technical certification and training for service technicians.
- *Proliferation of ISO- and dealer-owned service organizations.* Service organizations are growing rapidly in size and number. For most equipment categories, growth has been the highest in service organizations that are owned by independent service organizations. Consequently, ISO-owned service organizations represent expanding employment opportunities for service professionals, as do dealer-owned organizations in some technology segments. Conversely, manufacturers in these same industry segments are employing fewer service personnel as they outsource a greater portion of their service work.

AN ANALYSIS OF SERVICE ORGANIZATIONS

Up to this point, we have addressed the general framework of the service market and the demand structure of the U.S. service industry. In order to fully understand this dynamic market, it is also necessary to examine the characteristics of service organizations that currently operate in the service environment.

For the purposes of this analysis, BAI examined characteristics of service providers at two levels:

- *Service organizations* are internal, external, or independent business entities (independent companies, divisions, departments, etc.) that engage in providing service to one or more technologies or market segments.
- *Service establishments* are individual operating locations of service organizations (field offices, repair depots, call centers, etc.) that may or may not have some operational autonomy relative to their owner organization.

A service organization, then, may consist of one or more service establishments of various sizes and types. Typically, small service organizations operate one establishment, while large service organizations operate many establishments.

BAI's process for segmenting the service market in terms of service organizations is threefold. First, the ownership of service organizations in high-tech and related equipment categories will be examined. Second, the size distributions of service organizations and their owned establishments by technology segment are investigated and compared. Third, trends in the distribution of service establishments are examined to reveal key evidence of structural change in the U.S. service market.

Ownership Distribution of Service Organizations

The ownership of service organizations can be described as manufacturer owned, dealer or distributor owned, or ISO/TPM owned. BAI's estimates show that nearly 33% of all service organizations are owned by dealers or distributors, a figure that represents a decrease in the proportion in this category compared to past estimates and reflects the emergence of ISOs in many local and regional service niches previously occupied by dealers and distributors. Over 62% of service organizations are owned by ISOs, the largest single ownership category, and the remaining 5% are owned by manufacturers. A sharp increase in the proportion of ISO-owned service organizations has been observed in recent years, especially in the smaller size categories, as will be shown later. Figure B.7 summarizes the ownership of service organizations by equipment category.

Some equipment categories are supported primarily by ISO-owned service groups, while others are serviced mainly by dealer-owned service organizations. Very few high-tech equipment categories have a manufacturer as their primary service provider.

Equipment Class	OEM	Dealer	ISO/TPM	Total
Information technology	7853	32,122	24,397	64,372
Office products and equipment	1251	6103	259	7612
Telecommunications/datacom	886	16,335	25,767	42,988
Medical/scientific equipment	2,908	4333	904	8145
Process control/plant automation	4449	5896	533	10,878
Retail and food equipment	560	11,290	1677	13,527
Radio, television, appliance	366	18,223	1727	20,316
Building equipment and systems	3071	36,763	99,944	139,778
Aerospace/airline services	1415	725	1483	3623
Transportation (except air)	518	7247	12,942	20,707
Automotive and other vehicles	1963	20,717	128,318	150,998
Public utilities	0	0	7680	7680
Total	25,239	159,754	305,631	490,624

Figure B.7 **Estimated number of U.S. service organizations by equipment class and owner. (From Blumberg Associates, Inc., worldwide high-tech service industry database, Fort Washington, PA, with permission; U.S. Department of Commerce.)**

Dealers and distributors remain the dominant service provider category in a number of technology segments where they have traditionally played a large role:

- Retail and food service systems and equipment
- Radio, television, and appliances
- Medical/scientific equipment
- Office products and equipment

In addition, dealers and distributors are currently the majority providers but are losing share in the information technology and process control/plant automation segments. The information technology equipment category is populated by large numbers of both dealer-owned and ISO-owned service groups. In recent years, ISOs servicing the information technology industry have multiplied, as OEMs outsource more of their service work to multiple-technology, multivendor service organizations. In the case of process control/plant automation technologies, a number of OEMs have begun to pursue service strategies to help offset the thinning margins created by the gradual commoditization of their technologies.

The emergence and growth of ISOs in most other technology segments gives them a predominant position in:

- Telecommunications and data communications
- Building equipment and systems
- Transportation and automotive
- Utilities

While the building equipment, transportation/automotive, and utilities categories have been the traditional strongholds of ISOs, the telecommunications/data communications segment was dominated by OEMs and dealers/distributors as recently as the early 1990s. This technology segment has played host to a virtual explosion of both small and large ISOs as the installed base of public and private network equipment has expanded rapidly throughout virtually every industry and governmental organization, and even into the home environment.

The single remaining technology segment, aerospace and airline services, is almost evenly divided between OEMs and ISOs. While this is the only technology segment characterized by a relatively large OEM presence in terms of the number of service organizations, it is important to note that many of the largest service organizations in the overall service market are those operated by OEMs. In this sense, the ownership distribution of service organizations tells only one valuable part of the entire service market story.

Size Distribution of Service Organizations and Their Establishments

The size of a company's service force is directly related to three major factors: (1) overall size of the company, (2) type of ownership, and (3) equipment category that it supports. For example, companies with a large total employment size tend to have larger service forces. In addition, certain equipment categories require higher levels of support than others and are characterized by large service organizations. Figure B.8 presents the size distribution of the nearly 500,000 service organizations identified for all 12 technology segments.

A composite picture of BAI's independent survey research on service organizations shows that the percentage of total employment represented by the service force is directly influenced by the ownership type of the service organization. On average, approximately 26% of the total workforce of an OEM that operates a service organization is represented by service personnel. In contrast, service technicians comprise roughly 40% of the workforce of a similar dealer or distributor. Not surprisingly, ISO/TPMs have the largest service forces as a percentage of total employment. ISO/TPM service personnel represent 85% of the total workforce on average.

An analysis of the number of service technicians employed by each service organization reveals a large number of small service organizations supporting most equipment types. In the overall service market, the largest percentage of service organizations, nearly 60%, employ between 1 and 4 service technicians (see Figure B.8). Another 35% employ 5 to 50 service technicians, leaving only 5% of service organizations with 51 or more service personnel. While less than 700 service organizations employ more than 1000 service personnel, many of these are very large and are significant or dominant players in their primary market segments and niches. Although these general patterns hold across equipment categories, significant differences exist that are worth some discussion.

Three technology segments are skewed more heavily toward very small organizations than the general service market, with more than 60% having 1 to 4 service technicians:

- Information technology
- Radio, television, and appliances
- Automotive and other vehicles

Three other equipment categories tend to be supported by somewhat larger service organizations that employ 5 to 50 service technicians. These equipment classes register more than 20% of organizations in the 5–9 and 10–50 categories:

- Office products and equipment
- Process control and plant automation
- Retail and food equipment

Three technology segments contain an above-average concentration of organizations in this category:

- Medical and scientific equipment
- Aerospace and airlines
- Utilities

Although less than 1% of all service organizations have 501 or more service personnel, these organizations are often of the greatest strategic significance to companies contemplating the development of a new strategic

Size by Number of Firms

Equipment Class Serviced	1–4	5–9	10–50	51–100	101–500	501–1000	>1000	Total
Information technology	43,641	8816	9439	1305	957	100	114	64,372
Office products and equipment	3684	1703	1850	210	134	15	16	7612
Telecommunications/datacom	25,124	8486	7996	805	516	32	29	42,988
Medical/scientific equipment	2884	1719	2645	399	386	48	64	8145
Process control/plant automation	4472	2414	3227	397	314	29	25	10,878
Retail and food equipment	7319	2914	2927	240	117	6	4	13,527
Radio, television, appliance	13,307	3344	2643	532	452	23	15	20,316
Building equipment and systems	80,902	28,129	26,104	2435	1989	134	85	139,778
Aerospace/airline services	1640	647	950	168	156	18	44	3623
Transportation (except air)	11,422	4006	4053	578	531	60	57	20,707
Automotive and other vehicles	93,878	27,417	19,063	2475	8072	45	48	150,998
Public utilities	3740	1365	1514	492	364	49	156	7680
Total	292,013	90,960	82,411	10,036	13,988	559	657	490,624

Figure B.8   Size distribution of service organizations (number of organizations by service force size and industry supported). (From Blumberg Associates, Inc., worldwide high-tech service industry database, Fort Washington, PA, with permission; U.S. Department of Commerce.)

service organization, or enhancement of an existing one. Technology segments that have more than 200 of these very large service organizations include:

- Information technology
- Building equipment and systems
- Utilities

As discussed at the beginning of this section, a single service organization may own and operate multiple service establishments. These establishments may be external, such as branch offices, stand-alone repair depots, or call centers, or they may be internal, such as maintenance operations at different plants or regional technical support centers for information technology. Figure B.9 gives the size distribution of service establishments sorted by the size of the owner service organization for each technology segment. BAI estimates that the 490,624 service organizations operate 590,310 service establishments. As one would expect, almost a 1:1 correspondence exists between organizations and establishments among very small organizations (1 to 4 service personnel). In fact, when very small and small service organizations are combined (creating a category of 1 to 50 service personnel), the ratio of establishments to organizations only climbs to 1.06:1. At the other end of the distribution, organizations with more than 1000 service personnel operate an average of 41 establishments each, while organizations with 501 to 1000 service personnel operate an average of 17 establishments each.

STRUCTURAL TRENDS IN THE DISTRIBUTION OF SERVICE ESTABLISHMENTS

While comparisons of organization and establishment size distributions provide some insight into the current structure of the service market, the service establishment data are more useful in investigating the dynamics of service market structure. In previous studies, BAI presented data on the distribution of establishments in the service market. Figures B.10 and B.11 present comparisons of the distribution of service establishments in the early 1990s with the estimated 1999 establishment distribution used in this study.

The estimated total number of service establishments nearly doubled during the decade, from 303,282 to 590,310. Figure B.10 shows the dynamics of this growth in service establishments in terms of size categories. The number of service establishments owned by service organizations in both the largest (>1000) and smallest (1 to 4 and 5 to 9) categories increased by more than 100%. More modest increases (30 to 60%) occurred

Size by Number of Establishments

Equipment Class Serviced	1–4	5–9	10–50	51–100	101–500	501–1000	>1000	Total
Information technology	43,641	8964	10,784	2302	3354	1079	3077	73,201
Office products and equipment	4,133	1817	2357	485	657	126	1238	10,813
Telecommunications/datacom	35,253	11,734	9752	1090	1233	81	692	59,835
Medical/scientific equipment	2,884	1775	2910	476	572	287	462	9366
Process control/plant automation	4,472	2655	3872	993	1,099	456	375	13,922
Retail and food equipment	7,319	2972	3547	546	586	46	196	15,212
Radio, television, appliance	13,395	3467	3498	1764	3598	839	2280	28,841
Building equipment and systems	80,902	28,551	28,714	3799	5102	978	3654	151,700
Aerospace/airline services	1,640	653	1013	230	434	98	4441	8509
Transportation (except air)	11,422	4126	4837	1214	3014	1138	2311	28,062
Automotive and other vehicles	93,878	27,828	21,922	7301	16,144	3445	5041	175,559
Public utilities	3,755	1431	2083	1457	2608	843	3113	15,290
Total	302,694	95,973	95,289	21,657	38,401	9416	26,880	590,310

Figure B.9 Size distribution of service establishments (number of establishments by service force size of owner organization and industry supported). (From Blumberg Associates, Inc., worldwide high-tech service industry database, Fort Washington, PA, with permission; U.S. Department of Commerce.)

Year	1–4	5–9	19–50	51–100	101–500	501–1000	>1,000
1995[a]	114,267	47,514	60,134	16,131	29,226	23,933	12,068
1999[b]	302,694	95,973	95,289	21,657	38,401	9416	26,880
Change	+188,427	+48,459	+35,155	+5526	+9175	−14,517	+14,812
% Change	+165	+102	+58	+34	+31	−61	+123

[a] Based on late 1980s and early 1990s data.
[b] Based on middle and late 1990s data.

Figure B.10 Distribution of service establishments, 1999 vs. 1995 (total number of establishments and changes by size categories).

Equipment Class Serviced	Very Small (1–4) (%)		Small (5–50) (%)		Medium (51–500) (%)		Large/ Very Large (>500) (%)	
	1995	1999	1995	1999	1995	1999	1995	1999
Information technology	34.8	59.6	41.5	27.0	15.5	7.7	8.2	5.7
Office products and equipment	53.6	38.2	40.1	38.6	3.5	10.6	2.1	12.6
Telecom/datacom equipment	25.8	58.9	43.1	35.9	28.4	3.9	2.7	1.3
Medical/scientific equipment	28.0	30.8	45.3	50.0	25.8	11.2	1.0	8.0
Process control and plant automation	36.3	32.1	47.6	46.9	15.3	15.0	0.8	6.0
Retail and food service equipment	41.2	48.1	46.0	42.9	12.4	7.4	0.4	1.6
Radio, television, and appliances	30.0	46.4	27.3	24.2	20.6	18.6	22.5	10.8
Building equipment and systems	20.2	53.3	39.2	37.8	27.7	5.9	12.9	3.1
Automotive and aerospace[a]	47.2	50.4	30.8	28.5	8.7	13.4	13.4	7.8
Public utilities	7.7	24.6	44.4	23.0	33.1	26.6	14.9	25.9
Total	37.7	51.3	35.5	32.4	15.0	10.2	11.9	6.2

[a] In the 1998–1999 data, this category is divided into three: aerospace/airline, transportation, and automotive. They are combined here for comparison with the 1995 data.

Figure B.11 Distribution of service establishments, 1999 vs. 1995 (percent of establishments by service force size of owner organization and industry supported).

in the remaining size categories. At the same time, the number of establishments in the 501 to 1000 category fell by 61%. Evidence from industry-specific BAI market research strongly indicates growth in the number of service establishments across technology segments. Therefore, the contraction in the large organization category must indicate movement of these organizations and their establishments to either larger or smaller categories, rather than exit from the market.

In fact, these patterns reflect two concurrent service market trends:

■ Consolidation of service organizations and establishments is occurring in some segments of the service market. This structural change usually has taken the form of OEMs or large ISOs either acquiring or merging with medium-sized service organizations in order to gain service capabilities that would be too expensive to develop in-house.

■ Rapid growth in small independent service organizations is occurring simultaneously in other segments of the service market. This phenomenon is particularly pronounced in computer-related service segments, where highly skilled individuals or small groups who have been downsized by OEMs or ISOs form their own local or regional service and consulting firms.

Figure B.11 compares the percent distribution of service establishments over the 1990s in order to highlight the technology segments that fit these two major trends. If direct evidence of specific firms fitting these general descriptions exists, then these data indicate that a technology segment is experiencing consolidation if the percent of establishments in the largest categories is rising over time. Conversely, a significant emergence of small organizations is occurring if the percent of establishments in the small and very small categories is rising over time. These trends can occur concurrently if combined with a shrinking middle market.

Technology segments that have been exhibiting characteristics of consolidation over the past decade include:

■ Office products and equipment
■ Medical and scientific equipment
■ Process control and plant automation

Consolidation is most likely to continue in segments where there are economies of scale in service management or functions or where end-users are regional or national in scope. Industries such as large-scale manufacturing and health care are likely to fit this pattern.

Technology segments that have experienced a trend toward smaller organizations over the past decade include:

- Telecommunications/data communications equipment
- Information technology
- Building equipment and systems

Smaller organizations will grow in importance in segments where economies of scale are not important or where end-users tend to operate on local or limited regional levels. The general data communications, networking, and information technology service businesses fit both of these conditions rather well in all but the largest applications. However, much of the growth in smaller organizations in information technology can be accounted for by value-added dealer organizations. Although these companies often cater to niche businesses with very specific needs at present, large value-added retailers and OEMs are already making inroads in these areas and are likely swinging this segment toward consolidation in the long run. Building equipment and systems are certainly locally oriented, by definition.

The public utilities segment is the only one that has experienced concurrent consolidations and emergence of small ISOs over the past decade. Although these concurrent trends may persist for some time, it is likely that one or the other will emerge as the dominant pattern in this technology segment in the long run. Radical ongoing changes in the regulatory and competitive environments currently cloud the structural issues in the markets related to utility industries.

SUMMARY

Key strategic conclusions can be drawn from this analysis. An assessment of the trends influencing the field service industry reveals some important facts:

- Although the service market remains fragmented, end-users show an ongoing and increasing interest in a single point of contact for service. Thus, effective service providers need to strengthen their service portfolio internally or develop it through joint ventures, alliances, and mergers with other companies in the industry to include:
  - Multivendor service offerings
  - Multiple-technology service offerings
  - Offerings of services in all three service classes (basic, value-added/professional, and logistics/others)

- Particularly high growth opportunities are presenting themselves for value-added and professional services. Thus, service providers should target value-added and professional services as key areas for development and expansion that can provide the basis for increasing long-term service growth.
- Technology is changing rapidly in the industries supported by service organizations. Efficient service providers must predict and stay ahead of these changes through investment in research and development, training programs, and strategic assessments.
- The ability to provide network-related services is becoming more important. A service organization can improve its chances for success by strengthening its network service capabilities.
- Vendors supporting the service market (FSMS and field communications vendors, consultants, etc.) are expected to experience excellent product and service growth over the next 5 years. As service markets become increasingly more competitive and end-users expect increased service levels, service organizations will find these products and services critical to the sustained growth of their service businesses.

In the U.S. market for service, some types of services show particularly strong growth potential. Overall, the professional/technical services category shows the strongest increase through 2004; however, potential for growth can be found within each of the three major service categories (basic, value-added/professional, and logistics/others). Service organizations will benefit from developing these high-growth functions. Taking both size and growth into account, the most promising of these are:

- Maintenance and repair
  - Building automation, 16.0% CAGR
  - Process/environmental controls and networks, 13.9% CAGR
  - Voice/data integrated LAN, 10.5% CAGR
- Professional and technical services
  - Management consulting, 22% CAGR
  - Process control/plant automation, 22.4% CAGR
  - Network systems, 18.8% CAGR
- Logistics and other support services
  - Logistics support, 18.5% CAGR
  - Depot repair and parts, 13.0% CAGR

BAI's research related to the ownership of U.S. service organizations revealed a proliferation of ISO-owned service organizations. Increasingly, these groups represent a stronger source of competition for OEM-owned and dealer-owned service organizations. Many of the largest service organizations in some segments are OEM owned and are successful because they have become more efficient in order to face the challenge of the intensifying competition. This has involved elements such as extending service capabilities to provide multivendor or multiple-technology service and broadening service offerings beyond basic support.

Trends in the size distribution of service organizations and enterprises suggest two concurrent, but competing, influences on service market structure. Consolidation dominates segments where there are economies of scale in service management or functions or where end-users are regional or national in scope, such as large-scale manufacturing and health care. Smaller organizations are growing in importance in segments where economies of scale are not important or where end-users tend to operate on local or limited regional levels, such as data communications and networking and building equipment and systems.

Excellent opportunities for growth in the service industry can be found in the near future; however, a high industry growth rate cannot assure the success of every player in the market because the competitive environment is intensifying. Many new players (especially ISOs) are entering the market, and OEMs in some market segments are beginning to emerge as major strategic service market players. In addition, customers expect their external service providers to offer a complete line of services for a variety of installed technologies on a multivendor basis. It is crucial for each service organization to expand its service capabilities as much as possible while still maintaining control of the quality of each individual service. An expanded service portfolio, combined with well-targeted marketing and sales efforts will give companies an edge in today's competitive service industry.

Appendix C

BIBLIOGRAPHY

Adriaans, P. and Zantinge, D., *Data Mining*, Addison-Wesley, Reading, MA, 1996.

Berry, M.J.A. and Linhoff, G., *Data Mining Techniques: For Marketing, Sales, and Customer Support*, John Wiley & Sons, New York, 1997.

Blumberg, D.F., *Managing Service as a Strategic Profit Center*, McGraw Hill, New York, 1990.

Brown, S.A., *Customer Relationship Management: A Strategic Imperative in the World of E-Business*, John Wiley & Sons, New York, 2000.

Dyché, J., *e-Data: Turning Data into Information with Data Warehousing*, Addison-Wesley, Boston, MA, 2000.

Dyché, J., *The CRM Handbook: A Business Guide to Customer Relationship Management*, Addison-Wesley, Boston, MA, 2002.

Goldenberg, B.J., *CRM Automation*, Prentice-Hall, Englewood Cliffs, NJ, 2002.

Gordon, I., *Relationship Marketing: New Strategies, Techniques, and Technologies To Win the Customers You Want and Keep Them Forever*, John Wiley & Sons, New York, 1998.

Harvard Business Review on Customer Relationship Management, Harvard Business Review Press, Cambridge, MA, 1998.

Hughes, A., *Strategic Database Marketing*, 2nd ed., McGraw-Hill, New York, 2000.

Imhoff, C., Loftis, L., and Geiger, J.G., *Building the Customer-Centric Enterprise: Data Warehousing Techniques for Supporting Customer Relationship Management*, John Wiley & Sons, New York, 2001.

Immon, W.H., *Building the Data Warehouse*, John Wiley & Sons, New York, 1996.

Kimball, R., Reeves, L., Ross, M., and Thornthwaite, W., *The Data Warehouse Lifecycle Toolkit: Expert Methods for Designing, Developing, and Deploying Data Warehouses*, John Wiley & Sons, New York, 1998.

Linthicum, D.S., *B2B Application Integration: e-Business-Enable Your Enterprise*, Addison-Wesley, Boston, MA, 2001.

Martin, C., *Net Future: The 7 Cybertrends That Will Drive Your Business, Create New Wealth, and Define Your Future*, McGraw-Hill, New York, 2000.

Pine, J. and Gilmore, J. *The Experience Economy*, Harvard Business School Press, Boston, MA, 1999.

Quinn, J.B., *Intelligent Enterprise*, The Free Press, New York, 1992.

Reichheld, F.F., *The Loyalty Effect: The Hidden Force Behind Growth, Profits, and Lasting Value*, Harvard Business School Press, Boston, MA, 1996.

Seybold, P.B., *Customers.com: How To Create a Profitable Business Strategy for the Internet and Beyond*, Random House, New York, 1998.

Seybold, P.B., *The Customer Revolution: How To Thrive When Customers Are in Control*, Crown Business, New York, 2001.

Siebel, T.M. and House, P., *Cyber Rules: Strategies for Excelling at E-Business*, Doubleday, New York, 1999.

Sterne, J., *Customer Service on the Internet: Building Relationships, Increasing Loyalty, and Staying Competitive*, 2nd ed., John Wiley & Sons, New York, 2000.

Sviokla, J.J. and Shapiro, B.P., *Keeping Customers*, Harvard Business School Press, Boston, MA, 1993.

Swift, R.S., *Accelerating Customer Relationships: Using CRM and Relationship Technologies*, Prentice-Hall, Upper Saddle River, NJ, 2001.

Thorp, J., *The Information Paradox: Realizing the Business Benefits of Information Technology*, McGraw-Hill, New York, 1998.

Tiwana, A., *The Essential Guide to Knowledge Management: E-Business and CRM Applications*, Prentice-Hall, Upper Saddle River, NJ, 2001.

INDEX